Europe, India, and the Limits of Secularism

RELIGION AND DEMOCRACY

Reconceptualizing Religion, Culture, and Politics in a
Global Context

Series Editor:
AAKASH SINGH RATHORE is a Visiting Professor at the School of Social
Sciences, Jawaharlal Nehru University, New Delhi, an International
Fellow at the Center for Ethics and Global Politics, Luiss University,
Rome, and Director of the International Research Network on Religion
and Democracy (IRNRD), New York City.

This series is dedicated to the memory of Peter Losonczi (1970–2015),
the series' original editor and founder of IRNRD.

Europe, India, and
the Limits of Secularism

JAKOB DE ROOVER

OXFORD
UNIVERSITY PRESS

OXFORD

UNIVERSITY PRESS

Oxford University Press is a department of the University of Oxford.
It furthers the University's objective of excellence in research, scholarship,
and education by publishing worldwide. Oxford is a registered trademark of
Oxford University Press in the UK and in certain other countries

Published in India by
Oxford University Press
22 Workspace, 2nd Floor, 1/22 Asaf Ali Road, New Delhi 110002, India

First Edition published in 2015

Fifth impression 2023

ISBN-13: 978-0-19-946097-7
ISBN-10: 0-19-946097-3

Typeset in Adobe Jenson Pro 10.5 pt/13

by Tranistics Data Technologies, New Delhi 110 044
Printed in India by Replika Press Pvt. Ltd.

When revolutions fail, the dreams behind them live on.
His fight for radical change may have died, but his dream of a
better world never did.
This book is dedicated to my father, Willem De Roover,
for passing the dream on to us, so that we may do our bit to bring
it closer to realization.

Table of Contents

Series Note

During the last two decades, the formerly dominant status of the secularist paradigm has been undermined globally. Recent developments across different regions of the world (the Indian subcontinent, the Arab world, Europe) bear far-reaching political consequences, both within the regional as well as the global scenarios. Some authors, formerly secularists, speak of the emergence of a postsecular era, and it is by now a generally shared realization that the influence of religion can no longer be ignored as a determinative factor in the contemporary socio-cultural and political constellation. Reflecting on these developments, both in social and political science, an intensive body of work has been developing that addresses the complicated and dynamic nexus between components of these processes—religion(s), secularization, democratization, modernization, cultural transformations—in order to better understand and interpret the rapidly changing realities. Moreover, the process(es) of globalization and the consequences of the postcolonial condition make the exchanges and the mutual influences amongst world regions unprecedentedly rapid and intense. As a unique innovation, the series Religion and Democracy: Reconceptualizing Religion, Culture, and Politics in a Global Context combines interdisciplinary methods with an inter-contextual focus, with a new sensitivity for the palpable relevance of religion. It includes original works of pioneering scholarship that express and reflect the thematic and theoretical variability of the fluid and dynamic situation resulting from this dual process of 'postsecularization' on the one hand and 'globalization'/'postcolonialism' on the other. The main geographical focus of the series will be South Asia, predominantly India, with an eye on the earlier-mentioned global interplay.

Aakash Singh Rathore

Acknowledgements

The past ten years have been a lively period. There were beautiful and difficult, peaceful and turbulent times, but never a dull moment. During these years, new research groups in Europe and India came into being under the guidance of S.N. Balagangadhara (Balu). It has been a privilege and an honour to be witness to—and, hopefully, sometimes part of—the growth of his research programme.

Learning from a real teacher is not easy; at least, it has not always been easy for me. But what appears to be a struggle with the teacher is really a struggle of the student with his own ignorance. It often seems difficult to let go of the delusions about ourselves that we embrace so happily, even though they are the cause of our unhappiness. I feel a deep gratitude towards Balu for his guidance, generosity, patience, and thoughtfulness as a teacher, and (perhaps most of all) for his command of the art of being angry 'with the right person and to the right degree and at the right time and for the right purpose, and in the right way'.

It is impossible to describe all the ways in which the members of our core group in Ghent have helped, guided, and supported me over the years. Without Sarika, Nele, Marianne, and Sarah, this would not only have been a lonely journey but I would also be nowhere today. More than companions alone, they are stars that brighten the darkest of nights.

It has been a joy to travel along the roads of our research programme with so many comrades in India, Europe, and the US: Anil, Anne, Arun, Ashok, Ashwin, Ashwini, Chaitra, Divya, Dunkin, Emanuel, GSR, Jolien, Kannan, Kavita, Martin, Polly, Prakash, Praveen, Rajaram, Ramananda, Sadananda, Sandeep, Santhosh, Satya, Shankarappa, Shanmukha, Sufiya, Venkat, Vivek, Venkat ('vnr'), Willem, and many others. At different times and in different ways, the generosity of friends, family members, and colleagues in giving me their time, thoughts, and support proved invaluable. I owe much to all of you and look forward to the future that all of us will build together.

Finally, I would also like to thank the publishers of the journals and edited volumes where earlier drafts of sections of this book appeared, for their permission to include this material here. Earlier drafts of sections of Chapters 1, 4, 5, and 6 appeared in the following journal articles and book chapters: Sage Publications for 'John Locke, Christian Liberty, and the Predicament of Liberal Toleration', *Political Theory*, 36(4); Imprint Academic for 'Liberty, Tyranny, and the Will of God: The Principle of Toleration in Early Modern Europe and Colonial India', *History of Political Thought*, 30(1); Routledge for 'The Dark Hour of Secularism: Colonial Liberalism and Hindu Fundamentalism in India', in *Making Sense of the Secular: Critical Perspectives from Europe to Asia*, edited by Ranjan Ghosh (New York: Routledge, 2013) (all three essays co-authored with S.N. Balagangadhara); and Stanford University Press for 'Secular Law and the Realm of False Religion', in *After Secular Law*, edited by Winnifred Fallers Sullivan, Robert A. Yelle, and Mateo Taussig-Rubbo (Stanford: Stanford University Press, 2011).

Introduction

THE CRISIS OF SECULARISM

One need not be a prophet of doom to suggest that our coping with the cultural and religious diversity of humanity has seen little progress during the last century. From Iraq to Israel, India to the Balkans, Nigeria to Northern Ireland, Pakistan to Sudan, the list of plural societies disrupted by violent conflict between their different religious and ethnic communities is long. Yet, in this same period, some parts of the world were witness to the growing dominance and success of a particular way of solving the problems of diversity: the liberal model of religious toleration and the secular state.

Even though this model took various forms in the nation states that implemented it and among the political thinkers who elaborated it, these forms share a number of formal properties. The liberal model of secularism and toleration consists of a set of norms as to how a diverse society and its state *ought to be* organized. On the one hand, it claims that the state should be secular or religiously neutral. The state's policies and legal system cannot be based on any religious doctrine. Generally, religious authorities should stay away from political authority and vice versa. Under this model, the state is prohibited from endorsing the truth of any religion and from using its powers to enforce adherence to some religion. On the other hand, the liberal model insists that the right to religious freedom should be granted to all citizens. Each citizen ought to be free to believe and worship as he or she pleases, and all should respect this freedom and tolerate each other's forms of religious belief or unbelief. In this way, the model divides plural societies into two spheres: a political or public sphere, where citizens are subject to the laws and coercive power of the secular state, and another sphere, where they ought to be free to live according to their religious values or conceptions of the good life.

The liberal model met with considerable success in the nation states of western Europe and North America. After centuries of devastating wars of religion, these states enjoyed more than 200 years of relative peace among the religious groups in their societies. Systematic persecution and discrimination of groups considered 'heretic' or 'heathen' gave way to tolerance, religious freedom, and the granting of equal rights to all citizens. We should never underestimate this achievement.

In early modern Europe, human beings were burned, pilloried, mutilated, and denied access to all kinds of benefits for holding the wrong beliefs. As recently as 1826, a schoolmaster in Spain could still be executed for heresy because of his deist views.[1] Later in the same century, Protestant 'nativists' in the United States clashed with Catholics in violent riots and demanded exclusion of the latter from political office.[2] In 1886, a grand jury saw fit to have an American citizen sentenced on charges of blasphemy.[3] Liberal toleration may not have ended all forms of religious intolerance in the Western world, but it certainly provided a powerful instrument to prevent these from shaping state policies and laws.

---

[1]   Haliczer (1990), p. 357.
[2]   Jenkins (2003), pp. 27–8.
[3]   Sehat (2011), p. 1.

A Model in Crisis

Today the liberal model is under increasing pressure. Journalists and academics often blame this 'crisis of secularism' on the re-emergence of 'political religion' across the world: Hindu nationalism in India; political Islam in Turkey, the Middle East, and Northern Africa; Zionism in Israel; Protestant evangelicals in the US. The separation of politics and religion, they suggest, is being challenged by retrograde forces that once again seek their unity.[4] This account attributes the growing pressures on the liberal model to external factors that negate the norms of secularism. In doing so, it covers up major flaws *internal to* this model, which have come to the surface in recent decades.

First, liberal secularism did not deliver the goods it had promised when it was implemented in non-Western societies. Take the case of India. From the declaration of Independence in 1947, the country's first prime minister, Jawaharlal Nehru, made secularism part of the state credo; in 1976, the declaration that India is a 'secular' republic was added to the Preamble to the Constitution. But here the attempt to map the state onto the model of liberal secularism resulted in a rise rather than decline in conflict between Hindus and Muslims. Systematic violence between different communities has grown in frequency and intensity over the last six decades.[5] Some argue that the elitist imposition of secularism on Indian society lies at the root of the rising intolerance.[6] Others suggest that the situation should be blamed on the failure of Indian politicians to be truly secular and impartial.[7] Wherever the truth lies, the fact of the matter remains that the liberal model has failed to reproduce its European successes in India.

In countries like India, some intellectuals now reject liberal secularism as a typically Western invention that cannot be exported to other cultures. This does not mean they reject the model merely *because of* its Western

---

[4] Bhargava (2010), pp. 81–2; Hibbard (2010); Juergensmeyer (2008); Lilla (2008); Needham and Sunder Rajan (2007).

[5] Brass (2003), pp. 6–9, 60–70; Chandra, Mukherjee, and Mukherjee (2000), pp. 434–5; Nandy et al. (1998).

[6] Madan (1987), pp. 747–59; Nandy (1985), pp. 14–24.

[7] Brass (1999), pp. 370–1, 375; Chandra, Mukherjee, and Mukherjee (2000), pp. 438–9; Chatterji (1995), p. ix; Tambiah (1998), p. 427.

origins. Most of these intellectuals would not exclude basic physics, chemistry, or biology from their countries' educational curricula, even though these theories also hail from the West. The problem, they suggest, is that liberal secularism is so intertwined with a Western cultural context that it is bound to fail outside this context. For these thinkers, the liberal model lost much of its shine because of its failure to offer a viable framework for peaceful co-existence in plural societies outside the West.[8]

Second, in Europe also, the modus vivendi that crystallized within the outlines of the liberal model is beginning to show cracks. In the second half of the twentieth century, new migrant communities carried with them religious beliefs and practices that had earlier not been present in modern Europe on any large scale, especially various forms of Islam. The attempt to accommodate these groups within liberal secular states uncovered some limitations. In the name of secularism, certain practices of Muslim groups, such as the wearing of headscarves, were banned from the public sphere. Such policies had the effect of radicalizing some Muslims and creating antagonism towards the government and the majority population of the European nation states where they lived. They began to advocate a strict religious identity that included such controversial practices.

Many European intellectuals blame this on the nature of Islam and the fact that it does not allow for the separation of religion from politics. It is said that the Islamic world should go through its own Enlightenment in order to learn the art of separation.[9] Thus, the problem is again reduced to an *external* threat to the liberal model: because of their illiberal religious convictions, certain Muslim groups are not ready to accept the norms of secularism and toleration; therefore, they cannot currently be integrated into this model. Hence, so the reasoning goes, we need a democratic Islam adapted to liberal secular values.[10]

This explanation misses crucial dimensions of the growing diversity in European societies. Other groups face similar problems: to protect the neutrality of the public sphere, governments have disputed the right of Sikhs to wear turbans in schools, public offices, and other settings. The liberal model has also compelled such communities to take a particular

---

[8] See, for instance, Madan (1987); Nandy (1985), (1998b).

[9] See, for instance, Massie (2012).

[10] Buruma (2010).

form. In order to be recognized as proper religious communities by Western democracies, groups need to identify their 'religious beliefs' and appoint 'religious authorities' that speak for the entire community, even where they lack such structures. The traditions of these groups are not opposed to liberal secularism in any obvious sense. Yet, the liberal model faces great difficulty in accommodating such communities new to the modus vivendi that originally emerged in modern Europe.

Third, recent analyses show that the liberal model is plagued by conceptual problems. Its norms prescribe a particular relationship between the state and *religion*: the state ought to be neutral with respect to *religion*; citizens ought to be free to practice their *religion*; *religion* should not intrude into the public sphere. But what counts as religion? How do we distinguish the religious from the secular? Secular states and courts of law across the world have had great difficulty in determining the scope of religion. Still, they are compelled to take up this task in several types of cases: not only when groups claim exemption from specific laws or some special status in the name of religion, but also when civil authorities desire to ban certain symbols or modes of dress as religious intrusions into the neutral public sphere.[11]

Liberal states and courts are expected to be neutral towards all religions in their judgement as to what counts as religion. Yet, when they ban certain practices from the public sphere because these are 'religious', or determine that some practices are not 'religious' and do not fall under the scope of religious freedom, the failure to be religiously neutral appears inevitable. No state or court possesses an impartial scientific conception of religion; there are no shared secular criteria that enable one to identify and delimit the sphere of religion in a manner neutral to all religions. Consequently, judges and other secular authorities are bound to smuggle in some metaphysical or theological conceptions of religion.[12] That is, a specific religious language becomes the metalanguage to discuss and decide on matters of religion in courts of law and serves as the standard

---

[11] This matter will be discussed in detail in Chapter 1. For illustrations of the problem, see Greenawalt (2006), pp. 124–56; Jensen (2011), pp. 341–64; Sullivan (2007).

[12] On this practice of smuggling metaphysical positions into 'neutral' secular discourse, see S.D. Smith (2010), pp. 26–38.

to reject certain practices as not 'truly' religious. This calls into question the very claim to religious neutrality and secularity at the heart of the liberal model.

The coming chapters will closely examine these difficulties. At this point, we just note that the liberal model of secularism and religious toleration has lost much of the self-evident value it once had. Yet, the problems it was designed to solve remain as acute as ever: states around the world continue to confront tension and conflict between communities. How should we respond to the increasing failure of the liberal model to produce peacefully diverse societies? The situation compels us to start looking for alternatives elsewhere. Perhaps the flaws of the liberal model can be remedied. Even then, the growing complexity of plural societies across the world calls for the exploration of potential alternatives to this model.

The Asymmetry of Cultures

So far, political theory has presented the models crafted in the modern West as the best options for all other societies. There is a strong belief that all civilized countries ought to be liberal secular democracies abiding by norms of neutrality, toleration, religious freedom, and the separation of politics and religion. But it has become less credible today than before that the political models that happened to emerge in early modern Europe are the norm for all human societies. This stance could survive in a world of Western hegemony but is bound to crumble in our current 'multipolar' world.

In the early twenty-first century, our globe has seen fundamental shifts in its political and economic power configurations. The fact that it has become trite to declare that the hegemony of Western culture is coming to an end indicates the impact of these global shifts. The rise of Asian countries like India and China to world power is significant here. For the first time in more than four centuries, political leaders and thinkers from these cultures will play a central role in giving shape to global debates. The rise of Asia is likely to affect our political thinking, particularly that about the problems of diversity.[13]

---

[13] For an eye-opening account of these developments from an Asian perspective, see Mahbubani (2008).

In the twenty-first century, different cultures will meet as genuine alternatives for the first time—as forms of life that offer alternatives to each other.[14] This does not entail some 'clash of civilizations' where cultures will compete as rivals and one will emerge as victor. Rather, the current situation can be viewed in simplified terms: each form of life with some stability over time has approached and solved the problems of human existence in certain ways. Let us pitch our description of these problems at a high level of abstraction. In order to survive and flourish, human groups had to solve problems like political organization, creating an environment fit for human habitation, coping with human diversity and human suffering, and so on. Different cultures conceived of such problems differently and also developed different solutions. When such cultural forms of life meet, their approaches to the problems of human flourishing face each other as alternatives.

This opens up the possibility of choosing between such alternatives. Human groups will not be able to adopt cultures as wholes. Cultures are not like shirts that can be changed at will. However, we can imagine some society appropriating the solution that another has developed for certain problems of human flourishing. In fact, the last three centuries provide instances of this process. Many societies adopted the scientific theories, technological inventions, and political models originating in the modern West. The fact that this process happened one-sidedly should not prevent us from appreciating how it occurred: to some extent, through imposition by colonial states, but, where successful, it happened largely through imitation and experimentation.

It is likely that the twenty-first century will see such practical imitation and experimentation between cultures on a large scale. But the fact that we are still far away from this point calls for realism and reflection on the obstacles before us. On one hand, this process needs to be guided by theoretical reflection: intellectuals should reflect on the obstacles and differences between the forms of life that face each other as alternatives. Importantly, they will have to devise reasonable criteria for finding out which particular solutions to some specific problem of human flourishing are better than others.

[14] Balagangadhara (2012), p. 72.

On the other hand, the major obstacle is that the playing field is skewed. That is, cultural forms of life are not meeting as alternatives in the contemporary world. In the words of S.N. Balagangadhara, a peculiar *asymmetry* structures the encounter between cultures.[15] At a macro-level, the Western form of life is viewed as an alternative to all non-Western forms of life, while the latter are rarely seen as alternatives to the former. This is peculiar because the relationship of 'being an alternative to' always presupposes symmetry: if coffee is an alternative to tea, then tea is an alternative to coffee. Under today's asymmetry, however, it is perfectly reasonable to suggest that India should follow modern Western culture but it seems absurd to argue that Europe should emulate Indian culture.[16] Considering the currently dominant images of India, this would be like saying that Europe should implement the caste system, untouchability, dowry, arranged marriages, and political corruption—perhaps with a sprinkling of spirituality on the side.

Part of the problem is that the currently dominant descriptions of Asian cultures are those developed in Europe over the last three or four centuries. Since Edward Said's *Orientalism* (1978), we have reason to suspect that this body of descriptions is problematic: Western conceptions of Asian cultures tend to transform the latter into deficient variants of Western culture.[17] Balagangadhara characterizes this problem as follows: this body of descriptions reflects the Western cultural experience of other cultures.[18] That is, the descriptions describe *how one particular form of life has experienced other forms of life.*

Now, the experience that one culture has of another does not correspond to an objective factual description. Like any experience, it is structured by a background of prior attitudes and patterns of action and thought. As a body of descriptions, orientalism describes *such a structured cultural experience* and not just the empirical realities of Asia. It is the product of a systematic attempt of European minds to make sense of *their* experiences of Asian cultures. Significantly, this reflection on experience takes

---

[15] Balagangadhara (2012), p. 72.

[16] Balagangadhara (2012), pp. 72–3.

[17] Said (1978). For an overview of the debate concerning orientalism, see Macfie (2000). For important criticism of Said's work, see Irwin (2007).

[18] Balagangadhara (2012), pp. 34–59.

the form of apparent descriptions of other cultures. Yet these orientalist descriptions are shaped through and through by cognitive constraints and a conceptual apparatus characteristic of the Western form of life.[19]

Consequently, a cultural asymmetry lies at the heart of this body of descriptions. These conceptualize alternative forms of life from within a dominant cultural framework that reflects the reference points of one particular form of life. How can we surmount this obstacle and restore symmetry between cultures, when all we have to go by are the descriptions produced by one form of life, namely modern Western culture?

To appreciate the significance of this question, let us turn back to the theme of this study, namely, the limits of liberal secularism and its solutions to religious diversity. In the twenty-first century, a major task of political theorists will be to examine how Asian cultures offer potential resources for alternative solutions to such problems. The problem of diversity is particularly promising as a case in point. For centuries, Asian societies accommodated a diversity of religious, ethnic, and cultural groups much greater than that of Europe at any point during its history.

In India, a variety of Hindu, Buddhist, Jain, and Sikh traditions have lived side by side with Zoroastrian Parsis and different kinds of Jews, Christians, and Muslims for more than a millennium. Over the years, there were occasional conflicts between groups, more systematic clashes at times, and even decades of repression of certain traditions. Nevertheless, it is worth noting the following minimal fact: Indian society never disintegrated in spite of this diversity. Therefore, it *must have known* successful practices, heuristics, and mechanisms of coexistence between these groups. We need not romanticize this as pristine harmony but there is certainly a need to investigate these forms of coexistence and find out how they work. Once we gain insight into these forms of coexistence, these can then serve as conceptual resources for developing a new political theory of pluralism, which explicitly presents itself as an alternative to the liberal model.

Ideally, this is how a comparative political theory would go about its task, were it not for the obstacle of cultural asymmetry.[20] In this context, this

---

[19] Balagangadhara (2012), pp. 34–60.

[20] On the idea of a comparative political theory, see Parel (1992); Dallmayr (2004); March (2009); M.C. Thomas (2010).

obstacle takes a particular form. The liberal model is part of a larger normative framework. It is intertwined with other values like equality, freedom,
and human dignity, and also with clusters of commonplace ideas about the
nature of the human self and society. This framework crystallized in early
modern Europe from the sixteenth century onwards. In this same period,
European travellers and orientalists began to systematically describe the
societies and cultures of Asia. Through a process of selection and theoretical reflection, a fairly coherent set of dominant descriptions of Indian
culture came into being in western Europe. All of this happened within
the confines of a particular descriptive framework and its theoretical terms.

That is to say, European descriptions of India as the land of 'Hindu
religion' and 'the caste system' did not come into being independently of
the development of the liberal secular framework. The concepts of 'religion',
'freedom', 'equality', 'tyranny', and so on informing modern Western conceptions of Indian religion and the caste system were embedded in this emerging framework. Over the last two centuries, the resulting descriptions have
gained dominance and they continue to shape the study of India.[21]

If this is the case, the difficulty must be obvious: when trying to study
Indian culture and its traditions of coexistence as potential alternatives to
the liberal model, the descriptions one starts out with inevitably prevent
one from succeeding. The inevitability is caused by the fact that the available descriptions presuppose the liberal secular framework and frame
Indian culture in terms of its concepts and values. In other words, the
outer cognitive limits of the dominant political theorizing concerning
toleration and secularism overlap with those of our 'knowledge' about
India. Consequently, our current knowledge of India cannot possibly offer
the conceptual resources necessary to build an alternative to the liberal
model. The playing field where cultures meet as alternative forms of life is
fundamentally skewed.

A Different Route

Should we therefore simply ignore the liberal secular model while looking for alternatives? Such a radical step would be unwise and its success

---

[21] See Bloch, Keppens, and Hegde (2010); Dirks (2001); Inden (1990);
King (1999).

improbable. On one hand, whatever may be its flaws, the liberal model is a product of centuries of human experience and reasonable reflection. Rejecting it out of hand would be folly, for this would mean losing access to a rich tradition of reasoning that shaped many of our implicit and explicit ideas about the question of toleration. We would also lose the potential benefits of this model such as its more successful policies of impartiality and intellectual freedom.

On the other hand, discarding the liberal model is impossible, because its normative framework has structured the available descriptions of Asian cultures. We would not be able to access alternative forms of coexistence in these cultures without falling back into the very framework we intend to leave behind. Moreover, if we ignore the liberal model, what would the alternatives be *alternatives* to? We could not begin to demonstrate how such forms of coexistence have anything valuable to offer that is not already present in liberal secularism.

The route explored in this book is different. It shall take the constraints of the liberal model of religious toleration and the secular state as the focal point of its inquiry. The liberal secular framework of the modern West is subject to culture-specific cognitive limits that have also structured Western descriptions of Asian cultures. To be able to discover potential alternatives to the liberal model in Asia, we *simultaneously* need to develop alternative descriptions of such cultural forms of coexistence. The reason should be clear: we can only move beyond the cognitive limits of one by also going beyond those of the other. But before we can do so, we need to have clarity on the nature and causes of these limits.

Therefore, this book shall examine how the normative model of liberal secularism crystallized in modern Europe and how it determined the European understanding of another culture, namely India. Its focus will be on taking this first step: identifying the cultural constraints common to the liberal secular model and the Western understanding of India.

The different chapters will not have much to say about what an alternative model of pluralism and tolerance should look like. To take this next step, certain preconditions would have to be met: a different *kind* of research concerning Indian culture, society, and politics is needed, which is still in its infancy today. Currently, an international research group guided by Balagangadhara is in the process of developing the required type of hypotheses and descriptions. Within the confines of this book,

I can only offer a promissory note by saying that these research results will be made available over the coming years.

The reader will find an outline of the book at the end of the second chapter, after the theoretical framework guiding this study has been explained. Therefore, I have chosen not to summarize its seven chapters here. Before arriving at this outline, however, Chapter 1 reveals a fundamental problem at the heart of the liberal model of secularism and religious toleration and shows the practical implications of this problem in contemporary Europe and India. This problem points to some of the cultural limits of liberal secularism that will form the focus of this study. Chapter 2 reviews the different theoretical frameworks available for writing the story of liberal secularism and its cultural limits before it turns to sketching the research programme of which this book aims to be a part.

1. Limits of Liberal Secularism

Mysticism, when transposed from the warm twilight of myth and fiction to the cold searchlight of fact and reason, has usually little left to recommend itself. Its language, unless resounding within its own magic and mystic circle, will often appear poor and even slightly foolish ... Political mysticism in particular is exposed to the danger of losing its spell or becoming quite meaningless when taken out of its native surroundings, its time and its space.[1]

With these words Ernst Kantorowicz opened his celebrated study of medieval political theology. Written more than five centuries after the fact, they make one wonder how future generations will look back on the political mysticisms of our time. Much like the theory that attributed two bodies to the king, liberal secularism may face the danger of losing its spell or becoming quite meaningless when

[1] Kantorowicz (1997), p. 3.

taken out of its native surroundings, its time, and its space. Fortunately, in the twenty-first century, we do not have to wait another half millennium to find out if this is the case. Today's meeting of cultures compels us to examine how this political model fares outside its own circle well before future historians take up this task.

Is there any such thing as a liberal model of secularism? Modern nation states are home to different arrangements between the state and religion. France's *laïcité* (secularism) guarantees freedom of religious belief and exercise, but it also involves militant banning of religion from the public sphere. In the United States, the first constitutional amendment bars establishment of any state religion and protects free exercise so as to prevent the state from interfering in religion. In contrast, the Church of England remains officially established in the United Kingdom. The monarch is the head of the state *and* the church, while some bishops hold reserved seats in Parliament as Lords Spiritual. In India, state secularism has involved far-reaching intervention in certain traditions, such as state management of temples and the reform of Hindu law.

From a postmodern perspective, there are multiple 'secularisms' rather than one standard form.[2] Yet, from the variety alone, one cannot draw the conclusion that there is no such thing as liberal secularism.[3] These are variations on a model defined by a common set of norms and concepts such as the distinction between politics and religion. This model prescribes a particular relationship between the state and religion: the principle of separation says that the authority of each ought to remain confined to its own realm; that of equality demands that followers of all religions be treated equally; that of freedom states that citizens should be free to profess and practice their religion.

---

[2] See the introduction and several essays in Cady and Shakman Hurd (2010) and Jakobsen and Pellegrini (2008). Also see Asad (2003), pp. 5–6; Burchardt, Wohlrab-Sahr, and Wegert (2013); Khilnani (2007), p. 43; Tejani (2008), pp. 4–6.

[3] In fact, as Rainer Forst argues with regard to the concept of toleration, speaking about different conceptions or varieties of secularism presupposes a shared core meaning of the term 'secularism' and this core is the concept of secularism. See Forst (2013), p. 17.

Critics may object that some 'secularisms' do not share these properties: in the UK, the state lacks neutrality because of its ties to the church;
French laïcité is so anti-religious that it violates the principles of religious
freedom; the Indian state regularly intervenes in religious affairs. Such
criticism plays on another crucial property of the liberal model: *its normativity*. Because it is normative, it relates to factual instances in a peculiar
way. For any nation state that counts as an instance of liberal secularism,
one can always note that it is not really secular because it violates some of
the relevant norms.

Many differences among secular states in Europe and elsewhere have
their roots in the interplay between two distinct tendencies. The first
emerges from the concern to ban all expressions of religion from the
public sphere, politics, and education. This goes together with a general
suspicion towards the different forms of 'organized religion': all of these
are considered as potential threats to the public order. The second tendency is inspired by the conviction that the state should never interfere
in religion unless public order is at stake. The state should then allow all
religious communities in society to live by their own values and beliefs. In
the Anglo-Saxon world the second tendency is dominant, while the first
tendency has shaped French laïcité.

Yet, fundamental to all such manifestations of the secular state are
certain conceptual problems. This chapter will uncover one such problem
and trace its implications in various contexts. The first section characterizes the puzzle of the two spheres: how can we distinguish between the
public political sphere and the private sphere of religion? This puzzle takes
different forms in the Western world, all of which jeopardize the clarity
and coherence of the liberal model. The second section travels to India
and examines the forms taken by the puzzle in this part of the world.
The distinction between the religious and the secular turns out to be even
more problematic here.

The Puzzle of the Two Spheres

Liberal political theory may not attribute two bodies to the head of state
but it does postulate the existence of two spheres in social life. It suggests
that societies are divided into a public political sphere governed by the
state, and another sphere where we ought to be free to live according to
our own religious beliefs and values. The sphere of state coercion should

be secular. And as long as the rule of law is respected, the liberal state should refrain from interfering in the realm of religion and tolerate all religions.[4]

Recently, state neutrality has replaced individual autonomy as the essential liberal value.[5] This shift resulted from the late-twentieth-century liberal–communitarian debate. Liberalism demands that citizens confine their substantive conceptions of the good to their private lives, whereas the political community is governed in terms of a formal conception of justice. This is problematic, said critics, because many do not experience their ideas about the good life in this manner. They do not conceive of themselves as 'unencumbered selves' or 'autonomous individuals' but as members of a community sharing basic goals and values. These cannot be confined to the private sphere but should be taken into account in public political institutions. Besides, the liberal conception of the person does impose a substantive value: it compels citizens to become autonomous individuals, disposing of their commitment to community.[6]

In reply, liberal thinkers like John Rawls argued that individual autonomy was no longer constitutive of their project. Political liberalism does not deny the value of community but merely outlines its boundaries, given the fact of reasonable pluralism in modern democracies. Citizens can continue to cherish the substantive conceptions of the good they share with others. However, the plurality of these conceptions compels them to reach consensus on a political conception of justice that governs the state and its legal apparatus. This conception determines the basic structure of the society where various communities live and should, therefore, be impartial towards all substantive values, including individual autonomy.[7]

Political liberalism retains the twofold structure of earlier forms of liberalism: it still depends on dividing human existence into a personal sphere, where our comprehensive doctrines shape our lives and guide our actions, and a public sphere governed in terms of a free-standing political

---

[4]   B. Williams (1996), p. 22.

[5]   De Marneffe (1990), pp. 253–74; Dworkin (1985), pp. 191–204; Larmore (1990), pp. 339–60; Rawls (1996).

[6]   See Buchanan (1989) and Sandel (1998).

[7]   Larmore (1990) and (1999), pp. 599–625; Rawls (1996), pp. 1–207.

conception of justice. As human beings, we live in these two spheres and suffer from a corresponding split of identity: as 'citizens' we are subject to state coercion; as 'private persons' we are free. This generates a basic problem: how should we identify the two spheres?

Generally, this question has been understood as that of determining where to draw the boundary between the two spheres normatively: what should be the limit or scope of religious toleration and freedom?[8] Criminal behaviour such as murder, torture, or child abuse ought never to be tolerated but there are ambiguous cases also, from pornography to public smoking. While the question as to why one should obey the laws of the state is central to liberalism, the basic problem of liberal toleration is the following: How far into our lives can these laws reach? What criterion determines the scope of toleration? Where does the sphere of freedom end and that of coercion begin?

The Harm Principle

A major criterion used to delimit the sphere of state coercion from that of individual freedom is the harm principle: only practices that do not cause harm to others ought to be tolerated. This principle informs the widespread legal restrictions on religious freedom in the interest of public safety, health, and order. Individual freedom ends where harm to others begins.

Famously, John Stuart Mill introduced the harm principle in his *On Liberty* (1859). There, he intended to establish the limits of the power that could be legitimately exercised by society over the individual. He came up with 'one very simple principle' that should govern the state in its compulsion and control of individuals. The only end for which coercive authority can be exercised over the individual is self-protection and the prevention of harm to others. 'The only part of the conduct of anyone for which he is amenable to society is that which concerns others. In the part which merely concerns himself, his independence is, of right, absolute. Over himself, over his own body and mind, the individual is sovereign.'[9]

---

[8] Forst (2013), p. 23; McClure (1990), pp. 361–91; Mendus (1989), pp. 9–11; Warnock (1987).

[9] J.S. Mill (1987), p. 59, pp. 68–9.

This principle was to save democratic society from the tyranny of the majority. Since the nineteenth century, liberal politics and juris-prudence have invoked it as the standard to determine the scope of toleration.[10]

But there is a hitch to the harm principle: for its basic functioning, the question how we know whether our actions harm others becomes vital. If the principle comprised of physical harm alone, it would not help to fix the boundary between the spheres of freedom and coercion. Moreover, it is difficult to prove that even flagrant violations of liberty such as slavery cause direct physical harm, even if the slaves are 'treated well'. However, once we go beyond physical harm, the ambiguity of the harm principle surfaces. It is often impossible to tell whether an action of ours harms others. Severe criticism that hurts a person's ego may be seen as an attempt to ruin her psychological health or as an effort to help her become happier. This problem of indeterminacy threatens the harm principle since no viable criteria exist to determine when our conduct is harmful to others.[11]

The harm principle is useful as a heuristic for deciding where the state can legitimately intervene. On a case-by-case basis, this has proven to be effective: say, when parents refuse inoculation against diseases for their children on religious grounds, the state intervenes because this consti-tutes a significant risk of harm to these children. However, the principle cannot function as a general theoretical standard for distinguishing the sphere of personal freedom from that of state coercion, since we possess no clear and cogent theory of what constitutes psychological harm and harmful conduct. Consequently, the border between the two spheres becomes subjective. Depending upon our metaphysical beliefs about harm, the human psyche, and the integrity of human existence, we distinguish between the two spheres differently. At the normative level, it becomes impossible to separate them in any consistent and consen-sual manner.

[10] Dworkin (1985), pp. 335–72; Dyzenhaus (1992), pp. 534–51; Harcourt (1999), pp. 109–95; Skipper (1993), pp. 726–30. For critical analysis, see Vernon (1996), pp. 621–32.

[11] Dworkin (1985), pp. 336–7; Gray (1983), p. 49; S.D. Smith (2010), pp. 70–106.

A Split of Identity

What, then, is the status of the twofold structure of the liberal model? How can we clarify the distinction between the sphere of political coercion and that of religious freedom? If we want to explain the liberal model of secularism to the non-modern, non-liberal, and non-Western world, we cannot just assume that human lives have a 'natural' dual structure. We have to show how these two spheres can be retrieved in actual experience. The challenge is to provide a criterion that allows us to identify the two spheres at the empirical level. How to do so?

The political sphere is the domain of the state and its legal apparatus, whereas the private sphere of religion consists of what is left over. However, this does not allow us to identify the spheres, since any domain of our lives is subject to state laws at some point, while being free from them at other points. Our bedrooms may seem the most private spaces we can imagine, but if a husband abuses his wife in that space, the state is welcome to interfere.

Many theorists argue that 'the distinction between the public and the private ... is a slippery one, incapable of being established in a way that accords either with an adequate empirical description of the major institutions of modern society or with satisfactory normative justifications' and conclude that it concerns 'a shifting and uncertain boundary'.[12] Such remarks could be multiplied indefinitely.[13] However, to say that the boundary is constantly being renegotiated or that it is an essentially contested distinction evades the issue. The difficulty does *not* revolve around where the line is drawn between the spheres.

Consider the case of a country and its borders. The renegotiation of the borders does not make the country unidentifiable. Rather, the problem is to describe what lies within the borders. Even if its borders change, France remains recognizable as a distinct nation state. In the same way, the puzzle of the two spheres is not about the precise location of the boundaries. To make sense of the distinction, we should be able to recognize at least one of the two spheres. Either we possess a criterion to identify the private sphere of religion and distinguish it from its public political counterpart,

---

[12] Wolfe (1997), p. 195.

[13] Bailey (2002), p. 15; Casanova (1992), p. 17; Steinberger (1999), p. 293; Weintraub (1997), p. 2.

or vice versa. This criterion should describe the characteristic properties of at least one of the spheres.

Even where we suggest that the spheres are fluid and overlapping, it does not make much sense to speak of a public, political, and private religious sphere when we cannot distinguish between them. Liberal theories presuppose the validity of this distinction without being able to explicate it. This may be fine as long as such distinctions are confined to popular discourse but that ceases to be the case when they buttress a political theory. Perhaps we could argue that this distinction belongs to the basic intuitive ideas of Western societies and, consequently, there is no problem in implementing the liberal model here. This manoeuvre fails: not only have Western societies become home to communities that do not share the same cultural intuitions, but the model of liberal secularism has also been exported to non-Western societies.

This point is important in the context of claims about the free-standing position of liberalism. Political liberalism claims to have disavowed all controversial metaphysical doctrines. As Rawls put it, 'We apply the principle of toleration to philosophy itself: the public conception of justice is to be political, not metaphysical.' This political conception 'tries to draw solely upon basic intuitive ideas that are embedded in the political institutions of a constitutional democratic regime and the public traditions of their interpretation'.[14] Or, in Charles Larmore's words, liberalism should today be seen as 'strictly a political doctrine and not a general "philosophy of man", not a "comprehensive moral ideal"'.

Yet, Larmore argues, the liberal ideal 'relies on our being able to abandon "the cult of wholeness" and to embrace a certain differentiation between our role as citizens, free of status and ascription, and our other roles where we may be engaged with others in the pursuit of substantial ideals of the good life'. In that sense, Larmore continues, there is some point to talking of a 'liberal conception of the person', since the distinction between these two dimensions of human social life is largely confined to modern Western democracies.[15]

Larmore's reference to the lack of a liberal conception of the person in non-Western societies allows me to restate the puzzle of the two

---

[14] Rawls (1985), pp. 223–4.
[15] Larmore (1990), p. 345, p. 351.

spheres in a stronger form. Contemporary liberalism conceives of itself as a normative political model: its conception of justice tells us how the basic structure of society ought to be arranged. Perhaps we could confine its scope to the modern West. Even then, this model should remain intelligible and accessible to different groups living there. If not, they could never reach consensus on the political conception of justice. Even where the aim of liberalism is not to present 'a conception of justice that is true, but one that can serve as a basis for informed and willing political agreement between citizens viewed as free and equal persons', the minimal precondition is that this conception is intelligible and accessible to all reasonably intelligent citizens.[16]

Most non-Western cultures are ignorant of the liberal conception of the 'person'. To learn about its virtues, they should be able to make sense of this conception and its public–private distinction. That is, liberals need to explain how it is the case that each human lives in two spheres— one where we are citizens subject to coercive state laws and another where we are private persons free to live by our substantive conceptions of the good. The first step should demonstrate how to identify these spheres in human society. But, as already discussed, there are no widely shared and generally accessible criteria allowing us to recognize the spheres, let alone demonstrate their existence. So either liberal secularism is a viable political model and it should solve this problem, or the liberal conception of the 'person' is a piece of occult anthropology and then we can safely add liberal secularism to the political mysticisms of our time.

Symbols of the Secular

The puzzle of the two spheres is not a piece of sophistry without practical implications. Wherever liberal secular states grant religious freedom to their citizens and strive to keep religion out of politics, they need to determine the scope of religion. That is, states and courts of law require criteria to recognize practices or beliefs as *religious*. For instance, where secularism entails that religious symbols should be removed from public institutions, states first need to decide which modes of dress, jewellery, and objects count as *religious* symbols.

---

[16] Rawls (1985), p. 230.

Take the recent debates about the headscarf or hijab in several European countries. In the name of secularism, some argued that the headscarf is a religious symbol and that Muslim women should not wear it in state schools or when they work as civil servants. What rational grounds are available for deciding that the headscarf is a religious symbol?

An object can be a symbol only to some individual or group of people because they know what the symbol stands for. The symbolic function of some object is never the same to all. To whom does the headscarf count as a religious symbol? Not to Grace Kelly when she popularized the fashion accessory. Something is a religious symbol only to followers of the religion that identifies it as such. It is a specific interpretation of Islamic doctrine that transforms the headscarf from a piece of clothing into a religious symbol.

To those who are not members of this religion or do not accept this particular interpretation of the Quran, the headscarf remains a piece of clothing. To some it symbolizes the submission of women or Islamic attempts to take over public space in Europe; others respect it as a traditional practice of some communities.[17] But what is a symbol to one is not so to the other. Many view the headscarf as a piece of clothing—no more and no less. If such symbolism depends on individual points of view, how could a neutral secular state ever accept that the headscarf is a religious symbol, to be banned from public institutions?

Advocates of secularism could argue that the headscarf counts as a religious symbol to Muslim women who wear it. To them, the headscarf expresses certain religious beliefs; therefore, state representatives should view it in this way. This is dubious: how does wearing a headscarf demonstrate that the woman in question holds specific beliefs? She may as well wear it because the headscarf has become part of a struggle of Muslim minorities for equality and emancipation in European societies, because she feels more comfortable, or because her husband or parents prefer this.[18]

Generally, the argument that a symbol becomes religious when so considered by followers of a religion would work only if one is consistent: one should view all symbols of all religions as religious symbols and ban these from public institutions. How could the secular state then determine what objects count as religious symbols?

---

[17] Freedman (2004), pp. 11–16.
[18] Killian (2003), pp. 567–90.

In 2004, the French National Assembly enacted a law prohibiting the wearing of overt insignia and outfits whereby pupils express a religious affiliation in school.[19] The author of the law, French education minister and philosopher Luc Ferry, called for clear criteria to determine when headscarves, bandannas, or *beards* become religious symbols.[20] Indeed, when is a beard a religious symbol? When Muslims sport it? Preventing only Muslim men from growing beards would amount to discrimination. We could perhaps suggest that beards should be barred in cases where their wearers view them as religious symbols. But how can the state determine a man's motive for growing a beard? How can it distinguish between beards that grow for aesthetic reasons and those that are religiously inspired?[21]

The state could prevent all employees and pupils from growing beards but this policy goes against democratic freedoms. The only way out is to decide that beards of a particular shape and length count as religious symbols. No bureaucrat or pupil may have such a beard. Then the state faces the embarrassing difficulty of demonstrating that a beard suddenly becomes a religious symbol on the day the relevant collection of hairs reaches a particular length. This reveals the absurdity of the problem: it is impossible for states to determine from a neutral perspective when some object is a religious symbol. This is the case because there are no secular criteria to decide on the religiosity of symbols. Only specific religious teachings can transform objects into religious symbols. In this regard, the headscarf is similar to the beard.

The Secular Crucifix

The crucifix is as difficult a case as the beard and the headscarf. This symbol stood at the heart of the landmark case of *Lautsi v. Italy*, which came

[19] For explanations of this law and the French attitude towards headscarves, see E.R. Thomas (2006), pp. 237–59 and Bowen (2007).

[20] 'Laïcité: bandanas et barbes interdits', *Le Nouvel Observateur*, 22 January 2004.

[21] Similar problems concerning beards are now cropping up in British schools. See this URL: http://www.theguardian.com/world/2013/oct/03/muslim-boys-beards-breach-school-rules; last accessed 4 October 2013.

before the European Court of Human Rights in 2009 and 2011.[22] Soile Lautsi, an Italian mother of Finnish descent whose two sons attended a state school in Italy, contested the school's refusal to remove the crucifixes fixed to the walls of its classrooms. She filed a complaint before a regional administrative court, arguing that the school crucifixes constituted an infringement of the principle of secularism according to the relevant articles of the Italian Constitution. The court, however, held that the presence of crucifixes in classrooms violated neither the principle of the secular state nor the religious freedom of the complainant's children.[23]

The crucifix, the court argued, was indeed a Christian religious symbol, but it had also become a historical cultural symbol in Italy. It represents the identity of the Italian people. According to the court, key elements of the Enlightenment like the secular state, freedom, and equal rights derive from Christian teachings. There is a clear affinity between the 'hard core' of Christianity and the 'hard core' of the republican Constitution. Consequently, the crucifix is 'a symbol of a value system: liberty, equality, human dignity and religious toleration, and accordingly also of the secular nature of the State—principles which underpin our Constitution'.[24]

The court admitted that various interpretations could be given to the sign of the cross, including a strictly religious meaning. All such viewpoints were respectable but irrelevant in this case. The meeting of cultures in Italian state schools made it indispensable to reaffirm Italian identity 'even symbolically, especially as it is characterised precisely by the values of respect for the dignity of each human being and of universal solidarity'. Christianity, the judge claimed, is the sole religion that does not exclude the unbeliever, for it puts charity above all other values. As a Christian symbol, the crucifix cannot exclude anyone without denying itself; 'it even constitutes in a sense the universal sign of the acceptance of and respect for every human being as such, irrespective of any belief, religious or other, which he or she may hold'.[25]

---

[22] Case of Lautsi and Others v. Italy, 18 March 2011, European Court of Human Rights, No. 30814/06.

[23] For background information on the Lautsi case, see Andreescu and Andreescu (2010); Puppinck (2012); Temperman (2012).

[24] *Lautsi v. Italy*, paragraph 15.

[25] *Lautsi v. Italy*, paragraph 15.

When Lautsi appealed to the Consiglio di Stato (Council of State), this supreme administrative court agreed that in Italy the crucifix symbolized the religious origin of values like tolerance, mutual respect, and freedom of conscience. In the Italian Constitution, the court said, 'laicità' or 'secularism' is not proclaimed in express terms but derived from certain constitutional articles that deal with the inviolable rights of the person (Article 2), equality before the law (Article 3), the mutual independence of the state and the Catholic Church (Article 7), and the religious freedom of denominations and individuals (Articles 8, 19, and 20). To function within this legal framework, secularism had to take form under certain operating conditions, such as the Italian nation's cultural traditions and customs.

The meanings and purposes of the crucifix, the court pointed out, differ according to the place where it is displayed—'one can even deny its symbolic value and make it a simple trinket having artistic value at the most'. [26] In a non-religious context like a school, this symbol does not discriminate if it is capable of representing values of civil society. In Italy, the crucifix symbolically expresses the transcendent origin of constitutional values. It does not take anything away from the particular 'secular' nature of the Constitution, for these values may be endorsed 'secularly' by all.

On 3 November 2009, the *Lautsi* case came before the Chamber of the European Court of Human Rights. The Chamber rejected the Italian judges' reasoning and concluded that the displaying of crucifixes in state schools constitutes a violation of state neutrality. The religious meaning of the crucifix is predominant, it said, and associated with the majority religion in Italy. The state should refrain from imposing any beliefs, even indirectly, in places where persons depend on it. Any state has a duty to retain confessional neutrality in public education. The visible presence of crucifixes in state schools, the Chamber concluded, clashed with secular convictions and was 'incompatible with the State's duty to respect neutrality in the exercise of public authority, particularly in the field of education'.[27] Hailed by some as a victory for state neutrality,[28] this judgement provoked uproar in Italian and European public opinion.[29]

---

[26] *Lautsi v. Italy*, paragraph 16.
[27] *Lautsi v. Italy*, paragraphs 31–2.
[28] Andreescu and Andreescu (2010), p. 65.
[29] Puppinck (2010).

By insisting that the crucifix was the symbol of a particular faith, the Chamber had entered the debate about its true meaning. The Italian government, joined by third parties including twenty European countries, objected to this interpretation and argued that the sign of the cross was a 'passive symbol' lacking the impact of active conduct. It could be perceived not only as a religious symbol but also as a cultural symbol standing for the founding principles of Western civilization and democracy. The presence of crucifixes in classrooms was nothing more than 'a legitimate contribution to enabling children to understand the national community in which they were expected to integrate'.[30]

In response, the applicants argued that 'the crucifix was without a shadow of a doubt a religious symbol and trying to attribute a cultural value to it savoured of an attempt to maintain a hopeless last-ditch defence'. The principle of secularism requires state neutrality and a neutral space where everyone could live freely according to his own beliefs: 'By imposing religious symbols, namely crucifixes, in classrooms, the Italian State was doing the opposite.'[31]

In the end, the Grand Chamber of the European Court of Human Rights argued that the *Lautsi* case did not require it to rule on the compatibility between principles of secularism and the presence of crucifixes in state-school classrooms. Its task was more limited: to assess whether the school crucifixes conflicted with certain articles of the European Convention on Human Rights. The judges called on the principle of the margin of appreciation, saying that latitude should be left to each European Union member state in determining whether crucifixes are permitted in public schools. Reversing the earlier judgement, the Grand Chamber decided that the Convention had not been violated. Yet, to reach this conclusion, the judges again assessed the status of the crucifix as a religious symbol and concluded that it was essentially a passive symbol that did not actively indoctrinate or impose any particular religious views.[32]

[30] *Lautsi v. Italy*, paragraphs 36–40.
[31] *Lautsi v. Italy*, paragraphs 42–3.
[32] *Lautsi v. Italy*, paragraphs 71–2. For comments on the Grand Chamber's judgement, see Been (2011), pp. 231–5; Evans (2011), pp. 237–44; Fish (2011); Ronchi (2011), pp. 287–97.

In the *Lautsi* case, we see the logic of liberal secularism at work: secular states need to establish a neutral public space cleansed of religious symbols. But the scope of religion and the features that distinguish it are anything but clear. From a neutral perspective, the state cannot even determine which objects count as religious symbols. Consequently, in order to create such a space stripped of religion, the need emerges to enter the religious realm and take the theological position that certain objects are *religious* symbols conveying a particular message. This case brings to the surface the paradox of a secular court of law deciding on the religiosity of a symbol.

Secularism was not an abstract model that had appeared from nowhere, the Italian judges reasoned, but it had emerged from centuries of development within European Christendom. Shaped by the religious world where it crystallized, Italian secularism is a *Christian* secularism, which can be represented symbolically by the crucifix. To reach this conclusion, the judges had to engage in some heavy-duty theologizing. First, the regional court offered a theology of religions that explained how Christianity differs from other religions in that it cannot exclude unbelievers because it puts charity above faith. The Consiglio di Stato did not go quite that far but it did give interpretations of Christian teachings in order to argue that these correspond to the values constitutive of the secular state. In this way, *secular* courts of law participated in *theological* debates about the true message of a religion.

The judges were right in saying that an object like the crucifix is a symbol only according to the views of its beholder. It is a religious symbol only to those who know the theology of the cross. Take a Hindu onlooker. Unaware of the importance of theology to Christianity and its doctrines about the atoning death of Christ, he sees Jesus Christ as another swami or spiritual teacher, of which there are thousands in India. To him, Jesus attained the deepest meditative trance on the cross and could withstand pain and appear dead; his resurrection reflects the fact that Jesus returned from this state—all events fairly common in India.[33] When this Hindu

---

[33] This Hindu view of Jesus Christ is not fictional; see the observations of the Russian thinker and indologist Alexander Piatigorsky (1985), p. 211. Classical pagans like Celsus similarly viewed Jesus as a magician of some skill; see Chadwick (1953), I: p. 6, p. 10, and I: pp. 28–9.

looks at the cross, he sees it not as a religious symbol conveying certain doctrines, but simply as the sign of another swami. Hence, whether the crucifix is 'obviously' a religious symbol depends on its viewer.

Lautsi v. Italy was not the first case where judges had to decide on similar issues but only the latest in a string of cases in European countries.[34] Wherever the secular state is called on to decide on the religiosity of symbols, it embarks on a journey that ends up within the realm of religion.

Delimiting Religion in Law

Consider the following objection: admittedly, there are no neutral secular criteria to identify religion, yet, most citizens in the Western world share some understanding of what counts as religion. Even without clear criteria, judges and administrators have been able to distinguish between the two spheres in reasonable ways by relying on this consensus. Only philosophers are disturbed by the lack of watertight principles to separate the political from the religious.

This objection points to an important truth. Courts often determine what counts as religion. However, judges cannot be expected to develop some scientific theory that identifies and delimits the realm of religion. Instead, they express a consensus prevalent in society as to the scope of religion. To the best of their judgement, they should give reasonable answers to this question. These answers will be context-sensitive: they may differ depending on the society in question or religious communities involved in the case.

This is well illustrated by the Lautsi case. The Grand Chamber reversed the original decision and called on the principle of the margin of appreciation to suggest that the Italian public opinion should be taken into account. The absence of any European consensus on the question of religious symbols in state schools speaks in favour of that approach.[35] Thus, we see how judges come to judgements relying upon a local consensus about religion.

---

[34] Andreescu and Andreescu (2010), pp. 55–7.

[35] Lautsi v. Italy, paragraph 70. The Court also referred to other cases supporting this judgement: the Folgerø case concerning the religion syllabus in Norwegian schools and cases about the place of Islam in 'religious culture and ethics' classes in Turkish schools.

In this sense, one could argue, there is no need for any standard to delimit the realm of religion. However, this route involves several difficulties. First, it may lead to a tyranny of the majority. Any society's views regarding religion are shaped by the majority religion that has historically dominated that society. A practice not considered properly religious by the majority view will fall outside the scope of religious freedom. Or, similarly, a symbol or practice considered cultural rather than religious (because it belongs to the religion that shaped local culture) will be allowed entrance into state institutions. In this way, beliefs and practices of minority religions shall be marginalized. Considering that the principles of secularism mean to protect minorities, this would undermine the liberal model's very purpose.

Second, perhaps this modus operandi was effective as long as Western societies were relatively homogeneous in terms of religion. Then, some consensus could emerge among religious majorities like Protestants and Catholics and a few minorities like Jews and Muslims. In their reasoning concerning religious freedom, jurists could then express this consensus. Contemporary Western societies, however, have become more diverse than ever. In addition to the groups just mentioned, they are home to Buddhists, Hindus, Jains, Sikhs, neo-pagans, atheists, and so on. The chances of reaching a consensus on the scope of religion among these groups are slim. Several of these traditions do not even possess a conception of religion and its scope. Under these conditions, courts will end up privileging conceptions of religion shared by dominant groups and excluding alien views. Again, this undercuts the very purpose of state neutrality and religious freedom.[36]

A third difficulty arises if one insists that the state should leave the question as to what counts as religion to the religious communities. Judges can call on authorities or experts of the religions under consideration in order to determine whether some practice, belief, or symbol is indeed religious.[37] In this way, secular courts of law avoid theologizing and express the consensus within this community. Or do they? Again, there are several obstacles: in order to appoint experts and authorities, judges have

---

[36] For an argument to this effect, see S.D. Smith (1995), p. 68.
[37] For illustrations of this practice in American courts, see Sullivan (2007).

to decide that some form of life is indeed an instance of religion. Which criteria will allow them to do so, if they cannot decide what counts as religion? In the relevant community, there will be disagreement between different factions or experts. It will then be difficult for judges to find a consensus. Moreover, the step of appointing authorities that speak for a religion presupposes the structure of religions like Christianity, where such authorities exist. This approach compels any group to agree on certain beliefs and practices essential to its identity and appoint persons with the authority to represent these. Many communities and traditions do not share this structure.

In principle, none of these problems is unsolvable. It may be possible for a society and its legal system to develop ways of reaching consensus among a variety of groups concerning the identity and scope of religion. After all, courts are not asked to express an infallible consensus. In specific cases, their judgements should propose solutions to this problem equitable towards the parties involved. This shows that practical solutions might be worked out for the puzzle of the two spheres. However, such solutions will inevitably be limited in reach: any consensus about the scope of religion is valid only for a specific society during a specific period.

Take the case of the United State of America. No other nation possesses so rich and refined a body of jurisprudence on religious freedom and state neutrality. The First Amendment of the U.S. Constitution goes as follows: 'Congress shall make no law respecting an establishment of religion, or prohibiting the free exercise thereof.'[38] To assess whether some law or policy constitutes a violation of the establishment clause or a burden on the free exercise of religion, judges require a minimal understanding of what practices and beliefs are *religious*. For centuries, courts presupposed a Protestant consensus view in their judgements concerning religious freedom and non-establishment.[39] Considering the booming religious diversity of American society in the twentieth century, this approach could not last.

American legal theorists recognize the lack of clear criteria to determine what counts as religion as a major difficulty in interpreting the

---

[38] U.S. Constitution, Bill of Rights, First Amendment, https://www.law.cornell.edu/constitution/first_amendment (last accessed 25 June 2015).

[39] Beneke (2006); Sehat (2011).

religion clauses.[40] This has been especially troubling for granting exemptions from generally applicable laws in the name of religious freedom. When some individual invokes his religious beliefs to request exemption from some law, the state cannot accept all such claims at face value. To do so, as the Supreme Court noted in one of its landmark judgements, 'would be to make the professed doctrines of religious belief superior to the law of the land, and in effect to permit every citizen to become a law unto himself'.[41] In such cases, therefore, courts need to circumscribe religion to find out whether a law implies a burden on free exercise.[42]

Many thinkers argue that the criteria used by American courts to do so have been incoherent, ad hoc, and biased in favour of majority religions.[43] Others suggest that judges have developed a number of balancing tests and doctrines to delimit the scope of religion in reasonable ways.[44] Wherever the truth lies, this debate yet again demonstrates that the puzzle of the two spheres poses fundamental difficulties to the interpretation of liberal principles of secularism and religious freedom. If the liberal model keeps running into such difficulties within the Western world, one can only begin to imagine the troubles it encountered once it migrated to other cultures.

The Troubled Dream of Indian Secularism

Ever since the 1947 Independence Act and its partition of India and Pakistan, the question of secularism has been at the centre of the subcontinent's political struggles. The dream of India's first prime minister,

---

[40] From the vast body of literature on the religion clauses, see: Eisgruber and Sager (2007), pp. 22–50; Greenawalt (1984), pp. 753–816 and (2006), pp. 124–56; S.D. Smith (1995) and (2010), pp. 107–50.

[41] *Reynolds v. United States*, 98 U.S. 145 (1879), 5, cited in *Employment Division, Department of Human Resources of Oregon v. Smith*, 494 U.S. 872 (1990), 879.

[42] Gedicks (2006), p. 481.

[43] Eisgruber and Sager (2007), p. 29; for similar statements on the religion clauses in general, see Mansfield (1984), pp. 847–907, 848; S.D. Smith (2010), pp. 109–10.

[44] This is the position of Kent Greenawalt's multi-valued approach; see his (2006), pp. 124–56.

Jawaharlal Nehru, was to transform the country into a secular nation state. Communal bloodshed during partition only increased the confidence that secularism was the single viable option for India. With the rise of Hindu nationalism in recent decades, this issue has once again become as urgent as it was then. Religious conflict appears to have intensified from the 1992 destruction of the Babri Mosque in Ayodhya to the massacre of Muslims in Gujarat ten years later. Therefore, India needs secularism.

At least, that is what the secularists tell us. Indian society is characterized by its religious diversity, they claim, and therefore the state should be impartial towards all religions. In this view, the problem with the Sangh Parivar is that it strives to transform India into a religious nation state.[45] If this were to happen, the state would consistently take the side of the Hindu majority in conflicts and would no longer be able to curb violence as an impartial arbiter. In short, the fear of India's secularists is that the country will disintegrate if politics is not separated from religion: 'Secularism, for India, is not simply a point of view, it is a question of survival.'[46]

When such importance is attached to the idea of secularism, one would expect its content to be more or less clear. However, whenever Indian intellectuals attempt to pinpoint what secularism is, they end up in obscurity and confusion. In the 1970s, one author made the following remark: 'For the last two decades Indians have been talking of secularism, yet the term remains vague and ambiguous. One may, therefore, be justified in asking: what does secularism really mean—especially in the Indian context?'[47] Twenty years later, another author articulated a similar concern: 'Such a commonplace concept as secularism, with which the man in the street is so familiar and so used to, tends to acquire the character of a riddle, a puzzle, an enigma amongst intelligentsia.'[48]

Some point out 'the curious absence, the startling and significant vacuity of the notion "secularism" itself', and go so far as to claim that the notion has become 'a sort of mantra, a quasi-religious incantation.'[49] Others put it

---

[45] The family of Hindu nationalist organizations including the Vishwa Hindu Parishad (VHP), the Rashtriya Swayamsevak Sangh (RSS), and the Bharatiya Janata Party (BJP).

[46] Rushdie (1990), p. 19; see Chatterji (1995) for similar statements.

[47] Mushir-Ul-Haq (1972), p. 6.

[48] Sankhdher (1995), pp. 1–2.

[49] Rai (1989), pp. 2770–3.

mildly and say there is a tendency among Indian intellectuals to interpret the concept in their own subjective manner,[50] or they use more pointed terms: 'Like liberal Hindu gods who can take different forms and give a chance to the devotees to worship in any form they like, in India the concept of secularism has acquired so many interpretations and it now means different things to different groups of people.'[51]

The situation is no different in the courts. Confusion about the term 'secularism' surfaced in the 1994 Supreme Court *Bommai* judgement, where seven judges explained their views on secularism, each giving a different account. One judge concluded that 'the term "Secular" has advisedly not been defined presumably because it is a very elastic term not capable of precise definition and perhaps left best undefined'.[52] Whether Muslim or Hindu, rightist or leftist, these thinkers all agree that the term 'secularism' has acquired so many different meanings in India that it appears to have lost all meaning.

This section will argue that the semantic confusion surrounding the term 'secularism' masks a more fundamental problem in the Indian debate. Instead of being embedded in a well-structured theoretical framework, the notions of 'secularism' consist of a number of isolated normative propositions proclaimed as though these are self-illuminating. But the principles of the liberal secular state lack coherence and intelligibility in the Indian context. The puzzle of the two spheres takes an acute form, because the conceptual background necessary for making sense of the liberal principles of secularism and religious freedom is missing.

A Distinctive Secularism?

Over the last two decades, the Indian debate has focused on diagnosing the crisis of secularism.[53] Some authors conclude that factors internal to the secular state are to blame. Even though the Indian state professes to

---

[50] Khan (1994), pp. 370–83.

[51] Srikanth (1994), p. 39.

[52] *S.R. Bommai vs Union of India*, 1994 AIR 1918 at 29; cited in R. Sen (2010), pp. xxviii–xxix.

[53] Madan (1997); Pantham (1997); Bhargava (1998a); Ganguly (2003); Needham and Sunder Rajan (2007); Balagangadhara and De Roover (2007); B. Rao (2006).

be secular, they suggest it has not been impartial towards religion. The state intervened in the affairs of some religious communities while leaving others alone and used a tit-for-tat approach in dealing with the different communities.[54] Others argue that secularism has failed to take root in India because it was imposed on a deeply religious population by alienated Westernized elites.[55]

In response, it is argued that such critics presuppose one normative or 'transhistorical' model of secularism—an idealized version of the Western separation of church and state. Instead, this response continues, a specifically Indian form of secularism has come into being because of the historical conditions under which it emerged.[56] Secularism is a universal doctrine, Rajeev Bhargava asserts, since its basic constituents are constant, namely 'a separation of organized religion from organized political power inspired by a specific set of values'. But these elements can be interpreted in several ways. Therefore, secularism has no fixed content, but 'multiple interpretations which change over time'.[57] Indian secularism is distinct from Western secularism, such authors claim, for it was transformed in the process of responding to problems like caste discrimination and extreme religious diversity.[58]

India is supposed to be home to a different form and concept of secularism. So far we have characterized the liberal model of secularism in terms of a number of central concepts and principles and a basic problem that dogs this model. If secularism changed substantially in the Indian context, then the problem at the heart of its conceptual structure may no longer be relevant. In that case, Indian secularism should not face the difficulty of distinguishing between the public political sphere and the sphere of religion. Yet, it does. The distinction between the religious and the political

---

[54]   Brass (1999), pp. 370–5; Chatterjee (1998), pp. 353–66; B. Rao (2006), pp. 48–9; Tambiah (1998), p. 427. This assessment is shared by Hindu nationalists who accuse the Congress party and the Indian secularists of being 'pseudo-secularists' because of their failure to be impartial between Hindus and Muslims.

[55]   Madan (1998); Nandy (1985), (1998a), and (2007).

[56]   Chandhoke (1999), p. 42; Pantham (1997); Tejani (2008), pp. 4–6.

[57]   Bhargava (2007), pp. 21–2. See Mahajan (2002).

[58]   Gary Jacobsohn (2003, pp. 49–50) calls the result 'the *ameliorative* model', which 'embraces the social reform impulse of Indian nationalism in the context of the nation's deeply rooted religious diversity and stratification'.

plays as central a role in the Indian debate as it does in the Western debates. The same set of problems returns in a stronger form here.

For one, the relevant article of the Indian Constitution relies on the religious–secular distinction. Article 25 grants 'freedom of conscience and the right freely to profess, practice and propagate religion' but restricts this right by allowing the state to make laws 'regulating or restricting any economic, financial, political or other secular activity which may be associated with religious practice'.[59] Moreover, some Indian secularists provide definitions that leave no doubt as to the meaning of the term. Secularism calls for 'the demarcation of two realms of existence, the separation of church from state, of the sacred from the secular'; it requires the separation of the state from religion in general, from all faiths, or from any particular religious order; or it stands for the separation of religious and non-religious institutions.[60]

These are typical formulae of liberal secularism that generate the puzzle of the two spheres. If the separation of politics and religion is necessary, then one should be able to determine what properties distinguish the religious domain from the secular political domain in India. If there is no clarity on what makes some phenomena in society into *religious* phenomena or some institutions into *religious* institutions, then there is no point in stating that the religious ought to be separated (or equidistant) from the political.

The Constituent Assembly Debates

The foundations of the Indian secular state are located in the debates of the Constituent Assembly, the body that drafted the Constitution of India between 1946 and 1949.[61] Since most Assembly members agreed that India should become a secular democracy, they reproduced standard formulations of religious freedom and the secular state.[62] Yet, the trouble

[59] Bakshi (2011), p. 62.

[60] The quote is from Chatterji (1995), p. x. The other formulations can be found in Gopal (1993), p. 13; Sen (1996), p. 13; Bhargava (1998), p. 488.

[61] Bhargava (2008), p. 12; Chiriyankandath (2000); Jha (2002), pp. 3175–80.

[62] See *Constituent Assembly Debates* (*CAD*), Official Report, third reprint (New Delhi: Lok Sabha Secretariat, 1999), vol. 3, p. 488 and vol. 7, pp. 815–16.

in interpreting these surfaced whenever there was disagreement about their implications.

The most striking instance was the dispute about the question whether the secular state requires a uniform civil code.[63] This started when Mohamed Ismail, a Muslim representative, proposed to add the following proviso to Article 35, which said that the state would secure for its citizens a uniform civil code throughout the territory of India: 'Provided that any group, section or community of people shall not be obliged to give up its own personal law in case it has such a law.' Ismail defended his proviso as follows:

> Now the right to follow personal law is part of the way of life of those people who are following such laws; it is part of their religion and part of their culture. If anything is done affecting the personal laws, it will be tantamount to interference with the way of life of those people who have been observing these laws for generations and ages. This secular State which we are trying to create should not do anything to interfere with the way of life and religion of the people.[64]

Several Muslim representatives agreed that the secular state could not touch personal law because it ought not to interfere in matters of religion.

When others rejected this proviso as a direct negation of Article 35, the dispute turned to the correct interpretation of 'the secular state'. Another representative insisted that Indians seemed to have 'very strange ideas' about the secular state: 'People seem to think that under a secular State, there must be a common law observed by its citizens in all matters, including matters of their daily life, their language, their culture, their personal laws.' This is incorrect, he added, because, in a secular state, 'citizens belonging to different communities must have the freedom to practice their own religion, observe their own life and their personal laws should be applied to them'.[65] At the time of this debate, the idea that the same set of laws and rights should apply to all citizens, irrespective of religious affiliation, was not a 'very strange idea' but a central principle of the liberal

---

[63] These debates continue today along the same lines, see Larson (2001).

[64] *CAD*, vol. 7, pp. 540–1.

[65] *CAD*, vol. 7, p. 544.

secular state. If the state ought not to interfere with the ways of life of people, then legal uniformity would become impossible.[66]

Indeed, such reasoning led Muslim representatives to rejecting the attempt 'to have uniformity of law to be imposed upon the whole people' concerning civil matters as 'a tyrannous provision which ought not to be tolerated'.[67] In response, the lawyer K.M. Munshi remarked that democracies in the West had uniformity of law and were hardly tyrannies. Munshi also denied that personal law was part of religion. Expectedly, the dispute now took the form of disagreement about the scope of the term 'religion'. Munshi argued that 'religion' should be restricted to spheres that legitimately appertain to it, while the rest of life can be regulated by law.[68] The state was welcome to interfere in the *secular* affairs of any religion. But, as Ismail retorted, each community also disagrees on what was religious and secular: 'It is a question of difference of opinion as to what a religion should do or should not. People differ and people holding different views on this matter must tolerate the other view.'[69]

In this debate, Muslim representatives treated the principle that 'the state ought not to interfere in religion' as an isolated normative proposition and made use of a commonplace from Islamic theology to interpret it—the belief that the Shar'iah has been ordained by Allah, and not by human agency, and that humans should never modify it. Since religion covered all of God's revelation, they suggested, a secular state should not interfere in Muslim personal law.[70] Confronted by this interpretation, secularists in the Assembly could not draw upon any conception of religion that clarified the properties determining the religiousness of a practice or belief. They had to take recourse to other commonplaces to interpret this principle.

B.R. Ambedkar, the chief architect of the Constitution and advocate of social reform, borrowed the cliché from European orientalists that religion in India covers all aspects of life from birth to death: 'There is

---

[66] The rise of multiculturalism from the 1960s turned this into a contested idea, see Barry (2001).

[67] *CAD*, vol. 7, pp. 545–7.

[68] *CAD*, vol. 7, p. 548.

[69] *CAD*, vol. 7, pp. 721–2.

[70] The same argument surfaced in the infamous Shah Bano case of the 1980s. See Bajpai (2002).

nothing which is not religion and if personal law is to be saved, I am sure about it that in social matters we will come to a standstill.' He offered an alternative to seeing everything as religion: 'There is nothing extraordinary in saying that we ought to strive hereafter to limit the definition of religion in such a manner that we shall not extend beyond beliefs and such rituals as may be connected with ceremonials which are essentially religious.'[71] Ambedkar's proposal, however, generated a vicious circle, since his definition of 'religion' included the term to be defined. Without consensus on what religion was, there would also be disagreement on what was *essentially* religious.

Judging Hinduism

The puzzle of the two spheres wreaks havoc in India, because it is even less clear here than elsewhere how the religious and the secular are to be identified. The 'majority religion' of India is supposed to be Hinduism, but there is no clarity as to what Hinduism is, whether it is a religion or not, or even whether it exists or not.[72] In 1946, Nehru noted: 'Hinduism, as a faith, is vague, amorphous, many-sided, all things to all men. It is hardly possible to define it, or indeed to say whether it is a religion or not in the usual sense of the word.'[73] It must be extremely difficult, if not impossible, to identify something that is indefinable, vague, amorphous, many-sided, and all things to all men. But, when one does not succeed in identifying Hindu religion, how can one even dream of separating it from the state?

This constitutes a serious problem. Scholars agree there is no particular set of dogmas, beliefs, or practices that defines the Hindu religion.[74] Basically, the conclusion is that this religion does not have any properties

---

[71] *CAD*, vol. 7, pp. 781–2.

[72] There has been an extensive debate on these issues during the past three decades: see Balagangadhara (2005a), Bloch, Keppens, and Hegde (2010), Dubuisson (2003), King (1999), Llewellyn (2005).

[73] Nehru (1988a), p. 75.

[74] For some typical claims from the study of religion, see Dandekar (1971), p. 237; Flood (1996), p. 6; Michaels (2004), pp. 3–5; A. Sharma (2003), pp. 1–19; Zaehner (1969), p. 2. For typical claims by Indian judges, see R. Sen (2010), pp. 15–16.

(common beliefs, institutions, or practices) allowing one to recognize it. If Hinduism does not have such properties, how shall we determine when this religion intrudes into the political domain? When does a state become Hindu as opposed to secular? When the government publicly cites Rama as the prototype of the ethical king? Or when it consults an astrologer before making a political decision? When a puja ritual is done in parliament or when a Puranic story is told by state officials? Any answer to such questions will derive from the properties that distinguish the class of things Hindu from that of things secular. Since there is no consensus on this, one can fix this standard as one chooses. Accordingly, one can give one's own interpretation as to what it means for India to be a secular state.

Perhaps the consequences are best illustrated when the Indian judiciary invokes a number of definitions of 'Hinduism' and 'religion' to interpret laws related to religion. In 1952, the Bombay High Court had to interpret the constitutional religious freedom articles in the case of *Ratilal Panachand Gandhi vs State of Bombay*. Two petitioners had challenged the constitutionality of certain provisions of the Bombay Public Trusts Act of 1950, which allowed the state to regulate the administration of public religious and charitable trusts. They argued that Jain temples, which also fell under the scope of this trust, could only be used for specific purposes according to the tenets of Jain religion. Therefore, the Bombay Act contravened the constitutional articles of religious freedom.

The judge pointed out that the religious freedom granted by Articles 25 and 26 was restricted: 'It is not every aspect of religion that has been safeguarded, nor has the Constitution provided that every religious activity cannot be interfered with.' Drawing on a specific etymology of the term 'religion'—originally proposed by the Christian church father Lactantius—the judge suggested that this term should be understood in its strict etymological sense as 'that which binds a man with his Creator'. However, the petitioner's lawyer argued, Jains do not believe in any Creator and, therefore, the distinction could not apply to them. The judge responded as follows:

> But even where you have a religion which does not believe in a Creator, every religion must believe in a conscience and it must believe in ethical and moral precepts. Therefore, whatever binds a man to his own conscience and whatever moral and ethical principles regulate the lives of men, that

alone can constitute religion as understood in the Constitution. A religion may have many secular activities, it may have secular aspects, but these secular activities and aspects do not constitute religion as understood by the Constitution.[75]

If religion is constituted by the conscience and its moral precepts, then one cannot consistently argue that it does not encompass activities such as the administration of temples. Otherwise, one would have to allow that managing the finances of a temple, including potential embezzlement of its wealth, are actions outside the domain of morality and the conscience. But this does not make sense: according to any follower of a religion or tradition, such actions do belong in that domain. Consequently, since this judge argued that religion is constituted by 'whatever binds a man to his own conscience and whatever moral and ethical principles regulate the lives of men', such 'secular' activities would have to come under the realm of religion.

Still, interpreting religion in the 'strict constitutional' sense made the judge conclude that the administration of property (including temples) was not religious but a *secular* activity regulated by the state. Drawing on some definition of religion, the judge here determined for the followers of a tradition which aspects of that tradition were essentially religious and secular. In another similar case, the same court had stated that even the authority of a religious body in relation to its members had nothing to do with religion.[76]

When *Ratilal* and similar cases came before the Supreme Court of India, the bench rejected this interpretation of Article 25. A religion, it argued, 'is not merely an opinion, doctrine or belief' but 'has outward expression in acts as well'.[77] In the important *Shirur Mutt* case, the Supreme Court explicitly raised the issue: 'The question is, where is the line to be drawn between what are matters of religion and what are not?'[78] Drawing on a definition borrowed from an Australian court, the judges

[75] Ratilal Panachand Gandhi vs State of Bombay, 12 September, 1952, AIR 1953 Bom 242 at 4.

[76] D.E. Smith (1998), pp. 197–8.

[77] Ratilal Panachand Gandhi vs State of Bombay and Ors., 18 March 1954, 1954 AIR 388 at 1064.

[78] The Commissioner, Hindu Religious Endowments, Madras vs Sri Lakshmindra Thirtha Swamiar, 1954 AIR 282 at 1022.

suggested that a religion may not only prescribe an ethical code, but also 'rituals and observances, ceremonies and modes of worship which are regarded as integral parts of religion, and these forms and observance might extend even to matters of food and dress'. The court then attempted to provide a way out of the definitional quandary by arguing that 'what constitutes the essential part of a religion is primarily to be ascertained with reference to the doctrines of that religion itself'.[79]

This step shifts the problem to even more difficult questions: Which are the religions of India? Is 'Hinduism' one of them? 'Hinduism' consists of a range of traditions, all of which prefer different narratives, draw on different teachers, and emphasize different texts and customs. Which of these contains the doctrine that determines the essential part of Hindu religion? Perhaps one could propose that there are many different Hindu religions.[80] However, given the absence of fixed scriptures or doctrinal systems distinguishing these from each other, where will we find the doctrines about the essential parts of these religions? Given the non-existence of established ecclesiastical authorities, who will decide about this doctrine?

That these issues remain unresolved became clear in later cases, where the court argued that demonstrating that some practice was truly Hindu required that one produce its scriptural foundations. The next step was inevitable: judges claimed that certain practices that appeared to belong to some religion did not really constitute an essential and integral part of that religion. A community's claim could not always be accepted, for the 'essentially religious' might well be founded on superstition, ignorance, and misunderstanding of the true teachings of Hindu religion. As Ronojoy Sen shows in his work on religion in the Indian Supreme Court, Indian courts now took upon themselves the task of reforming Hinduism back to scriptural purity and discarding all 'superstitious accretions' added to its original core.[81]

To conclude, Indian judges have decided what religion is, what is secular and essentially religious about certain practices, and what is truly religious as opposed to superstitious. At its most disquieting, this modus operandi takes the form of the so-called 'doctrine of essential practices',

[79] 1954 AIR 282 at 1025.
[80] Stietencron (2001).
[81] See R. Sen (2010), pp. 49–67.

which allows the Supreme Court to reform religions and dispose of all 'non-essential' practices according to a normative picture of rational religion.[82] As many have noted, the criteria used to settle these issues are deeply flawed, even though they bestow upon Indian judges a religious authority greater than that of any high priest.[83]

At this point, we can come back to the confusion surrounding the idea of secularism in India. Fundamentally, this is caused by the lack of theoretical clarity in the religious-secular distinction. Moreover, the term 'secularism' has grown to be a keyword in Indian political discourse to refer to any kind of situation where different groups of people co-exist: if they get along well, this is because of secularism; if they fight and kill each other, they are in need of the antidote of secularism. Anything that allows different kinds of people to live together can be called 'secularism'. The notion has become as vague as it possibly could: it is defined as 'a state of mind, almost an instinctive feeling, such as existed, by and large, for many centuries in India when Hindus, Muslims, Christians, Parsis and followers of other faiths lived side by side in general harmony',[84] or as 'a respect for differences cutting across class, caste, community, and gender, in which religion is a component in the shaping of identity but not the determining criterion'.[85]

Instead of examining and theorizing the ways in which different communities have succeeded or failed to live together peacefully in India, one takes recourse to the obscure language of secularism. Consequently, the discourse of liberal secularism prevents one from understanding the problems of pluralism in India, instead of helping to solve them. The urgency of these problems today makes it all the more painful that some continue to believe that they can be resolved by endlessly repeating the mantra that 'the political' should be separated from 'the religious'.

*   *   *

[82] R. Sen (2010), pp. 40–72.

[83] Mehta (2008), pp. 65–88; Chatterjee (1998), pp. 359–60; Derrett (1968), p. 447, p. 534; Dhavan and Nariman (2000), p. 259; Galanter (1971), pp. 467–87; D.E. Smith (1998), pp. 196–201.

[84] Gopal (1993), pp. 19–20.

[85] Bharucha (1998), p. 6.

This chapter has revealed a problem at the heart of the liberal model of secularism and religious toleration, namely that of identifying the sphere of religion and distinguishing it from the public political sphere. This split between two spheres—one of political coercion and the other of religious freedom—is essential to the liberal model. Yet political theorists and jurists take it as a pre-theoretical given requiring no explanation, even though the distinction between the two spheres is anything but clear.

The idea of secularism, both its advocates and opponents acknowledge, emerged in the modern West.[86] This fact leads secularists and anti-secularists in India to very different conclusions. The latter argue that secularism has become a sterile concept in India because of its alien origins.[87] The former disagree. Charles Taylor writes: 'The Christian origins of the idea are undeniable, but this does not have to mean that it has no application elsewhere.'[88] Mushirul Hasan agrees: 'The central issue is not the Western provenance of an idea but its place and relevance in a plural society.'[89] The sociologist Andre Beteille has similar reservations: 'Surely, the test of an idea or an institution should be its capacity to meet our present needs and not its provenance' and 'geography can never be a decisive test of the social value of an idea or institution.'[90]

It would indeed be problematic to argue that the Western origins of liberal secularism rule out its relevance in India. Not only does this type of argument commit the genetic fallacy, we also know from human history that ideas are rarely the exclusive property of one culture. The liberal model emerged as a solution to certain problems that people faced in living together. Given its apparent success in Europe, there was good reason for other plural societies to adopt it. Consequently, the fact that an idea migrated from one culture to another cannot in itself constitute a problem.

[86] Madan (1998), p. 754; Mahajan (2002), p. 35; Nijwahan (1995), pp. 183–8; D.E. Smith (1963), p. 22; Taylor (1998), p. 37; Vanaik (1997), p. 29.

[87] This point of view is taken by Gandhian anti-secularists like Madan and Nandy, and shared by some Hindu nationalists: Madhok (1995), pp. 110–22; Nijwahan (1995), pp. 183–8.

[88] Taylor (1998), p. 37.

[89] Hasan (1996), p. 202.

[90] Beteille (1994), p. 560.

However, the issue raised by the anti-secularists does not concern the origins of secularism but its spectacular failure in India. To paraphrase Kantorowicz, they suggest that the language of liberal secularism, unless resounding within its own magic and mystic circle, often appears poor and even slightly foolish. That is, the liberal model seems to lose its spell and become quite meaningless when taken out of its native surroundings, its time, and its space. These critics suggest that the reason for this failure lies in the close ties between this model and the cultural and religious context where it originated. This suggestion is certainly worth examining.

2. Stories of Liberal Secularism

What enabled Europe to escape from an era of state persecution and wars of religion into one of religious tolerance and secular states? Some argue it took centuries of warfare and suffering before post-Reformation Europe discovered that preserving a society's religious unity had become impossible without continuous bloodshed. They present the rise of the liberal secular state in the West as a lesson for humanity.[1] Others insist that such a magical 'rise' never occurred. Tolerance is the result of compromises between communities and the management of aversion—a modus vivendi largely inspired by pragmatic concerns. Liberal toleration, they point out, goes hand in hand with its own modes of intolerance and involves a condescending attitude towards those who are different.[2]

---

[1] See, for instance, C. Taylor (1998) and Schneewind (1997).

[2] See, for instance, Brown (2006), p. 6. See Forst (2013) for an analysis of these conflicts over toleration.

Both perspectives have merit. On one hand, from the seventeenth century until today, the transformation of the Western world in matters of religion has been spectacular. Its societies saw an expansion of the scope of toleration from a limited number of Christian confessions to all varieties of belief and unbelief. The legal framework and policies of liberal secular states aim to be religiously neutral. The majority of the population appears to have become tolerant of many religious differences considered unacceptable in past centuries. Compared to many parts of the world, the West has seen few violent religious conflicts during the last seven decades.

On the other hand, intolerance of heterodoxy always remained present in Western societies. In the colonial era, Europe presented itself as a morally superior civilization that should replace the cultures of the colonized. Anti-Semitism was a destructive force in the first half of the twentieth century and it is on the rise again. Ethno-religious conflicts between Protestants and Catholics continued in Northern Ireland well into the 1990s. In West Germany, a *Berufsverbot* (professional disqualification) operative until 1985 banned communists and other 'radicals' from professions like teaching and the bureaucracy—a measure similar to the earlier treatment of religious 'dissenters'. The growing hostility towards Islam in the West draws upon the age-old Christian rejection of this religion as a fanatic theocratic ideology. From this perspective, liberal toleration has few lessons to teach: some other cultures have shown a much greater capacity to accommodate human diversity.

The challenge facing any account of the emergence of liberal toleration and the secular state is to make sense of both perspectives. It needs to account both for the observation that the Western world witnessed a spectacular rise of religious toleration during the last three centuries and for the perception that Western culture is distinctly intolerant of differences when compared to many other cultures. This chapter draws upon this challenge to assess the value of the different theoretical frameworks that try to account for the crystallization of the liberal model.

It first looks at classical accounts that present the rise of toleration as a distinctive dimension of the modern West. From nineteenth-century Whigs to contemporary liberals, these accounts have changed little in substance. Next, the chapter examines the critical genealogies of the second half of the twentieth century. In the wake of the two World Wars, some thinkers questioned the illusion that the West had gone through a process of progress resulting in secular modernity. Modernity, they said, constituted no radical break with the pre-modern past but instead had its origins in the secularization of Christianity. In response, others set out to defend the legitimacy of modernity against its detractors. Recently, more refined accounts materialized but these also show a remarkable lacuna: they have little to say about the relationship between the secular West and other cultures like those of Asia. Finally, the argument turns to the alternative framework that guides this study namely, the research programme developed by Balagangadhara over the last three decades.

Classical Accounts

For centuries, the dominant Western view looked at the relationship between different cultures in terms of an evolution of religion. It was believed that religion was a singular phenomenon with a common substratum evolving over time. In the eighteenth century, Enlightenment thinkers began to characterize the history of religion as a growth process. Beginning with the savage state, 'Man' had proceeded in everything from the concrete to the abstract—from the veneration of powers of nature, through polytheism, to monotheism.[3]

During the nineteenth century, the heyday of evolutionism, authors stated unambiguously that different religions should not merely be considered as varying forms of a single general type, but also as successive stages in one process of development, where the later stages include and presuppose the earlier stages. From its primitive origin, religion travelled through different stages represented by various cultures. Finally, it reached the climax of Western modernity, which (according to some) gave religion a rational form or (according to others) outgrew religion altogether.[4]

The same type of scenario also shaped the historiography of toleration. In the 1920s, a work titled *The Liberation of Mankind* had 'mankind' move from the Greeks, through the Renaissance and the Reformation, to Voltaire and the day 'when tolerance shall be the rule, when intolerance shall be a myth like the slaughter of innocent captives, the burning of widows, the blind worship of a printed page.'[5] Guided by the idea that

---

[3] Herbert of Cherbury (1663) and (1768); Hume (1976).
[4] See Caird (1894), p. 40; Spencer (1898); Tylor (1970).
[5] Van Loon (1926), pp. 306–7.

human history embodies progress, this scheme determined the Western understanding of the relations between different cultures well into the twentieth century: the modern West was the apex of human development, the end to be aimed at by all other cultures, which counted as equivalents of earlier stages of Western culture's historical growth.

Whig Historiography

In an essay first published in 1931, Herbert Butterfield noted that the 'Whig interpretation of history' had distorted modern historiography in major ways. The Whig historian 'stands on the summit of the 20th century, and organises his scheme of history from the point of view of his own day'.[6] For instance, the Protestant bias of such historians had transformed the medieval period into 'an era of darkness' that kept humanity tongue-tied by clerical authority until the Reformation inaugurated its liberation.

The Whig fallacy, Butterfield argued, confronts historians with a double bind: either they write general histories organizing the past as evolutionary progress towards the present, thus producing 'a gigantic optical illusion', or they end up being immersed in history for its own sake, soon 'concentrated upon the most useless things in the world—Marie Antoinette's ear-rings or the adventures of the Jacobites'.[7] According to Butterfield, the misstep of Whig history is its wish to go beyond the one simple assumption historians can make, namely that the whole of the past, including all its complexity of movement and entanglement of issues, has generated the whole of the complex present.

The ways of progress are 'crooked and perverse', 'twisting and turning', so Butterfield argued. They certainly do not move along a straight path to some *telos* (end or goal). Religious liberty is a case in point: its origin is often traced to Luther and Protestantism from where it purportedly progressed to the present age. Such interpretations depend on 'a hundred quotations torn from their context and robbed of their relevance to a particular historical conjecture'.[8] In reality, historians can only demonstrate

---

[6] Butterfield (1965), p. 13.
[7] Butterfield (1965), p. 29.
[8] Butterfield (1965), p. 18.

that today's religious liberty is a consequence of the whole past, travelling by meandering tracks and born of strange conjunctures.[9]

Many noted the relevance of this critique to the history of toleration, often written as though toleration expanded gradually but naturally to its current climax.[10] As an example, consider W.K. Jordan's monumental work on the development of religious toleration in England, first published in 1932.[11] Today, critics read this work as a catalogue of the errors of Whig historiography: it presents a teleological narrative with a predetermined end (the triumph of toleration), ignores the contingency of historical events, and makes these seem 'inevitable'. Jordan also neglects the theological contexts within which advocates of toleration wrote and transforms them into 'modern, secular liberals'.[12]

These interventions by Butterfield and others made an important point. Narratives about 'the rise of the modern West' cannot ignore all kinds of anomalies and hope to retain credibility. They present Western modernity as the telos of a 'universal history of humanity', the endpoint of a journey now to be undertaken by all other cultures. However, while the Western world witnessed revolutionary progress in science, law, and other fields, it has also faced major difficulties in domains where other cultures appear to be doing better. Europe has confronted recurrent threats to its capacity to accommodate genuine diversity; it produced extreme violence and inhumanity during the era of colonialism and the World Wars; and it is witness to increasing unhappiness and anxiety among its citizens. So the twenty-first century is in need of an alternative account of the relations between the modern West and other cultures.

To develop such an account, however, we cannot just dismiss the experience of the great numbers of Europeans and Americans who viewed their past as progress towards the achievements of the present. Past historians also realized that this did not happen in a 'straight line' but took centuries of struggle and setbacks. Like us, they faced the fact that we

---

[9] Butterfield (1965), p. 19, p. 22, p. 45.

[10] Coffey (2008); Wolfson (1996).

[11] Jordan (1965).

[12] Coffey (2000), pp. 1–3. Similarly, the author of another classic, Joseph Lecler (1955), denies any connections between early modern arguments for toleration and the Protestant beliefs of their authors; instead, these arguments are taken to prefigure contemporary liberal values.

inevitably look at the past from the present and craft a narrative pattern where the past gives rise to the present. We cannot assume that these historians hallucinated when they wrote 'Whig' accounts of the rise of Western liberalism, or when they perceived the outlines of contemporary liberal values in early modern thought.

If they were indeed mistaken, an alternative account should 'save the phenomena'. That is, it should not only tell us how and why they made these cognitive mistakes, but it also needs to account for the way in which generations of Western intellectuals have perceived the emergence of their culture and its liberal-democratic values.

The Great Separation

The model that transforms other cultures into earlier stages in the growth of Western culture remains alive today. In the introduction to his major work *Political Liberalism* (1996), John Rawls traces the historical origin of liberalism to the Reformation period and its long controversies over religious toleration:

> [T]he success of liberal constitutionalism came as a discovery of a new social possibility: the possibility of a reasonably harmonious and stable pluralist society. Before the successful and peaceful practice of toleration in societies with liberal institutions there was no way of knowing of that possibility. It is more natural to believe, as the centuries-long practice of intolerance appeared to confirm, that social unity and concord requires agreement on a general and comprehensive religious, philosophical, or moral doctrine. Intolerance was accepted as a condition of social order and stability.[13]

Here, Rawls ignores the history of many societies beyond the Western world. Between 1153 and 1155, a monk travelling through the Mongol Empire observed 'that members of virtually every religious group known to the Mediterranean and Eurasian worlds—he mentions Christians (Nestorians, Armenians, Russians, Alans, and Georgians, as well as Romans) and non-Christians (Muslims ('Saracens'), Uigurs, and 'pagans' of many varieties) alike—may be found in territories under Mongol

---

[13] Rawls (1996), pp. xxvi–xxvii.

domination'. These groups, he noticed, lived side by side with minimal conflict.[14]

This was no exception. The Indian subcontinent is called 'the world's oldest and most interesting "living laboratory" of religious pluralism': a variety of Hindu, Buddhist, and Jain traditions coexisted with Christians, Jews, Muslims, and Parsis from the end of the eighth century CE. This diversity also included streams of thought that denied the existence of any deities.[15] Of course, Indian society also knew occasional and sometimes persistent clashes between communities, but systematic persecution and oppression on the basis of comprehensive doctrines was absent.

Such societies did not need liberalism to discover the 'new social possibility' of 'a reasonably harmonious and stable pluralist society'. They *never* held the 'natural' belief that 'social unity and concord requires agreement on a general and comprehensive religious, philosophical, or moral doctrine'. But, according to Rawls, they had to await 'the successful and peaceful practice of toleration in societies with liberal institutions' to see that intolerance is not a condition of social stability.

How could a thinker of Rawls' stature come to such patently false ideas? In order to make sense of his reasoning, we need to postulate a background presupposition: all plural societies face a similar predicament, namely a conflict of comprehensive doctrines. They do so because traditions and communities are isomorphic in the sense that they are all constituted by comprehensive doctrines aiming at general agreement on their claims. In other words, Rawls' claim that the success of liberal toleration reflects humanity's discovery of a 'new social possibility' makes sense, *if and only if* all plural societies are variations on the structure of post-Reformation Europe. They should consist of a variety of religious communities, each of which revolves around a set of comprehensive doctrines and strives for general dominance of these doctrines.

Rawls is not alone. In a recent work, Mark Lilla argues that the revolt against political theology in the West generated *something unprecedented*: the birth of a new form of political reasoning free from disputes over divine revelation. Since *we* (modern liberals) wrongly assumed 'that

---

[14] Nederman (2000), p. 56.
[15] Coward (1987), p. xi; Basham (1969), pp. 264–8, pp. 345–7.

human beings had learned to separate religious questions from political ones', Lilla suggests we need reminding of a simple fact:

> In most civilizations known to us, in most times and places, when human beings have reflected on political questions they have appealed to God when answering them. Their thinking has taken the form of political theology. Political theology is a primordial form of human thought and for millennia has provided a deep well of ideas and symbols for organizing society and inspiring action, for good and ill.[16]

Modern Westerners find the survival of political theology ('discourse about political authority based on a revealed divine nexus') in other civilizations difficult to understand, because they have reached *the other shore*, the realm beyond the separation of politics and religion. 'When we observe civilizations on the opposite bank, we are puzzled, since we have only a distant memory of what it was like to think as they do.' These civilizations all confront the same questions concerning justice, political legitimacy, and rights and obligations, but answer them by referring to divine authority, a mode of reasoning now alien to modern liberals.[17]

Lilla presumes that non-Western cultures are alike in that they justify the legitimacy of political institutions in terms of divine authority and revelation. This reflects a deep ignorance of civilizations like those of Asia. The many non-Abrahamic traditions of Asia lack the notions of 'God', 'divine revelation', and 'divine authority'. True, inspired by Christian schemes of thought, Europeans have consistently spoken of the 'gods' of Asian religions; some Asians also adopted such English words to translate terms from their own languages. Still, God—a Sovereign Creator ontologically separate from the universe that is governed by His will—is alien to the indigenous traditions of Asia.

Could one not say that Asians have another conception of 'God' or believe in several 'gods'? Consider this counter-question: why use the same term to refer to two sets of entities as different as these? On one hand, we have a supernatural, ontologically separate, omnipotent, omniscient, omnipresent, perfectly good, and trustworthy Sovereign Creator whose will is embodied by the cosmos; on the other, a variety of beings, part of

---

[16] Lilla (2008), pp. 3–4.
[17] Lilla (2008), pp. 3–5.

nature and living *in* the cosmos, who have some exceptional capacities but can also be prone to deception, thieving, capricious behaviour, unpredictable emotions, and human-like frailties. These are not merely different entities—their properties are mutually exclusive. How can they belong to the same set?

Naturally, one can always use one word to refer to very different objects and give it two radically different meanings ('god$_1$' and 'god$_2$' or, in its original version, 'the true God' and 'false gods'). But then one has only two options: either consistently commit the fallacy of equivocation or qualify all usage of these terms and cognates like 'divine', 'revelation', 'theology', or 'theocracy'. Since authors like Lilla do not take the second route, they must be travelling along the first.

The problem becomes clear once we turn to the notions of 'divine revelation' and 'divine authority'. In the Hindu traditions, devas and devis ('deities', if you wish) have all kinds of conversations with humans but these are not considered 'divine revelations'. It is not because Shiva, Krishna, or Kali state something that it is accepted on 'divine authority'. Historic declarations by some king might say that his kingdom is 'Ramarajya' (the period of peace and prosperity when Rama ruled) but this does not grant 'divine authority' to the ruler. In contrast, in the religions of the Book— that is, Judaism, Christianity, and Islam—anything stated by God counts as divine revelation. A king rules by divine right whenever God is taken to have dispensed a fraction of His sovereignty to him.

Beyond the so-called Abrahamic religions, one cannot speak of 'political theology' as though this is a common type of political reasoning based on divine revelation. The authority attributed to some deities in Asian traditions is so radically dissimilar from the sovereignty attributed to the biblical God that they cannot count as different kinds of 'divine authority'. Lilla admits that political theology may not be a feature of *all* societies:

> Yet in countless other civilizations, revealed political theologies developed to explain and justify the exercise of political authority. The number of gods they imagined were many, as were the political arrangements they justified. But there is an underlying structure to this vast array, and a place within that structure reserved for Christian political theology.[18]

[18] Lilla (2008), p. 23.

Each political theology, he claims, develops an account of legitimate politi-cal authority in terms of a revelation about the nexus between God, man, and the world. There are three distinct ways to conceive of this nexus: the immanent God of the pantheist, the remote God of the gnostic, and the transcendent God of the theist. All three are stable pictures. In Christianity, however, the transcendent Father sent his Son into the world. This divine movement transformed the picture of God and gave rise to a number of theological tensions, which generated doctrinal con-flict and eventually erupted into the Reformation.[19]

Against this background, Lilla writes, a new approach to politics emerged, relying on human nature instead of divine revelation: 'A Great Separation took place, severing Western political philosophy decisively from cosmology and theology. It remains the most distinctive feature of the modern West to this day.'[20] By pronouncing this Great Separation, Lilla's account inevitably transforms the political traditions of non-Western cultures into representatives of earlier stages of Western politics. These still organize political life and conduct political argument on the basis of divine revelation and so become instances of 'political theology', stuck on 'the other bank' of the river, where 'the Great Separation' has not yet occurred.

To sum up, Lilla's characterization of political theology is off the mark for cultures beyond the Judeo-Christian and Islamic world. Still, he speaks of 'countless other civilizations' where political theology rules the roost. Basically, he reproduces the evolutionary scheme that projects the mod-ern West as the apex of human history. In this respect, Lilla's account is representative of the still popular 'liberation of mankind' genre, which has the whole of humanity journey through a universal history that happens to coincide with the Western culture's dominant self-understanding of its own history.[21]

---

[19]   Lilla (2008), p. 17, p. 23, pp. 24–54.

[20]   Lilla (2008), p. 58.

[21]   In Jonathan Israel's words, 'If the Enlightenment marks the most dra-matic step towards secularization and rationalization in Europe's history, it does so no less in the wider history not just of western civilization but, arguably, of the entire world. From this, it plainly follows, it was *one of the most important shifts in the history of man.*' Israel (2001), p. vi, italics mine.

Critical Genealogies

'All significant concepts of the modern theory of the state are secularized theological concepts.' So the controversial legal theorist Carl Schmitt famously wrote in 1922. Concepts had moved from theology to political theory, he added, with the omnipotent God becoming the omnipotent law-giver.[22] Even though Schmitt has become a controversial thinker, his thesis about the secularization of political theology lives on in various shades.[23]

With roots going back to Hegel, the idea that modern secular culture resulted from the *Verweltlichung* (secularization) of Christianity crystallized further during the twentieth century.[24] Today, many authors continue to trace the origins of secular modernity to Christianity, but it is unclear what implications this has for the relation between our present-day secularism and the Christian models of the past.[25] If it merely concerns a question of *origins*, it would be an instance of the genetic fallacy to argue that the Christian origins of secularism show that it is flawed. If it concerns a matter of *influence* of one on the other, it is unclear how this is relevant to the cognitive status of secularism. After all, religious ideas also influenced and inspired Newton in his search for the divine order in the universe, but the cogency and coherence of his theories are not dependent on these ideas. But there is also a third option: What if there is a relation of *dependency* between today's secularism and Christian religious doctrine?

The Secularization of Theology

Secularization, the historian Heinz Schilling suggests, 'is a fundamental process within the development of modernity, and to describe it adequately we need to take seriously the original religious and ecclesiastical contents of [the] social and mental structures that entered into the modern mind in secularized forms.'[26] In the period following the Second

---

[22] Schmitt (1985), p. 36.

[23] For instance, see Bethke Elshtain (2008); Riley (1986); Schilling (1991), p. 42, p. 60.

[24] See the overviews in Monod (2002) and Latré (2010).

[25] C. Taylor (2007); Gillespie (2008); Glover (1984); G. Smith (2008).

[26] Schilling (1991), p. 42, p. 60.

World War, this version of the secularization thesis had been given a new lease of life by Karl Löwith in his *Meaning in History* (1949). This work argued that the 'occidental conception of history, implying an irreversible direction toward a future goal ... is essentially a Hebrew and Christian assumption that history is directed toward an ultimate purpose and governed by the providence of a supreme insight and will'.[27]

Löwith traced the transfers from theology to philosophy in the work of a series of thinkers from Augustine to Marx. Concepts from modern philosophy reproduced Christian ideas, he said, but also disposed of their theological substance and thus hollowed out these ideas. 'The whole moral and intellectual, social and political, history of the West is to some extent Christian, and yet it dissolves Christianity by the very application of Christian principles to secular matters.'[28] Secularization consists of universalizing Christianity's formal schemes, while also retaining its very kernel. Consequently, the fundamental rupture in the emergence of the West is not that between Christianity and modernity, but that between Greco-Roman pagan culture and Christian religion. The transition from the Christian to the modern 'is only a secularization of the Christian *saeculum*'.[29]

This thesis gave birth to a genre of writing that revelled in revealing how a particular set of modern ideas secularized a prior set of theological ideas. Authors produced propositions of the form 'B is the secularized A': 'The modern work ethic is secularized monastic asceticism; The world revolution is the secularized expectation of the end of the world; The president of the Federal Republic is a secularized monarch'.[30] Against this background, Hans Blumenberg developed a critique of the category of secularization in his *Legitimacy of the Modern Age* (originally published in German in 1966).

Blumenberg pointed out that the secularization thesis of Löwith and others had a simple structure: it claimed that some distinct substance, properly belonging to a Christian-theological framework, had been

---

[27] Löwith (1949), p. 54.

[28] Löwith (1949), p. 202.

[29] See Gasché (2014) and Blumenberg (1983), p. 28; the '*saeculum*' in Christianity refers to the historical period between the Fall and the Second Coming of Christ.

[30] Blumenberg (1983), p. 4.

transformed into a secularized form.[31] But did such distinct substances, transposed from theological ideas to their 'secular' counterparts, really exist? For any relevant conceptual structures, Blumenberg argued, one could point out as many differences as similarities between the so-called theological original (say, Christian eschatology) and the secularized version (modern progress). In fact, Löwith's category of secularization presupposes 'an identity of substance' and thus, a continuity between the Christian and the modern world. Therefore, it fails to account for discontinuities in history and autonomous developments and innovations.[32]

The category of secularization rejected 'the alleged break between modern rationality and its past as ideological'.[33] To re-establish the legitimacy of modernity, Blumenberg produced a different genealogy of the modern understanding of progress: it was one instance of the new stance of human self-assertion characteristic of modernity. There is indeed continuity between modernity and Christianity, he admitted, but not in the form of secularization. Rather, modern thinking has inherited a set of puzzles originally solved by theology and its interpretations of Scripture. In the modern age, the theological answers were discarded but not so the original questions. Independent and innovative modern answers now 'reoccupied' the positions left by the displacement of Christian theology.

Here, Blumenberg appears to affirm certain dimensions of the secularization thesis.[34] After all, any question puts limits on what counts as an answer. The conceptual structures giving shape to a question also constrain the outer limits of its potential answers. How could one then be sure that modern 're-occupied positions' had indeed become independent of the theological concepts that structured the original questions? This certainly happened in some cases. As said, Newtonian physics started out as an attempt to answer some variant of the following question: 'What is the order put by God into the universe?' Yet one does not have to believe in God or the divine order to understand Newton's theory of gravitation. Could the same be said for the conceptions of sovereignty,

---

[31] Blumenberg (1983), pp. 15–20; Wallace (1981), p. 69.
[32] Gasché (2014), p. 340.
[33] Blumenberg (1983), p. 25.
[34] As noted by Monod (2002), pp. 275–6.

rights, toleration, or religious freedom? These appear to have a different relationship to the theological questions from which they emerged, because they often draw on the very same terms as the original theological reasoning. How could one demonstrate that the resulting theories are independent re-occupations of Christian positions?

In this context, non-Western cultures come into the picture. To establish the independence of some set of ideas from Christianity and its theologies, these ideas should be intelligible and accessible to relatively intelligent people from all cultures. The ideas in question should not rely on any set of culture-specific metaphysical notions, however implicit these may be. If this is the case, intellectuals from other cultures should not only be able to understand such ideas (like sovereignty, the secular, the self, and so on) but also to develop them in productive ways in order to solve certain problems. Asian intellectuals have certainly been able to do this with concepts from mathematics, physics, or biology, which are also of Western stock. But have concepts from Western social and political thought shown a similar potential to solve the societal problems of other parts of the world?

The Disenchantment of Politics

There are more reasons to address the relations between the modern West and non-Western cultures. One, such cultures offer a contrast to the West's secular world, certainly more alive than its own 'pre-modern' and 'pre-secular' past. This should allow us to more clearly characterize the distinct structures and limits of the modern Western form(s) of life. Two, any contemporary account of modern secularism faces the challenge of making sense of the world in which we live today: a world where Asia is playing an increasingly central role. To understand the place of Western modernity in this world, we are compelled to conceptualize its relation to Asian cultures.

As Charles Taylor puts it, there are two different takes on 'modernity': the cultural and the acultural approach. A cultural theory of modernity 'is one that characterizes the transformations that have issued in the modern West mainly in terms of the rise of a new culture', with 'its own specific understandings, for example, of person, nature, the good'. An acultural theory describes these transformations in a culture-neutral way as a process that any traditional culture could undergo or for which any culture could serve as 'input'—for instance, the account that sees modernity as the growth of reason.[35]

Taylor clearly prefers the cultural approach. Hence, a reader of his magnum opus *A Secular Age* (2007) would expect that he adopts this approach and looks at the emergence of secular Western culture in terms of its *specific* understandings of things like the person, nature, or the good. Does he take into account cultures beyond the West and their differences with the West, when he theorizes the characteristics and crystallization of what he calls 'the secular age'?

In his introduction, Taylor distinguishes between three senses of 'secularity': secularity$_1$ means that religion is retreating from public space; secularity$_2$ is the decline of religious belief and practice; secularity$_3$ refers to the fact that belief in God has now become one among several options. He notes that all three depend on a reference to religion, and asks: but what is 'religion'? This term, he says, 'famously defies definition, largely because the phenomena we are tempted to call religious are so tremendously varied in human life'. Taylor suggests a prudent route. Since we are only trying to understand 'a set of forms and changes which have arisen in one particular civilization, that of the modern West—or in an earlier incarnation, Latin Christendom—we see to our relief that we don't need to forge a definition which covers everything "religious" in all human societies in all ages'.[36]

Within the West, the crucial shift is the move from a world where the place of 'fullness' was self-evidently understood as 'beyond' human life or transcendent, to an age where this is challenged by other accounts that place it 'within' human life and make it immanent. Therefore, Taylor suggests, we can limit ourselves to reading 'religion' in terms of the transcendent–immanent distinction. He admits that 'religion' cannot be generally defined in these terms and that this distinction could even be unique to the Western world: 'So defining religion in terms of the distinction immanent/transcendent is a move tailor-made for our culture. This may be seen as parochial, incestuous, navel-gazing, but I would argue that this is a wise move, since we are trying to understand changes in a culture for which this distinction has become foundational'.[37]

---

[35] C. Taylor (1995), p. 24–5.
[36] C. Taylor (2007), p. 15.
[37] C. Taylor (2007), pp. 15–16.

In spite of its prudential justification, there is something not quite right about this definitional move. First of all, how can it make sense to define 'religion' in a particular way confined to some society? Consider an analogy: a physicist claims to have discovered that the gravitational field of some planet in the universe has radically changed. The phenomena we are tempted to refer to as 'gravitation', he says, are so 'tremendously varied' in the universe that we cannot find a general definition. Since he is only trying to understand changes in the gravitational field of this specific planet, he decides to prudentially define 'gravitation' in a particular way confined to this planet. Drawing on this definition, he then concludes that its gravitational field has indeed declined fundamentally. The tome written by this physicist would be considered gibberish. To understand changes in the gravitational field of some planet, one cannot depend on some stipulative definition of 'gravitation' valid only for this planet. One needs a theory that explains what gravitation *is* (as a phenomenon) and encompasses any gravitational field.

In spite of the differences between the natural sciences and the humanities, this analogy reveals some problems in Taylor's proposal. There are two options: either the phenomenon of religion is present in all (or most) human societies, or the many phenomena in human societies that we refer to with the term 'religion' are really different phenomena. In the first case, we could then sensibly speak of a secular age (or society) in contrast to a religious age (or society) by theorizing the distinctive properties of both. We could also account for the shift from a religious age (or society) to a secular one in terms of these properties. The result would be a general theory of secularization.

In the second case, it is indeed prudent not to use the same term 'religion' to refer to these different phenomena. Taylor's prudence should then confine him to speaking of 'Latin Christendom' only and its shift towards 'secularity'. After all, the changing relation between the immanent and the transcendent is a shift *within* the Christian religious world. Under these conditions, the religious and the secular age could be contrasted in terms of the theological immanent–transcendent distinction. But then Taylor cannot claim to offer a generally accessible account of the Western world and its shift towards secularity; instead, he is engaging in Christian-theological meta-reflection.

However, drawing upon the conceptual language of Christian theology to theorize the emergence of the secular age has implications for understanding the cultures and societies of the non-Western world. Looking at the earlier accounts of the evolution of religion and the rise of 'secular modernity' in the Western world, these always relied on an implicit or explicit reference to the non-Western world. For instance, they said that the West separated religion from politics, whereas the rest had not yet succeeded in doing so.

Take the work of Marcel Gauchet, another cultural theorist of modernity.[38] In *The Disenchantment of the World*, Gauchet characterizes religion in its primitive form as a system that historically existed among all human groups: it places the founding events of the group in a radically separate and different primordial past of the ancestors whose legacy should now be reproduced in every detail. It generates an attitude of complete acceptance of the world as it is and a refusal to transform it. The first religious revolution in history occurred when the State came into being, because this incarnated among humans what had been separated from them: 'What was originally excluded became embodied within society where the founding law now had its representatives, administrators, and interpreters.'[39]

In the axial age, the period between 800 and 200 BCE, religion developed a new formal structure, common from Greece through the Middle East to China and India. Essential to this new structure of axial religion was the distinction between the immanent and the transcendent. It created a split within 'the ought-to-be' between 'the law of belonging, the immediate and characteristic requirements of the group' and the call of 'the Other' or 'the Supernatural'—'the demand for the essential and the worthy, indifferent to circumstances, united and unchanging'.

In other words, axial religion produced a split between the divine norms of the other world as opposed to the human demands of this world. From now on, there was something new that went beyond human obligation. Because the divine norms transcend any worldly demands, there is always the constant possibility of conflict between them, and therefore, of questioning and challenging the current state of affairs. Building on this transcendent-immanent split of axial religion, Gauchet suggests, Christianity emerged as 'the religion for the exit from religion'. This religion both emerged from religion and eventually allowed for its superseding. Briefly, Protestantism allowed for the very disposal of the

---

[38] See Cloots, Latré, and Vanheeswijck (2013).

[39] Gauchet (1999), p. 14.

transcendental by having it gradually drift away from humanity, thus giving Western modernity its specific shape.[40]

The basic structure of Gauchet's account reproduces the notion of the evolution of religion. He does not value the steps from 'primitive' through 'axial religion' to Christianity as 'the religion to exit from religion' as an evolution of religion to higher stages. But his account does share the same structure. First, he postulates that religion is a singular phenomenon with a common substratum that has historically existed among all peoples. Second, he attributes the structural split between the immanent world and the normative transcendent world to all axial 'religions' from Judaism and Platonism through Confucianism to Buddhism and the Upanishads. Finally, this allows him to present Christianity as the culmination of a process of religious change, as the 'exit' from all that came before.

Gauchet inherits the first postulate from centuries of Christian-theological reasoning that took for granted the existence of a singular phenomenon of religion among all nations ('God's gift to humanity', 'the *sensus divinitatis* engrained in the human soul', or 'natural religion'). The second claim is a projection of the internal structure of Christianity, namely its fundamental split between the transcendent and eternal will of God ('the world as it ought to be') and the state of the actual world ('the world as it is'), onto other traditions that lack this structure.[41]

To realize how problematic this idea of axial religion is, one need only reflect on the fact that experts insist that classical Chinese and other Asian languages lack the vocabulary to express such normative statements: there is no moral 'ought' (neither prudential nor obligatory) to be found in these languages.[42] This has the implausible consequence that the 'axial religions' of Asia lacked the conceptual language to express the split between the factual immanent and the normative transcendent, which is supposed to have determined their basic structure.

Consequently, Taylor has good reasons to suggest that we limit the immanent–transcendent distinction to Latin Christendom. However, the difficulty does not go away. Basically, Taylor suggests that the best route

---

[40] Gauchet (1999), pp. 48–9; Cloots Latré, and Vanheeswijck (2013), p. 4.

[41] See Section 'An Alternative Framework' and Chapter 4.

[42] For instance, see Rosemont (1988) and Balagangadhara (1988) and (2012), 82–4.

available to us is using the language of Christian theology ('immanent', 'transcendent', 'this world', 'the other world', 'fullness') as a meta-theoretical language to understand shifts within the modern West. But what one ultimately gets as a result is Western-Christian self-description. Given that the use of this theological language in the past transformed other cultures into inferior variants of the West, this cannot end merely by limiting oneself to self-description. It will continue to entail an implicit description of the other.[43]

In fact, Taylor indicates the danger of this kind of approach when he develops a critique of the 'subtraction stories' of secularization. These view secular modernity as the residual kernel that remains after discarding the impact of religion on human nature. Subtraction stories assume the following: there is a common 'neutral' core of human experience and existence, different religions added different layers of beliefs and practices to this core, and secularization in the West gradually cast off these superfluous layers and uncovered the fundamental structure of human experience and existence without religious additions. Yet, Taylor argues, Western secular culture is not simply the product of discarding Christianity and uncovering the secular. It was shaped by the internal dynamics of Latin Christendom, including its long history of reform movements and its attempts to reorder society according to a single rational model.[44]

Indeed, the self-understanding of the modern secular West assumes that there is a basic structure of human experience and existence, and that Christianity (or any other religion) was only an add-on to that basic humanity. From this perspective, the cultural experience of the modern West is structurally equivalent to the fundamental human experience.

---

[43] This becomes clear whenever Taylor forays beyond the boundaries of Latin Christendom. For instance, when he discusses the 'early religion' of Paleolithic and Neolithic times, he postulates the 'ubiquity of something like a relation to spirits, or forces, or powers, which are recognized as being in some sense higher', and says that 'religious life' was 'inseparably linked with social life' in these societies. As we will soon see, such claims presuppose Christian-theological beliefs as to the cultural universality of religion (see Section 'An Alternative Framework').

[44] C. Taylor (2007), pp. 25–218; Warner, VanAntwerpen, and Calhoun (2010), p. 15.

Once the Christian religious layer has gone, it is as though one gets 'the human experience'. There is no awareness that the modern Western form of life is subject to its own particular set of constraints and limitations when compared to other forms of life.

The 'subtraction story of secularization' goes hand in hand with the asymmetry of cultures discussed in the introduction. From the perspective of the modern West, other cultures cannot experience the human world radically differently. The otherness of other cultures is merely that they have added *another layer* to a basic human structure: some a Hindu layer, others a Buddhist layer; some a Chinese coating, others an African. Hence, modern Western culture cannot have anything to learn from these other cultures. The subtraction story confirms this self-understanding: secularization simply constitutes a gradual retrieval of basic human structures from underneath the Christian layers.

Inevitably, this transforms non-Western cultures into variants of Western culture—or to put it more accurately, into variations of the West's conception of itself. According to the resulting descriptions, the formal structure underlying all cultures becomes the same. Take Europe and India. Each culture has its own religion or worldview: Europe has Christianity and atheism, whereas India has Hinduism and Buddhism. These worldviews consist of sets of beliefs: Europeans believe they have only one life, whereas Indians believe in reincarnation. Their ethics revolve around norms and values: Europeans hold individualist and egalitarian values whereas Indians hold the traditional values of a collectivist and hierarchical society. Their practices and institutions are supposed to be expressions of such beliefs and values: liberal democracy in Europe; the caste system in India. Their societies are held together by a foundation of laws and governed by political authorities. In other words, all cultures differ in the same way.

The basic approach is this: while there is variety in the content of their beliefs, practices, norms, and laws, the formal structure of all cultures remains invariant. Within this framework, the asymmetry of cultures remains in place. Other cultures can only offer different beliefs, norms, and customs to the West. Some of these may be appealing and worth adopting: say, Native American beliefs about mother earth, Indian yoga and meditation, or the custom among some tribal groups to allow adolescents to have several years of free sexual relationships before choosing a life partner. But the West cannot learn from other cultures in ways that would change it fundamentally. It can adopt exotic content but it can do no more, since the form of all other cultures is identical to its own. In contrast, other cultures can and should learn from the modern West, because its beliefs (the sciences), its norms (liberty and equality), and its institutions (liberal democracy and social justice) offer superior content to fill out the form.

An Alternative Framework

In contrast to its rivals, the research programme developed by S.N. Balagangadhara over the last three decades does address the critical question of the relation between contemporary Western culture and the cultures of Asia. He formulates this in terms of cultural difference: How is Western culture *culturally* different from Asian cultures? Which culture-specific constraints are characteristic of contemporary Western forms of life? How have these constraints determined the Western understanding of other cultures?

Surprisingly, Balagangadhara comes to the conclusion that the central characteristic of contemporary Western culture does not lie in its secularity but in its religiosity. It is a *religious* culture par excellence. That is, Christian religion is the determining factor and force that has gradually given rise to the Western culture as a distinct configuration of learning. This is where some of the most fundamental cultural differences between Western and Asian culture are located: the former is religious, whereas the latter is not.

Naturally, this highly counter-intuitive point can be reached only after a long conceptual journey. This section will give a staccato report of that journey to sketch how Balagangadhara's research programme offers an alternative framework for understanding the emergence of liberal secularism.[45]

No Culture without Religion?

What are the theoretical and empirical foundations for the common belief that religion is a cultural universal? How do we know that each culture

---

[45] The section draws upon Balagangadhara (2005a), (2005b), (2010), (2012), and some of his unpublished notes and lectures. See Shah (2014) for an essay concerning Balagangadhara's research programme.

has its own religion (or world view) and that it can be characterized in terms of a distinct belief system? Balagangadhara raises these questions as challenges to the contemporary study of religion.

Let us first address the empirical foundation. From the very beginning, the observations of European missionaries and travellers visiting other societies were shaped by a basic conviction, namely that the biblical God had gifted religion to humanity and that all peoples, therefore, had some form of religion (either pure or corrupted). In some parts of the world, travellers raised doubts as to the presence of religion. Certain nations in the Americas, Asia, and Africa, they said, appeared to have no religion at all. But later scholars argued that such observations reflected a lack of real understanding and a flawed definition of 'religion'. In fact, *there could not but be religion* among all human nations.[46]

Building on this theological foundation, European scholars imagined various forms of false religion that defined the cultures of these exotic regions. In the case of India, growing sophistication led to the observation that it had several such religions constituted by distinct belief systems and rites. Thus, 'Hinduism', 'Buddhism', 'Sikhism', and 'Jainism' were born. In the course of the nineteenth century, explicit theological predicates of truth and falsity disappeared from orientalist writings about India. Yet, the theological foundations necessary to postulate the existence of religious entities like 'Hinduism' and 'Buddhism' were never challenged.

These conceptual entities consisted of specific building blocks. Through a process of systematic reflection and filtering on the European reports sent home from India, their observations were made compatible with clusters of commonplace ideas widely shared across European societies, most of which came from Christian theology. Among these ideas was the belief that each culture had its own religion. Scholars went in search of the scriptures, doctrines, sacred laws, gods, priests, and religious rites characteristic of the various 'religions of India'. Sanskrit and Pali texts were taken to be scriptures and sources of religious doctrine; social practices had to be founded in these doctrines.

Balagangadhara shows how the Western cultural experience of India crystallized along these lines. More than being concepts alone, 'Hinduism', 'Buddhism', and similar 'religions' were also *experiential entities*

---

[46] De Roover (2014).

that structured European travellers' experiences of India. These entities shaped their horizon of expectation and constrained the common sense European reasoning about Indian culture and society. As conceptual patterns, the notions of 'Hinduism', 'Buddhism', 'Sikhism', and so on became the preconditions of order in the Western experience of India. Without postulating such religions, Europeans and North Americans would confront 'a blooming, buzzing confusion' in the societies of the subcontinent.

What then are the *theoretical* foundations for the belief that all cultures have religion? From David Hume onwards, Western scholars attempted to build 'naturalistic' explanations of religion, but these are irremediably flawed.[47] On one hand, Balagangadhara points out, they presupposed the truth of their *explanandum*, namely that all cultures have religion. Looking to explain why religion is a universal property of humanity, they produced a variety of ad hoc speculations specifically invented to account for this 'fact', which cannot be tested in any way. These thinkers postulated a series of properties that supposedly 'could not but cause religion': fear of the unknown, the primitive search for explanations of the world, the I–Thou split of human consciousness, the structure of our brain, the solidarity necessary for group survival, and so on. On the other hand, these explanations of religion relied on earlier descriptions of non-Western cultures by adopting these as self-evident facts about the world. Yet the basic structure of those descriptions consisted of clusters of commonplace ideas deriving from Christian doctrine. Consequently, all such explanations reproduce theological claims as 'scientific facts'.[48]

Even the very concept of religion, Balagangadhara demonstrates, is a theological concept that precedes all theorizing about its putative object. Thus, the contemporary study of religion has inherited the problems of reproducing Christian religious ideas in secular guise. Its theorizing continues to depend on the pre-theoretical assumption that religion exists in all human cultures. It remains unclear how we can distinguish 'the religious' from 'the secular'; what defines 'scriptures' as opposed to other texts; how acts of 'worship' are different from other behaviour and 'priests' from other respected figures; by what criteria one can recognize a 'god', 'deity', or 'supernatural being'; and how the indigenous traditions of Asia

---

[47] Preus (1987).
[48] Balagandhara (2005a), 143–73; De Roover (2003).

could be variants of the same phenomenon as Christianity and Islam. These conceptual difficulties are caused by the fact that theoretical terms embedded in a particular religious framework ('religion', 'worship', 'priest', and such like) are used as though they have somehow become theory-neutral observational terms.[49]

All of this leads to a fundamental set of questions: How could theological ideas survive in secular guise and thus determine the Western experience of—and reflection on—other cultures like that of India? What explains the stubborn belief that explaining another culture requires excavating its religion and belief system? Does religion exist at all, and if yes, what is its distinct structure?

The Dynamic of Religion

Balagangadhara builds a theory of religion that not only resolves these problems but also predicts new facts. To fully understand this theory, a close study of its claims and consequences is required; here, I can only sketch its outlines.[50] Religion, Balagangadhara proposes, is *an explanatorily intelligible account of the cosmos and itself* and the only religions we currently know of are Christianity, Islam, and Judaism. What does this mean?

In the attempt to understand human behaviour, two types of accounts have emerged: one type points to an individual's reasons or intentions to make a particular set of actions intelligible ('John chases after goblins because he believes they exist and follow him everywhere'); the other postulates causal relations to explain the same set of actions ('John chases after goblins because something is wrong with the chemical balance of his brain due to excessive use of hallucinogens').

Now imagine an account that does both at the same time. It claims that a particular set of actions can be made intelligible by explaining the causes of the actions. To allow for this, the causes and reasons behind the actions need to coincide, or in other words, the actions should perfectly embody the reasons for acting. This is impossible for human beings, since

---

[49]   De Roover and Claerhout (2010).

[50]   A more elaborate account of his theory of religion can be found in Balagangadhara (2005a) and (2010).

our reasons or purposes are separated from our actions by a substantial gap. But it is possible for a very different kind of being and his actions. The set of actions is the universe: all events that ever occurred, are occurring, and shall occur. The agent is the universe's sovereign creator, God. His actions—namely the cosmos or universe—are perfect embodiments of His will or purpose. God's reasons for acting perfectly coincide with his actions.

As an explanatorily intelligible account, religion does not explain all events in the cosmos in terms of God's purposes, but it does transform the cosmos into an explanatorily intelligible entity. That is, within the framework of a religious account, it makes sense to look for the reasons behind events or the meaning of life, and to try and discover the order underlying the phenomena. The cosmos is explained as an expression of the plan and order instituted by the Creator. Since religion is itself part of the cosmos, it must also reflect the structure of God's will. That is, it must account for itself. This is possible because it claims to be the account whereby God reveals His will; in religion, He discloses His will to humanity—His sentient creatures—so that they can worship Him and submit themselves to His purpose. In this sense, religion accounts for the cosmos *and* itself by explaining both as embodiments of the divine will, purpose, reason, or plan.

The forte of Balagangadhara's hypothesis is that it makes sense of the experience of religious believers and the reasoning of theologians as both crystallized over the centuries. His focus is on understanding the Christian religion and its role in the emergence of Western culture. How does the thesis that religion is an explanatorily intelligible account of the cosmos allow us to understand these phenomena?

First, consider his hypothesis concerning the double dynamic of religion. Inevitably, each explanatorily intelligible account makes a particular kind of truth claim: it is the one true account of God's will, because it has been so revealed by Him. Naturally, this truth claim cannot be confined to any particular group. The Creator's will encompasses all of humanity and hence, any particular religious account (any account of God's will) strives for universality. As a consequence, every religion is subject to a peculiar tension. On the one hand, as an account of God's will or purpose, it always needs to be *a particular account* that reveals His will or purpose to humanity. On the other hand, any such account also needs to lose all particularity: it cannot but become *the one explanatorily intelligible account,* the general all-encompassing revelation of God's will, accessible to all and exclusive of none.

This tension at the heart of religion can be clarified in terms of Christianity. God reveals Himself in Jesus Christ, who is the focal point of its particular account. He is the Saviour and the only route to salvation for humanity; surrendering to God's will equals having faith in Christ. This entails that the particular message of the Gospel should be spread among all human nations. But the particularity of this message inevitably functions as a constraint on its universalization. For instance, its specific doctrines (God's sacrifice of His only son to atone for human sin, the crucifixion and resurrection of Jesus, the Eucharist, the Trinity, and so on) confront potential converts with difficulties of understanding and credibility. This brings us to the other side of the coin: a religious account aspires universality and its specific doctrines become obstacles here. To achieve such universality, it has to become increasingly generic.

The double dynamic of universalization is a consequence of this tension in each religion. One, it strives to spread its particular account through the moment of proselytization, whereby a religion spreads the distinct doctrines that reflect God's will. Two, to achieve universality, any religious account needs to become as generic as possible and this generates the moment of secularization, whereby a religion casts off its distinct doctrines as obstacles that prevent it from universalizing itself. The never-ceasing interplay between these two moments shapes the dynamic of universalization of every religion. These are not two separate moments, for neither can resolve the tension at the heart of religion: at every point, the moment of proselytization recurs in the moment of secularization and vice versa.

Secularization Reconsidered

The double dynamic of religion accounts for the fact that Christian religious ideas are being reproduced in secular guise in the Western intellectual tradition. Balagangadhara develops a rich hypothesis about the form that secularization takes in the realm of ideas. Whereas proselytization consists of articulating ideas in the framework of a specific religious account and its theologies, secularization entails untying such ideas from this specific theological framework.

At this point, two technical terms need to be introduced. 'Tropes' are recurrent patterns in a tradition of thought; in the case of Christianity, they are the conceptual patterns that recur in its theological reasoning. 'Topoi' constitute a particular kind of commonplace idea, which plays a central role in the conceptual world of a society. They are commonplace ideas that have been elaborated in the form of theories or hypotheses. A commonplace idea can become a topos in at least two ways: it can either become a conceptual building block of a new theory or it can play the functional role of a heuristic that allows one to develop new theories or hypotheses.

Consider two examples. First, as Schmitt and Elshtain point out, religious ideas about God as the sovereign of the cosmos gave rise to the worldly claim that the king is sovereign over his kingdom, or that the nation, parliament, or individual can be sovereign. The cluster of ideas concerning sovereignty forms the core of a number of political theories in the Western intellectual tradition. This is an instance of the first route that can transform commonplaces into topoi.

The second example is of a different nature: the biblical account of the flood and Noah's ark generated the belief that Noah's sons had populated the earth and all nations could be traced back to them. This idea gradually entered the European intellectual world. Later it began to play an important role in the emergence of comparative and historical linguistics and led to the formulation of theories about language families.[51] This illustrates the second route where commonplace ideas play the role of heuristics in the formation of new theories.

In this second example, the theories in question eventually became independent of the theological ideas: the scientific hypotheses about language families are intelligible, accessible, and refinable without presupposing any of the biblical beliefs about Noah's sons. In the first example, however, secular notions of sovereignty cannot simply be cut loose from their religious background. This background appears necessary to make sense of the very idea of sovereignty.[52]

This is related to another important characteristic of topoi: they exhibit some sort of structure or coherence. They are not isolated ideas but consist

---

[51] Trautmann (1997).
[52] Van Duffel (2007).

of clusters of interlinked ideas. Taken together, all these clusters do not form a coherent whole. Their mutual relationships are variable. It could be a relationship of relevance or irrelevance, compatibility or incompatibility, coherence or incoherence, and dependence or independence. However, the fact that topoi operate in clusters has a major consequence. More often than not, one cannot understand one set of ideas without drawing on other related sets of ideas. Because of this, topoi often continue to depend in some way on the theological tropes from which they emerged. Accordingly, as the tropes remain present in the background of a culture's conceptual world, they give coherence to the 'secular' clusters of ideas and constitute their conditions of intelligibility.

These technical terms allow us to succinctly formulate the hypothesis on secularization: secularization is the process whereby *tropes* of a particular theology are transformed into *topoi* of a culture or society. That is, recurrent patterns in a religion's traditions of theological reasoning are secularized into the clusters of commonplace ideas that constitute the social, political, and cultural theorizing of a culture or society.

What are the strengths of this hypothesis? First of all, it does not require the kind of hard and fast distinction between 'religious' and 'secular' ideas that is impossible to draw. New tropes of some theological tradition could very well derive from 'secular' topoi already present in a culture; in the form of topoi, originally theological ideas can give rise to new scientific concepts. Theological tropes and secularized topoi interact in much the same way as the dialectic between the two moments of secularization and proselytization.

Second, Blumenberg's relevant objections to Löwith's secularization thesis are met. Indeed, it does not make sense to suggest about a variety of ideas that 'B is the secularized A' as though there is a one-to-one relationship between the substance of a theological idea and its secular counterpart. Balagangadhara's hypothesis concerning the moment of secularization shows the complexity involved: tropes are patterns of reasoning that become commonplaces of a culture and can then be transformed into topoi that constitute social and political theories. Both tropes and topoi consist of clusters of ideas which are articulated and interpreted in many ways and combined and recombined to build different theories.

Topoi also function as heuristics for the formulation of independent theories and thus the moment of secularization of the double dynamic of religion does account for innovations and the generating of new ideas. It is not necessarily the case that the secularized set of ideas B becomes unintelligible without the background of the religious set of ideas A. The relationship among topoi and between topoi and tropes can take several forms, which can now be elaborated by refining Balagangadhara's hypothesis.

Third, this explanation of secularization is able to make sense of historical facts. As Ann Moss has shown, one of the concerns of medieval Christendom was the spreading of theological knowledge among the populace. This resulted in sermons and *florilegia*: a kind of handbook for producing sermons, consisting of quotations from the Bible, the church fathers, respected theologians, and pagan philosophers, indexed and classified in terms of topics relevant to the life of the believer. This classification followed fixed levels of theological authority. Scripture came first, then certain church fathers, and later theologians. Passages from classical philosophy could serve only as illustrations of truths already established.

Out of this tradition grew a new genre of texts and mode of learning: that of the commonplace books. These books emerged during the Renaissance and were associated with the educational programme of humanism. They dominated European education throughout the sixteenth and seventeenth centuries. Students and scholars kept notebooks divided into headings and sub-headings, under which exemplary quotations from various sources were brought together and fitted into the conceptual framework of Christianity.[53] Thus, theological ideas were transmitted in society as commonplaces about the human and the divine. In the development of early modern social and political theories, these commonplaces were then transformed into topoi: they became building blocks for the theorizing of thinkers from Bodin to Bayle and from Hobbes to Helvetius.[54]

Fourth, the hypothesis on the double dynamic of religion is not confined to the realm of ideas. It offers a more general account of the emergence of the secular world in Western-Christian societies. That is, it shows how Christianity generates a 'secular' *Lebenswelt* (lifeworld), ordered by a series

---

[53] Moss (1996).
[54] De Roover, Claerhout, and Balagangadhara (2011).

of religious patterns, structures, and attitudes. The result is a Christian secular world where political life, urban patterns, social relations, and everyday practices are reorganized by the secularization of this religion.

For an illustration of this dimension of secularization, consider Balagangadhara's account of the monasticization of daily life in post-Reformation Europe, elaborated in Chapter 3. The monasteries of early medieval Christianity had developed a Christian form of life based in Scripture: the process of *conversio* or gradual conversion to God. In this process, monks were called upon to obey God's will in the form of monastic rules. Inevitably, they failed to do so and discovered the darkness at the heart of their existence. Nevertheless, they could never cease the attempt to obey God and had to travel through the same circle again and again. They gained an ever-deeper awareness of human sin and the inconceivable fact that God loved them in spite of their iniquity. Thus, they also realized that only God could give them true faith and righteousness.

Gradually, this monastic process of conversion began to shape the life world of lay believers. Eventually, the Protestant Reformation claimed that every Christian had to undergo conversion, turn to God in the same way, fail to live up to His will because of sin, and ultimately realize that only total surrender to God helps. Balagangadhara suggests that the secularization of this process of conversion gave shape to Western normative ethics (the incessant attempt and failure to do what one ought to do) and thus, monasticized Western daily life. This process continues unto this day. Progressively, human existence and all its domains are being 'normed' in the Western world: normativity expands and encompasses more and more dimensions of human existence from the political to the erotic.

This is but a rough sketch of Balagangadhara's theory of religion and its double dynamic, but its potential to generate new accounts of the emergence of liberal secularism must be clear. The crystallization of this political model during the last few centuries can be understood in terms of the two moments of proselytization and secularization that constitute the historical unfolding of Western Christianity. The double dynamic of religion produced a model for coexistence that allowed different Christian confessions to live together in relatively peaceful ways. Once we have a better understanding of this process, we will also be able to raise the issue of the relationship between liberal political theory and Christian political theology from a new perspective.

A Religious Culture

How does Balagangadhara's theory establish that Western culture is a *religious* culture? One dimension of its religiosity is determined by the double dynamic of religion. However, this leads to a second more fundamental dimension: Christian religion has generated Western culture as a distinct configuration of learning.

The fundamental problem of human existence is that of learning to survive in the world and creating a habitat where human beings can live and flourish. Balagangadhara argues that the human species produced different kinds of knowledge and associated learning processes to do so. One is theoretical knowledge: knowledge *about* what exists in the world. This knowledge takes the form of beliefs and claims about phenomena. The prototypical examples of theoretical knowledge are the natural sciences. Another form of knowledge is practical or performative knowledge. This is knowledge embodied by actions, which allows us to build human relationships and go about in the world and with each other.

These two and several other kinds of knowledge are present in all cultures and societies. However, constitutive of a culture is the configuration established among the types of knowledge. Here, religion comes in. As an explanatorily intelligible account, it becomes the root model of order: its explanation embodies God's order and the object of its explanation (the cosmos) does the same; hence, a religious account perfectly mirrors the structure of the object it seeks to explain. In this sense, religion is the prototype of all explanation. As the root model of order, religion makes theoretical knowledge into the dominant form of knowledge. Theoretical learning becomes the meta-learning process of a culture: that is, explanation and description become the means through which one learns to learn. Thus, a configuration of learning comes into being.

Religion is an entity that orders the relationship between different kinds of knowledge and thus generates a configuration of learning. Western culture is one such configuration, where theoretical knowledge is dominant. Here, this type of knowledge subordinates to itself all other forms of knowledge, including practical knowledge. This happens because theoretical learning, or learning *about the world*, becomes the meta-learning process of a culture. The dominance of theoretical knowledge impacts all domains of life: in order to build a good society, one needs a political theory to explain what such a society would look like; to be a good mother, a woman has to know what a good mother is; a city should be planned in terms of a conceptual scheme; art embodies ideas or concepts; our lives should be meaningful and planned, and so on.

This dominance of theoretical learning has also determined Western cultural attitudes towards other cultures. The assumption is that human beings cannot orient themselves in the world without a belief system or representation of the world. Consequently, in order to go about with people from another culture, one needs to know what the central beliefs of that culture are: its religion, world view, or belief system. When one encounters alien practices, one desires to understand the reasons *why* people participate in these practices. Practices are connected to beliefs in a particular way: they are viewed as expressions of beliefs. Hence, one can always raise the issue of justifying a practice in terms of the underlying reasons or beliefs and ask whether these beliefs are true or well founded.

Recently, Balagangadhara has taken further steps in theorizing the dominance of theoretical knowledge in Western culture. He points out that human practices cannot be founded in reason. Practical knowledge does not have its foundation in theoretical knowledge. It has its own domain, namely that of human relationships. But reason does have another role to play in the growth of human practice: that of reflecting on practice, constraining its potential excesses, rejecting some practices, and reordering the relation among different practices. Here, reasonableness becomes crucial. Reasonableness is the attempt to make the common-sense ideas, heuristics, and attitudes of a culture as compatible and coherent with each other as possible. This never-ending pursuit enables reason to rearrange practices and ideas in such a way that a better, more reasonable, pattern comes into being.

Balagangadhara contrasts reasonableness to rationality, a tendency, or a project (and its associated set of attitudes) dominant in the Western intellectual traditions. Rationality is the attempt to found practice in reason. This project emerged from Christian theology and its goal of founding human practice in truth, in the biblical God's revelation of His will. Theologians desired to justify practices in terms of particular interpretations of Scripture. Next, secularization transformed this into a general inclination to justify actions by referring to reasons or to found practices in beliefs. One of the results is the stubborn conviction across the Western world that one can reform human societies and practices along the lines of some conceptual model or set of rules. In spite of the failure of past attempts to realize this, the cultural project of rationality has never been abandoned.[55]

At this second level, Balagangadhara's research programme offers a promising framework for examining the emergence of the liberal model. This model appears to be a part of the project of rationality, for it tries to find a conceptual foundation for coexistence. Its basic drive is the desire to identify some common ground or independent framework, however minimal, which should enable different communities to live together. Its basic assumption is that a society needs a shared framework in order to allow for the coexistence of communities. However, the ongoing attempt to formulate such a common framework also accounts for the peculiar intolerance at the heart of the liberal model: any tradition or community that does not fit into this framework, or refuses to conform to it, is rejected or compelled to change.

Cultures without Religion

How does Balagangadhara's account allow us to understand the differences between Western and Asian cultures? His work focuses on Indian culture, but much of what it says is valid for Asian cultures in general. Unlike the West, he argues, Asia is home to cultures without religion.

It must be clear from the foregoing that Hinduism, Buddhism, Jainism, and Sikhism are fictitious entities. They exist in the libraries and minds of the Western world but not among the people whose religions they are supposed to be. That is, these concepts describe patterns and entities in the cultural experience of the West, which do not correspond to the patterns in the Asian traditions' experience of themselves. Of course, these traditions do exist. However, their different elements are not related to each other in the way the discourse about 'the religions of India' presumes.

Instead of religions, these are traditions. Such traditions are not constituted by beliefs or founded in reasons. They consist of the practices and practical knowledge of a community handed down from generation to generation. They are generally approached as 'ancestral' traditions. Since the religious connection between practice and belief does not exist in these traditions, it does not make sense to ask why people participate

---

[55] See, for instance, Scott (1999).

in practices. The answer commonly given to such questions shows this: 'because our ancestors did so' or 'because my parents taught me to do things this way'. In other words, the demand that one justify traditional practices in terms of reasons is equivalent to imposing a concern of religion onto such traditions.

Because of the absence of doctrinal foundations, traditions have a particular kind of flexibility. It is not the case that any practice is justified (or compulsory) because it has been transmitted by ancestral generations or taught by one's parents. At any point, one can formulate good reasons to change, select, or put an end to some practice(s). What is transmitted from one generation to another is modified and adapted to the times. Yet, tradition is also characterized by a particular kind of conservatism. As it is the totality of practices transmitted by a group from generation to generation, which also constitutes the group, one does need good reasons to change some practice(s).

The emphasis on correct practice that is so characteristic of Asian cultures is a manifestation of their configuration of learning. Here, practical or performative knowledge is dominant. In these cultures, ritual plays the role that religion plays for Western culture: it is the entity that structures the relationship among different forms of knowledge and learning. 'Ritual' refers to actions without meaning, purpose, or goal. While individuals participating in a specific ritual may give a variety of reasons or beliefs to account for the ritual, the ritual action is independent of these reasons. Ritual is pure action. As such, it generates a configuration of learning where all forms of learning, including theoretical knowledge, are subordinated to practical knowledge and its learning process. Practical or performative learning is the meta-learning process that dominates Asian cultures. This learning process takes the form of mimetic learning: one learns predominantly through mimesis or by imitating actions.

One implication is that reasonableness is highly developed in the intellectual traditions of Indian culture, while rationality is largely absent. These traditions do not attempt to give a foundation for practice in reason. The role attributed to reason is very different: that of systematic reflection upon practices, and modifying, rearranging, or constraining them wherever there are good reasons to do so. It is only after the encounter with Western culture and its emphasis on giving rational foundations for practices that members of the Indian traditions began to feel the need to produce the 'scientific reasons' behind their practices.

Some Potential Objections

Balagangadhara's work has met with some objections. Three sets of claims keep recurring in the writings of his critics: (*a*) He defines 'religion' in a way that takes Christianity as the prototypical model of religion and then infers that the traditions of India cannot be religions. Thus, he himself presupposes a theological definition of religion.[56] (*b*) His theory of religion ignores the tremendous internal diversity within Christianity and confuses a Protestant-Deist model with the basic structure of religion.[57] More generally, his argument 'seems to have little space for situating the *internal* conflicts within cultures, the million diversities that make us doubt whether "cultures" exist as stable objects of knowing'.[58] (*c*) He exaggerates the differences between Judaism, Christianity, and Islam, on the one hand, and the Asian cultural traditions, on the other hand, and ignores their many family resemblances. Hence, he fails to see that all of these do belong to the category of religion when it is broadly defined.[59]

All three objections betray a misunderstanding of Balagangadhara's theory and larger research programme. Consider the first: he is said to presuppose that 'the Abrahamic religions are the sole model for the concept of religion', which 'leads him to claim that any major features they share, and only those, are crucial'. He then builds on these criteria 'to exclude anything Asian from the category'.[60] Similarly, he supposedly concludes that Hinduism is not a religion by using 'a definition of religion' that 'is explicitly modelled upon Christianity'.[61] The critics in question suggest that the academic study of religion has left behind such narrow notions of religion. We now realize that not all religions are like Christianity. Instead of arguing that religion is a Western-Christian notion, which 'cannot have any valid cross-cultural meaning', 'all competent scholars' are aware that 'exact analytical definitions like those in the natural sciences cannot be formulated for "religion" ..., because only polythetic definitions relying on

---

[56] Fuller (2012); Guthrie (1996); Larson (1997); Sweetman (2003).
[57] Almond (1996), p. 144; Sweetman (2003), p. 339.
[58] Das Gupta (2005), p. 16.
[59] Fuller (2012).
[60] Guthrie (1996), p. 163.
[61] Sweetman (2003), pp. 337–9.

"family resemblances" among significant characteristics can be employed cross-culturally'.[62]

How valuable is this type of objection? These authors confuse between a definition and a hypothesis. Definitions tell us how we use a word and which objects it refers to. In the case of 'religion', a definition should address this referential task of identifying which things are referred to when this word is used. The act of defining this word cannot give us any understanding of the structure or properties of religion and does not have any empirical consequences (as is the case for defining any other word, say 'species' or 'psychosis'). It merely points out the phenomena that are to be theorized. The result of this second process of theorizing is a hypothesis, which characterizes the properties or structures of a phenomenon.

When one confuses between defining a word and theorizing a phenomenon, as these authors do, one faces a dead end: it is as though the aim of a definition is to classify objects and decide whether or not they belong to a particular category. But this generates disputes that cannot be settled. Imagine a scholar who defines 'religion' as a belief in supernatural beings or non-empirically verifiable entities. Another points out that ancient Greek religion does not involve supernatural beings (since Greek *theoi* [deities] belong to the natural world); hence, 'religion' requires another definition. The first author then says that theoi are non-empirically verifiable entities; therefore, ancient Greek traditions do belong to the category of religion. But then the second points out that many particles predicted by theoretical physics are not empirically verifiable; hence, theoretical physics would also be a religion according to this definition. Our second author could then point out that we need a definition focusing on family resemblances.

This exchange illustrates the problem: when one confuses the task of defining 'religion' (by pointing out its referent) with the task of classification, one ends up in disputes as interminable as disputes about taste. Scholars keep inventing definitions that should accommodate their intuition that all cultures have religion or that some tradition is 'not really a religion'. The resulting definitions are inadequate and increasingly vague. Consequently, we now face a cemetery of discarded definitions of 'religion' and scholars who try to justify this situation by saying that one cannot expect 'exact analytical definitions'.

---

[62] Fuller (2012), p. 665.

When Balagangadhara suggests that religion is an explanatorily intelligible account of the cosmos and itself, he is *not* providing a definition but a hypothesis. Naturally, as a first step in the process of theory building, the term 'religion' needs to be defined so that we know which object(s) should be theorized. We could say that 'religion' has no referents in the world, but this is an epistemic decision that cannot be taken *before* developing a theory. Instead, Balagangadhara suggests the following: we provide an *ostensive* definition of 'religion' by pointing out an instance of how we use the word. Minimally, 'religion' refers to Christianity, since Christianity has used the word to refer to itself and to certain others. In that sense, Christianity is taken as a prototypical example of *what we refer to when we use the word 'religion'*.

But this does not imply that the characteristics of Christianity are those of religion. To avoid making this mistake, Balagangadhara characterizes the constraints that any hypothesis about religion should live up to. First, Christianity has used the term 'religion' to refer to itself and to certain others as its religious rivals: Islam, Judaism, Roman *religio*, Hindu traditions, and so on. This has resulted in a particular set of descriptions invoking the term 'religion'. Second, Islam and Judaism not only recognized themselves in such descriptions, but also provided similar descriptions of each other and of Christianity. Moreover, they described the same others (Roman religio in the case of Judaism, Hindu traditions in the case of Islam) as religious rivals. Thus, using whatever word they may have used, they share a basic notion of religion with Christianity. Third, the followers of Roman religio and the Hindu traditions recognized neither themselves nor Islam and Christianity in these descriptions. In fact, they showed a remarkable indifference and blindness towards the idea that all of these were religious rivals. Any hypothesis about religion should be able to account for this set of historical facts. That is, it should explain as to why the Semitic religions recognized each other and the same others as religious rivals, while 'pagan' traditions failed to recognize themselves and the relevant others in these descriptions.

One could attempt to develop the required hypothesis about religion by means of an inductive approach: that is, studying the vast body of descriptions that Christianity, Islam, Judaism, and the 'pagan' traditions have given of each other and then trying to infer a hypothesis that accounts for all these descriptions. But this would be a cumbersome process and its success would be highly doubtful. Instead, Balagangadhara takes a different route: that of formulating a hypothesis and deriving its logical and empirical consequences so as to test whether this hypothesis is able to account for past phenomena and predict new facts.

Since this hypothesis does not rely on induction (inferring some common structure of religion by culling over the available descriptions), it does not build on any 'Christian' definition or 'Abrahamic' concept of religion. Rather than being founded in any such concept or definition, it is formulated independently. Consequently, its relation to the available body of 'Abrahamic' and 'pagan' conceptions of religion is different. These function as tests or constraints for the hypothesis: it should account for both sets of conceptions in one move without ad hoc modifications. And it does.

The second objection is equally misguided. A hypothesis about the structure of a phenomenon does not deny that there can be many diverse instances of this phenomenon. Evolutionary theorizing concerning a species called *Homo sapiens* does not ignore the tremendous variety among human beings. Similarly, the hypothesis that all religions share the structure of an explanatorily intelligible account does not deny that each religion has internal diversity. Different schools, strands, and theologians in Christianity (or Islam or Judaism) give different accounts of what it means for the cosmos to embody God's purpose or for human beings to worship Him. However, these strands remain within particular limits. They cannot deny, for instance, that the universe is infused with a divine order, purpose, or plan.

Still, Balagangadhara's theorizing not only accounts for the common structures of religion, but also for the internal differentiation that results from its double dynamic of universalization. Different strands emerge from the interplay between the two moments of proselytization and secularization. Of course, this hypothesis cannot explain the details of the specific theologies developed by individual Christian thinkers, but it can make sense of their common concerns and conflicts. Moreover, this theory is able to show how the secularization of a religion inevitably gives rise to progressively vague and generic accounts, which do not always explicitly refer to a sovereign creator, God.

Finally, the third objection: Balagangadhara exaggerates the differences and denies the similarities between religions like Christianity and Islam and the traditions of Asia. If one recognizes the family resemblances, one cannot but admit that they are just different *kinds* of religion. This objection is best tackled by means of an analogy.

At first sight, it may appear obvious that whales are the same kind of organisms as, say, sharks, lampoonfish, groupers, and so on. They all seem to be fish: all live in water, swim, and spend long stretches of time under water. When we learn that whales are different because they do not lay eggs but give birth to live young, this may lead to the following qualification: whales are a different *kind* of fish. As such, they have certain distinct properties: they breathe through blowholes rather than gills; they are endothermic while most fish are exothermic; they feed their young through mammary glands; and they have body hair.

Scholars could view these as properties of *a different kind of fish*. To anyone who says whales are not fish but a very different kind of organism, one could then repeatedly point out the properties shared by whales with other fish: they are vertebrates, aquatic, and have fins and a tail. Given these family resemblances, one can continue to insist that they must be fish, merely of a different kind. In the absence of a theory, such classificatory discussions are never-ending.

Once evolutionary theory began to develop, it became clear that the differences between fish and whales are fundamental and make them distinct kinds of organisms. Whales are mammals. But only the framework of evolutionary theory (or another theory) can show why these differences are so vital. In fact, such a conceptual framework is required for us to filter certain properties and view them as relevant similarities, family resemblances, or salient differences. Even more important, this framework has us relate certain properties to each other in a coherent pattern.

Given this analogy, the following point must be clear: the fact that Asian traditions like those of India have properties or family resemblances in common with Christianity, Islam, and Judaism can never constitute evidence for the claim that all of these are variants of the same phenomenon of religion (but just different kinds of religion). Similarly, merely pointing out the differences between Asian traditions and the Semitic religions does not constitute evidence for the claim that these two are distinct kinds of phenomena (and not different kinds of religion). Again, this disagreement can only be settled in terms of a theory.

This generates a question: Which theory made it so self-evident that the Asian traditions and Semitic religions are the same kind of phenomenon, given the striking differences between them? This self-evidence depends on the secularization of the conceptual framework of Christian doctrine. Against this background, it is obvious that these must all be variants of religion. For generations, this background framework has caused us to filter out certain 'salient properties' of these traditions and describe them in a particular way. And it then has us relate these 'family resemblances' to each other in an apparently coherent pattern. Eventually, this descriptive pattern makes it obvious that what goes on in a Hindu temple is very similar to what goes on in a Catholic Church (namely, divine worship) or that devas are the same kind of being as God.

Balagangadhara's alternative theory of religion challenges this background framework and demonstrates how the Asian traditions and Judaism, Christianity, and Islam are not variants of the same phenomenon. Generally, attacking such a new framework by giving arguments and counter-arguments is not a fruitful endeavour. Indeed, one can always point out that its alternative hypotheses do not correspond to the self-evident 'facts' of the old framework. However, the real test of an alternative research programme does not lie in potential objections to some of its particular claims. It lies in its capacity to be elaborated, refined, clarified, and tested in order to make better sense of the world.

The Route Ahead

This chapter aimed to contrast Balagangadhara's research programme to some of the frameworks available for telling the story of the emergence of liberal secularism in Europe and India. The remainder of this book will try to give an alternative account by drawing upon this new theoretical framework. The research programme's basic hypotheses and conceptual tools should allow us to deal with the problems identified in the introduction and the first chapter. They also predict the routes where solutions can be found.

First, to get a handle on the conceptual structures of the liberal model and its central puzzle of the two spheres, I look into the process whereby tropes of Christian political theology were transformed into topoi of liberal political theory. The first task will be to identify the recurrent patterns of theological reasoning that gave shape to early modern thinking about the questions of religious freedom and toleration. We need to find out how these conceptual patterns derive from dynamics within Western Christendom. This is what Chapter 3 sets out to do.

Second, there is the question as to how and why European political thinkers felt the need to build a normative framework for resolving conflicts between religious communities in European society. The urge to create and enforce such a shared framework for religious coexistence must be related to the increasingly dominant tendency towards rationality in Western-Christian culture. Chapter 4 looks into the crystallization of the normative framework of toleration, its relation to specific religious dynamics within post-Reformation Europe, and the fundamental intolerance located at its heart.

Third, the moment of secularization of Christianity's double dynamic of religion has played a central role in the formation of Western political thinking. If that is the case, the issue arises as to how secular the liberal model of the secular state and religious toleration really is. Is it indeed 'secular', that is, non-religious or neutral? To address this issue, Chapter 5 studies the conceptual relations between the Enlightenment discourse on religious toleration and the theological debates that had preceded it in the sixteenth and seventeenth centuries.

Fourth, the thesis that Western culture is a religious culture has two vital consequences. On the one hand, many of the topoi and ideas common to European societies may turn out to be culture-specific ideas that fail to make sense outside the framework of Christian religion. This entails that these ideas should encounter unexpected problems of unintelligibility and sterility when they travel to cultures beyond the West. On the other hand, the public institutions and policies that crystallized in Europe will have similar links to the religious dynamic that constitutes Western culture. When such institutions and policies are implemented in a completely different socio-cultural setting, this will have unpredictable effects on social and cultural life, which may be wholly unintended. To examine the importance of these two consequences, Chapters 6 and 7 travel to colonial and postcolonial India and assess how the liberal model and its secularism discourse have fared in this new socio-cultural setting.

Finally, the conclusion will try to explicate some of the lessons we can draw from this alternative story about the emergence of the liberal model of secularism. What should an alternative model of pluralism look like? Rather than address this question directly, I will do so indirectly by reflecting upon some of the flaws of the liberal model that should be avoided by any future alternative.

3. The Political Theology of the Two Kingdoms

Christs Kingdom is of another World, and requires none of the Policy of this to manage it; it ought to be kept pure and unmixt, being clear of another nature: We see Oyl in a Vessel of Water will not mix, but keep its Body intire to itself, no more ought Spirituals to be mixt with Temporals. But these Spiritual Politicians have mixt Heaven and Earth together, confounded the World with their Policy, and so jumbled things together, that Christianity is almost lost in the Composition, so that men know not where to find it.[1]

W here did the separation of human society into a political sphere and a religious sphere originate? Which conceptual background made this into a significant and sensible distinction? To find answers, we need to travel far back into the history of Western Christianity. The distinction between the temporal and the spiritual, or

---

[1] Anonymous (1688b), p. 17.

this world and the other world, has been essential to Christianity and its understanding of human existence from the very beginning. According to the Gospel, Jesus not only said, 'My kingdom is not of this world' (John 18:36 [King James Bible]), but also instructed his followers to 'render to Caesar the things that are Caesar's, and to God the things that are God's' (Luke 20:20 [KJB]; Mark 12:17 [KJB]).

Building on the biblical distinction between two worlds, the early medieval pope Gelasius I identified two powers for the government of humanity: *regnum* or the royal power, which dealt with material temporal matters, and *sacerdotium*, the priestly power, which cared for spiritual and eternal matters. Medieval thinkers often put this in terms of a metaphor of two swords, each of which had its own sphere of activity.[2] This distinction between the temporal and the spiritual would play a crucial role not only in the Papal Revolution that shook medieval Christendom, but also in the Protestant Reformation that was to transform early modern Europe.

This chapter introduces the hypothesis that the conceptual foundations of the liberal model of religious toleration and secularism were laid by a specific theological framework developed during the Protestant Reformation. It will trace the crystallization of this political theology of Christian freedom and the two kingdoms. Freedom in Christianity was a function of the process of conversion or gradual submission to God's will. Originally, only monks and priests were supposed to go through this lifelong process, which gave them spiritual freedom and the authority to guide the laity.

The Protestant Reformation monasticized daily life by transforming the monastic process of conversion into a general process that was to shape the lives of *all* believers. Here, the moment of secularization took the form of breaking down the walls of the monastery and the Church so that Christian modes of living and institutional structures could reshape the secular world. Along with the secularization of these components of medieval Christianity, however, the Protestant Reformation also generated its own conceptions of true religion. These consistently rejected the trappings of the Roman-Catholic Church and its priesthood as false religion, that is, human additions to divine revelation.

---

[2] Bethke Elshtain (2008), pp. 29–55; Morris (1989), p. 17.

Out of this transformation emerged the Protestant theology of Christian freedom. This was a normative theological framework, which claimed that all believers ought to be free from human interference in the spiritual realm. By implication, this theology also divided human existence into two realms or kingdoms: the spiritual kingdom, where no man could rule but God alone, and the political kingdom, where the believer should always obey secular authorities. Across Reformation Europe, the political theory of the two kingdoms would constitute the basic framework for debates concerning religious toleration and freedom.

Conversion, Law, and Liberty

What does it mean to be a Christian? This question has kept Christian thinkers busy from the time it became clear that Christ's second coming was not imminent. Once Christianity began to dominate the Roman Empire, martyrdom no longer sufficed to define the true Christian. What divine purpose lay behind the prolonging of the phase between Christ's sacrificial death and the advent of the heavenly kingdom? How should Christians live in the saeculum, this temporal worldly age that would last until the second coming of Christ?[3]

The Process of Conversion

The aim of the Christian was submission to God, this much was clear. The true Christian lived to obey his Creator and submit his own purposes to the divine purpose. In early medieval monasteries, this aim brought about the genesis of a process that structured the lives of the monks, the process of *conversio* or conversion. In this lifelong process of reform or regeneration, 'man turned to God and was reformed to His image'.[4]

From a theological perspective, the basic idea was that human nature had been created in the image of God. But original sin corrupted this nature and humanity became the slave of the sinful flesh. The soul lost its command of the body.[5] As a consequence, human beings are all too

---

[3] See Markus (1988) and (1990).
[4] Ladner (1967); Morrison (1992); Tellenbach (1993), pp. 102–3.
[5] Augustine (2000), p. 13.

easily seduced by the devil to live carnal lives and give in to the desires of their sinful bodies. All they care for is food, property, sex, and the satisfaction of self-interest. Monks were aware of the disorder of this life and of human guilt, and wished to escape from sin by becoming truly spiritual. The escape route was the process of conversion, which could recover the divine spark of potentiality still remaining in the human being.[6]

The monastic orders elaborated and institutionalized this process of conversion in various ways, but everywhere it shared certain properties. First, there was the role of monastic rules. Monks fought 'the devil within' and could no longer give in to the carnal desires of their bodies. Instead, they lived according to a strict ascetic discipline imposed by monastic rules, which were presented as God's own law.[7] A central function of these rules was to make the religious aware of the depth of human depravity. The rules were so strict and demanding that monks could not but fail to live up to them. The resulting experience was one of persistent failure to obey God, which kept reminding monks of their sinful nature: they were miserable wretches before Him, who nevertheless loved them and gifted them His grace.[8]

The second property is the belief that God's grace in Christ is the one force that can save sinful humanity from ruin. Not our human selves, but the Spirit and its gift of grace bring about conversion. As Augustine wrote, it is this importation of the Spirit of grace that elevates our will, without which the teaching of God's law is but 'the letter that killeth', only holding us guilty of transgression.[9] Divine grace alone can regenerate the soul and make the old man into the new, giving him the freedom to resist the seduction of sin and the clutches of the devil.[10]

Third, this process divides both the world and the human being into two realms. The temporal and the spiritual were viewed as two distinct worlds. One was the secular material world of earth, also referred to as 'this temporal world', which would last until the second coming of Christ. The other was the eternal spiritual world, also named 'the other world' or 'the heavenly kingdom'. This corresponded to a fundamental split in

---

[6] Morrison (1992), p. 29.

[7] P. King (1999), p. 76, p. 96, p. 387.

[8] See the description of this process in Balagangadhara (2005b).

[9] Augustine (1995a), p. 91.

[10] Tellenbach (1993), p. 106.

human existence: as bodies, we live earthly lives; as spirits, spiritual lives. The monks were expected to turn to God by moving away from the temporal carnal world to the eternal spiritual world.

True Christians lived in a perpetual struggle in which the spirit tried to control the flesh. Slowly, the spirit should become less carnal and the body more spiritual.[11] In his *Epistle to the Romans*, the apostle Paul had given a central role to this struggle between spirit and flesh in his explanation of the Christian faith. The law serves to reveal human sin: 'Therefore by the deeds of the law there shall no flesh be justified in his sight: for by the law is the knowledge of sin' (Rom. 3:20–23 [KJB]). But one cannot escape from sin through human efforts to obey the law. Only those who are in Jesus Christ, 'who walk not after the flesh, but after the Spirit', could be saved from destruction through sin' (Rom. 8:1 [KJB]).

Inevitably, believers would fail to attain full spirituality in their lives here on earth. The process of conversion could never be complete, for the hold of sin on humanity is too strong. Yet the lives of true Christians had to be shaped by never-ending reform.[12] The extent to which the believer was converted in this life on earth determined the degree of his freedom. 'Libertas' in early and medieval Christianity was the equivalent of submission to God's will. In so far as one was subject to God, one would no longer be subject to human authorities on earth. Men were free to the extent they had submitted themselves to God. The resulting freedom was the ability to resist the seduction of sin, given by God's grace in Christ.[13]

The church fathers elaborated this idea of Christian liberty in terms of a contrast between the Law of the Old Testament and Christ in the New Testament. Humanity desires good and strives by its own efforts to attain the good, regarding this as the command of the Law. But it becomes clear that we cannot live up to the Law. It is simply beyond our reach. Through His sacrificial death, Christ gained divine grace for man and through the gift of grace man obtained the power to do good from inner necessity. Thus, Christ overcame the compulsion and bondage of the Law by removing the reason for their existence.[14]

---

[11] Augustine (2000), p. 20
[12] Ladner (1967), p. 31; Morrison (1992), p. 75.
[13] Augustine (1995b), p. 472.
[14] Tellenbach (1991), pp. 4–5.

Freedom of the Church

In 1077, Pope Gregory VII forced the emperor of the Holy Roman Empire, Henry IV, to kneel in the snow near the Italian castle of Canossa and had him beg for papal absolution. This dramatic moment in the history of Western Christendom symbolized the power that would be possessed by the papacy during the next centuries. It was the culmination of a long, sometimes violent, struggle concerning the relation between secular authority and the religious authority of the Church.[15]

In the preceding centuries, monastic Christianity had harboured two tendencies: withdrawal from the world and reform of the world. The second tendency entailed that monks, who had reached a higher spiritual position, also gained the authority to 'convert' earthly society. They were asked to become bishops and leaders of the church. Thus emerged a trend to reform society by transforming it according to the image of the monastic community. The papal reform or revolution sounded the victory of this tendency within Western Christendom.[16]

Before the tenth century, the monastic world had gone through an attempt to unify the rules of various monasteries, centred on the Rule of Saint Benedict. In the eleventh and twelfth centuries, a reform movement intended to make the monasteries even more uniform and strict.[17] The institutional structures of the monastery functioned as models for the reform of the church in this period, which in effect amounted to *a monasticization of the Church*.

On the one hand, a common and coherent body of law was created out of the various monastic rules and ecclesiastic laws of Western Christendom. The result was the new comprehensive system of canon law that would govern the Church for centuries to come.[18] On the other hand, the papal reform was the culmination of an important change in Western Christendom: rather than the monk, the priest became the principal figure of Christian religion. Christianity turned into *a religion of the priest*. But priesthood was also modelled on the monastic life, in the sense

---

[15] Bethke Elshtain (2008), pp. 45–7.
[16] See Berman (1983); Morris (1989), pp. 98–9; Tellenbach (1991), p. 164.
[17] P. King (1999), pp. 103–58.
[18] See Berman (1983); Kuttner (1980).

that the priests had to go through the same process of vocation, reform, conversion, and purification.[19]

How did the priest gain spiritual authority? The idea of freedom as subjection to God became crucial to the medieval conception of the hierarchy. The extent of an individual's submission to God made him either ruler or subject.[20] According to the Church's theologians, not all men were capable of attaining the same spiritual standard. The clergy was superior to the laity, like adults were to children. Because of their asceticism, the monks went furthest in the subjection to God and thus occupied a high place in the holy hierarchy. But this hierarchy would become a reality only in the next world.

In contrast, the clerical hierarchy of the Church was to lead the people of God in this world. Thus, the libertas attained by priests and bishops corresponded to a superior position in this earthly life. As Cardinal Humbert put it:

> Anyone then who wishes to compare the priestly and royal dignities in a useful and blameless fashion may say that, in the existing church, the priesthood is analogous to the soul and the kingship to the body, for they cleave to one another and need one another and each in turn demands services and renders them one another. It follows from this that, just as the soul excels the body and commands it, so too the priestly dignity excels the royal or, we may say, the heavenly dignity the earthly. Thus, that all things may be in due order and not in disarray the priesthood, like a soul, may advise what is to be done.[21]

This analogy to the soul's command of the body symbolized the aims of papal reform. Priests and monks were 'the religious', forming 'the spiritual estate' as opposed to 'the temporal estate'. The clergy was not only superior to, but also responsible for the laity. The Church came to be identified primarily with the clergy, whereas the laity became the flock guided to salvation by its shepherds.

According to the papal reformers, the mystery of ordination had raised the priests above ordinary humanity. Therefore, it was obvious to them

---

[19] Tellenbach (1993), p. 128.
[20] Tellenbach (1991), p. 41.
[21] Excerpted in Tierney (1964), p. 42.

that the Church had to be free from lay domination.[22] Until the eleventh century, many Christian churches had been the property of temporal rulers (the so-called *Eigenkirchen*). Priests were selected, instated, and paid by these laymen. Similarly, the ordination or investiture of bishops was in the hands of the Emperor and other lay authorities. This was intolerable to reformers like Cardinal Humbert and the monk Hildebrand, who would later be appointed as Pope Gregory VII. They argued that clerics could not possibly be invested with a church by laymen, since the latter were spiritually inferior to the former. The laymen had to be content with the position properly theirs in the ecclesiastical order, 'the passive position of a minor who cannot act for himself'. With the battle cry of 'libertas ecclesiae' (freedom of the church), the reformers set out to restore right order in the Christian world and free the Church from all forms of lay domination.[23]

In this sense, the hierarchical relationship between the religious (priests) and the secular (rulers) depended on the process of conversion. The temporal world was the kingdom of bondage, where men were doomed to live under the yoke of Satan and sin. Responding to their vocation, priests turned away from this world towards the spiritual kingdom of God. Through this process, they attained Christian freedom, reached a superior position in the hierarchy, and gained spiritual authority over the laity.[24] The Holy Spirit conferred the gift of grace upon the priests, since they were true servants of God. Through the spiritual leadership of the priest, the layman could then share in this divine grace. Priests became channels of God's grace to the laity.

Once it had become widely accepted that the vocation of priests gave them spiritual authority, the church hierarchy was reinforced: the priests performed sacraments, took confession, and prescribed penance. The Church prescribed orthodox belief and surrender to the priestly hierarchy as the sole route to salvation. Its authority included the power to discipline the laity in this temporal world through a range of measures

---

[22] Tellenbach (1991), p. 134.

[23] Tellenbach (1991), p. 111, p. 126; see also Tierney (1964), p. 40.

[24] See the letter by Pope Gregory VII to the Bishop of Metz, justifying his deed of deposing and excommunicating King Henry IV, excerpted in Tierney (1964), pp. 69–70.

like excommunication and execution. Hence, it was unthinkable that the hierarchy of priests be subject to the laws of temporal authorities. Instead, the Church 'set out to reform both itself and the world by law'.[25]

The Spiritual and the Secular

The papal reform had revolved around the relationship between the secular powers and the spiritual authority of the clergy. However, it is important to note that this was not a battle for the power and scope of religious authority as against a secular authority standing independently from the religious. The conceptual distinction between the 'spiritual' and the 'secular' had always been drawn *within* the religious framework of Christianity.[26] It corresponded to the division of the world into an invisible eternal realm and temporal earthly realm and that of the human being into spirit and flesh. At the close of the papal reform, the prominent theologian, Hugh of Saint Victor, summed up the foundations of its political theology:

> There are two lives, one earthly, the other heavenly, one corporeal, the other spiritual. By one the body lives from the soul, by the other the soul lives from God. Each has its own good by which it is invigorated and nourished so that it can subsist. The earthly life is nourished with earthly goods, the spiritual life with spiritual goods. To the earthly life belong all things that are earthly, to the spiritual life all goods that are spiritual ... Among laymen, to whose zeal and forethought the things that are necessary for earthly life pertain, the power is earthly. Among the clergy, to whose office the goods of the spiritual life belong, the power is divine. The one power is therefore called secular, the other spiritual.[27]

This demonstrates the extent to which the spiritual–secular distinction depended on an elaborate theological edifice. Without the support of a cluster of Christian-theological notions—soul and body, the earthly and spiritual life, divine power and the kingdom of Christ, and so on—this distinction would dissolve into thin air.

[25] Berman (1983), p. 83.

[26] Similar points are made by S.D. Smith (2010), pp. 112–17 and by Stolzenberg (2007), pp. 30–1.

[27] Hugh of Saint Victor, *De Sacramentis Christinae Fidei*, excerpted in Tierney (1964), pp. 94–5.

Rather than being general categories of human society, 'the spiritual' and 'the secular' were theological terms embedded in this larger framework. Christianity attributed these two spheres to all human societies, but this again was a theoretical claim of its theological anthropology. In other words, a specific religious framework not only drew the distinction between the spiritual and the secular but also determined the scope of these two realms.

Faith, Conversion, and the Freedom of a Christian

From the twelfth century onwards, popular movements began to reject the papal reform's goal of a hierarchically organized church intervening in every area of life. Common to these movements was a deep concern for the sin and salvation of individual believers. Penitence had become an obsession of popular preaching and lay religiosity in late medieval Christendom. Distress about the need for contrition and conversion grew among the believers. This concern for the spirituality of lay believers generated distrust towards the priestly hierarchy as mediators between the laity and God. In this 'age of anticlericalism', the populace challenged the avarice of the clergy and the tyranny of the church. Many pointed out that the priests were not truly spiritual but slaves of carnal desire.[28]

Anticlerical sentiment was intertwined with the growth of lay piety. Groups of lay people gathered together for spiritual comfort and social support by means of private worship and gospel study. In order to become truly spiritual, they emulated the asceticism of the monks.[29] Thus, the strictures and structures of monastic conversion began to shape the lives of these lay believers. The process, however, lost some of its typical features while spreading in society. Most notably, the need to live in a monastery and submit oneself to monastic rules disappeared. This secularization of the process of conversion or its diffusion in lay society generated the great heresies of the fourteenth and fifteenth centuries. Gradually, it gained the momentum needed to erupt into the Protestant Reformation of the sixteenth century.[30]

[28] Elm (1993), p. 13; Moore (1987), p. 19; Moore (1994), p. 69; Moore (1995), p. 27; Thayer (2002).

[29] Glover (1984), p. 21; Reventlow (1984), pp. 23–7; Moore (1987), p. 21.

[30] Glover (1984), pp. 45–6.

The Monasticization of Daily Life

Whereas the Papal Revolution had extended the monastic process of conversion to the church and its clergy, the Protestant Reformation now extended it to all Christians. In this way, it initiated a monasticization of daily life. The Reformers' anticlericalism was closely related to the expansion of conversion. As a process that now structured the lives of lay believers, it eroded the foundations of the clerical hierarchy. Often, laymen believed they were more genuine about the ascetic apostolic life than clerics. Stories about lecherous priests and gluttonous monks gained popularity. More and more, the Church was considered an impediment to the flourishing of true Christian faith and its process of spiritual conversion. Instead of conforming to clerical authority, lay believers were expected to go through an individual process of subjection to God's will, modelled on the monastic process of conversion. The result was the Protestant Reformation's conception of faith.

This conception consisted of several steps. In the first step, a Christian should try and live up to the law of God. The purpose of these attempts, however, is to reveal the nature of human sin. No matter how hard we try, we cannot resist the seduction of sin and continue to violate God's law.[31]

Persistent failure to live up to the law brings us to the second step. We begin to despair of our own ability to do good. In his *First Sermon at Wittenberg* (1522), Luther stressed this: 'In the first place, we must know that we are the children of wrath, and all our works, intentions, and thoughts are nothing at all'.[32] To John Calvin, it was equally obvious that we should realize that God alone can do good and that we rely on Him at all times.[33] Without this kind of self-knowledge, there can be no knowledge of God. We first have to become aware of 'the world of miseries' within ourselves, to be stripped of all confidence in our own ability, before we can receive knowledge of God.[34]

---

[31] See Luther's early text, *The Heidelberg Disputation* (1518), in Luther (1989).

[32] Luther (1989), p. 414.

[33] Calvin (1960), vol. 1, p. 13.

[34] Calvin (1960), vol. 1, pp. 35–6.

The third step is reached when the believer realizes that God promises to save him in spite of sin. In Christ, God has given the promise of grace. Once we despair of our own ability, we become aware that God's work alone can save us. Righteousness is attained only through absolute faith in Christ. The worst thing a man can do is to believe in his own or other men's achievements in the search for grace and righteousness before God. We do not depend on ourselves but on something outside ourselves, the promise and truth of God, which cannot deceive.

The final step is to yield completely to the Lord's promise of grace in Christ. This surrender is true faith and genuine subjection to God's will. But the believer should remain aware that even this is not his own work. It is the work of the Holy Spirit in the soul. Conversion of the will can be effected by divine grace alone.[35] Thus, the believer becomes but the passive recipient of God's grace.

Luther's reading of Scripture revolved around this gradual process of conversion. In his central tract *The Freedom of a Christian* (1520), he divided the Word of God into two significant parts: commandments and promises or Law and Gospel. The commandments express God's will for humanity. Although they tell us what we ought to do, they never give us the power to do it. In fact, they are intended to make us aware that we *cannot* do good as human beings, since we can never ourselves succeed in fulfilling the Law. These laws are only to make us despair of our own ability.[36] This is where the second part of Scripture comes to our aid. It tells us that in Christ we are promised grace, righteousness, peace, liberty, and all things. Simply through faith in Christ, these promises declare, we can fulfil all commandments and subject ourselves to God's will.

The Protestant Reformation extended the medieval process of conversion to all believers. Before, the monks and priests had been the true Christians because of their vocation and conversion. Now God called *all* believers to conversion. *All were priests.* Through this monasticizing of everyday life, Christianity began to pervade society at a much deeper level than it ever had before. At times, the Reformers explicitly stated this goal. A Lutheran pastor suggested that every household had to be transformed

---

[35] Calvin (1960), vol. 1, p. 289, pp. 294–7.
[36] Luther (1989), p. 600.

into a monastery.[37] Calvin remarked that every family of the pious ought
to be a church.[38] By stripping it of its restrictive monastic features, the
basic schemes of the monastic way of life could structure the experience
of all believers, instead of that of priests and monks alone.

Spiritual Freedom and Temporal Law

The Reformation's transformation of Christian freedom undermined the
justification for the authority of the clerical hierarchy. In the medieval
understanding of libertas, the spiritual–temporal distinction had corresponded to that between clergy and laity. Because of the process of conversion and purification, priests commanded laymen much like the soul
should control the flesh. If the lay believer turned from the carnal to the
spiritual world in the same way as priests and monks, then he should also
gain the freedom corresponding to this submission to God's will. Luther,
Calvin, and other Reformers all agreed on this point. 'Christian freedom'
became the rallying cry of the Protestant struggle against what they called
'the tyranny of the papacy'.

The Protestant teaching of Christian liberty claimed that faith makes
us free from spiritual laws because these become redundant. Since God
alone can bring about the faith that allows us to come to justification before
Him, human actions and laws possibly lead to redemption. No law or work
ought to be considered necessary to salvation. This would mean we set up
our own human selves as idols, instead of having faith in God. In other
words, Christian faith releases our souls from the bondage of all human
works and laws, for these are made unnecessary to man's righteousness and
salvation. This was the basic message of Luther's *Freedom of a Christian*
(1520). 'Yes', Luther concluded, 'since faith alone suffices for salvation, I
need nothing except faith exercising the power and dominion of its own
liberty. Lo, this is the inestimable power and liberty of Christians.'[39]

Luther's companion Philip Melanchthon explained the nature of
Christian liberty in his *Loci Communes Theologici* (1521), the first systematic theological work of the Lutheran Reformation:

---

[37]   Karant-Nunn (1997), p. 40.
[38]   Calvin, *Commentaries on Genesis I* (part 25, § 12).
[39]   Luther (1989), p. 607.

Christianity is freedom, because those who do not have the Spirit of Christ cannot in any way perform the law; they are rather subject to the curse of the law. Those who have been renewed by the Spirit of Christ now conform voluntarily even without the law to what the law used to command. The law is the will of God; the Holy Spirit is nothing else than the living will of God and its being in action (*agitatio*). Therefore, when we have been regenerated by the Spirit of God, who is the living will of God, we now will spontaneously, that very thing which the law used to demand ... Therefore, freedom does not consist in this, that we do not observe the law, but that we will and desire spontaneously and from the heart what the law demands.[40]

This clarifies the idea: as sinful human beings, we necessarily fail to submit ourselves to the will of God. Therefore, the divine will has to act in us in the form of the Holy Spirit and bring about faith in our hearts. Thus, the Spirit gifts us 'new birth' or conversion: our souls are regenerated and cannot but live up to the law. The will of God now lives in us, so to speak.

Again and again, the magisterial Reformers emphasized that the power and liberty of the Christian are of a *spiritual* nature. As followers of Christ, we are free in spirit. But, in this mortal life on earth, we also have a body. The flesh must be disciplined so that it remains subject to the spirit. Luther stressed that the freedom of Christians does not go beyond the spiritual and that they should obey the laws of the temporal authorities so long as these do not infringe upon faith.[41] True Christians always remain free from every human law, since faith allows them to do everything out of pure freedom.

Calvin agreed. In a chapter on *Civil Government* in the *Institutes*, he wrote that some men, after hearing the Gospel's promise of freedom, think they cannot benefit from this freedom as long as any human authority rules over them. Such men wish to reshape the world to a new form, without courts, laws, or magistrates. 'But whoever knows how to distinguish between body and soul, between this present fleeting life and that future eternal life, will without difficulty know that Christ's spiritual Kingdom and the civil jurisdiction are things completely distinct.'[42] The freedom of

---

[40] Melanchthon (1969), p. 123.
[41] Luther (1989), p. 621.
[42] Calvin (1960), vol. 2, p. 1486.

the Christian should be limited to the spiritual sphere. In the temporal, he always had to obey the laws of human authorities.

In the spiritual realm, the Reformers insisted, freedom from human authority should be complete. Since all Christians should undergo the process of conversion, there could be no superior class of priests constituting the spiritual estate. In another famous tract, *To the Christian Nobility of the German Nation* (1520), Luther wrote that this distinction between the spiritual and the temporal estate was the invention of power-hungry men. Like so many other doctrines and practices of the Roman-Catholic Church, it was but a human fabrication falsely superimposed onto God's revelation.

All Christians, Luther argued, are of the spiritual estate and the only difference between them is one of office.[43] They are all equally priests, bishops, and popes. All respectable occupations are Christian vocations. Those who preach the gospel and perform the sacraments are not a separate and higher group embodying spiritual power. Because of their abilities, they are elected by a community of Christians to perform these tasks. Some are the stewards of the mysteries of God, but in the Church, he added, this stewardship has been developed into an idolatrous tyranny, as though laymen were not also Christians. Thus, the liberty of the Christians had been replaced with a false bondage of human works and laws.[44]

The Idolatry of Law

The Protestant notion of Christian freedom entailed that all human laws imposed on the Christian in the spiritual sphere went against true religion. To think that one can serve God by following the laws prescribed by monastic orders or priestly hierarchies now became the worst kind of idolatry. Human laws and works functioned as restrictions on true faith, the work of the Spirit in our souls. False religion was to prescribe human laws as though these were necessary for salvation.[45]

---

[43] Luther (1989), p. 12, pp. 14–15.

[44] Luther (1989), p. 608.

[45] For example, see Luther's *Avoiding the Doctrines of Men* (1522) in Luther (1999), vol. 35.

From this point of view, the Reformers rejected the traditions, rites, and canon law of the Church as idolatry and false religion. Zwingli liked to refer to canon law as 'canon twaddle'.[46] An entire chapter of Calvin's *Institutes* carries the title 'The Power of Making Laws in Which the Pope, with His Supporters, Has Exercised upon Souls the Most Savage Tyranny and Butchery'. These spiritual laws, Calvin asserted, invaded the kingdom of Christ and oppressed Christian liberty: 'They say the laws they make are "spiritual", pertaining to the soul, and declare them necessary for eternal life. But thus the Kingdom of Christ ... is invaded, thus the freedom given by him to the conscience of the believers is utterly oppressed and cast down.'[47]

The main problem, Calvin continued, was that these human laws were prescribed as *spiritual* laws, binding souls inwardly before God, 'as if enjoining things necessary to salvation'. If these laws are passed to lay scruples upon us, 'as if the observance of these laws were necessary of itself, we say that something unlawful is laid upon conscience. For our consciences do not have to do with men but with God alone. This is the purpose of that common distinction between the earthly forum and the forum of conscience.' The whole case, Calvin concluded, rests upon the fact that 'if God is the sole lawgiver, men are not permitted to usurp this honor'.[48]

This account of Christian freedom from spiritual laws gave rise to a notion that would be central to the pleas for toleration across early modern Europe: the notion of liberty of conscience. The disastrous effect of *Menschensatzungen*—human inventions presented as religious precepts—was their snatching away the freedom of conscience. In the *Loci Communes*, Melanchthon equated Christian liberty to freedom of conscience, for Scripture asserted that the conscience should not be bound by anything going beyond its rules. The papal laws should be endured like any injustice or tyranny, as long as they did not threaten the conscience. Those who allow freedom of conscience to be snatched away by such human traditions become slaves of men: 'For as Christian freedom is freedom of conscience, so Christian slavery is the enslavement

---

[46] Cited in Ozment (1991), p. 58.
[47] Calvin (1960), vol. 2, pp. 1180–1.
[48] Calvin (1960), vol. 2, pp. 1180–6.

of conscience.'[49] This conscience, it should be clear, is not some general human aptitude or faculty to distinguish right from wrong. No, it is the divinely engrained faculty that conveys the will or command of God to the believer in a particular situation.

Importantly, the principles of Christian freedom and the priesthood of all believers constituted a normative framework that gave shape to certain descriptions of the Church. The Church became a reverse image of the Reformation: it was the embodiment of Christian slavery and spiritual tyranny, the very negation of the principles of freedom and equality of all believers before God, and justification by faith alone. In the following centuries, the resulting description of the Roman Church would spread across Europe. It was viewed as a den of corruption, headed by depraved clerics who wished to dominate and manipulate the laity with fabricated religious precepts.

Even though this image is often explained in terms of the 'corruption' of the Church in late medieval Europe, it should be clear that it did not result from any empirical study of European society. Its descriptive terms—'spiritual tyranny', 'idolatry', 'corruption', human fabrications', 'false religion'—were not empirical terms but deeply normative theological concepts. Rather than reflecting the factual condition of late medieval Europe, the framework of Christian freedom filtered out certain facts, construed these in particular ways, and thus produced descriptions of the Church as an abysmal failure to live up to genuine biblical norms.

The Theory of the Two Kingdoms

According to the Reformers, it was insanity to think that priests were a superior spiritual estate with the authority to rule the temporal estate. All men lived in the spiritual and the temporal sphere at the same time. Entering the domain of political theology, Luther described these spheres as two kingdoms, 'the temporal, which governs with the sword and is visible; and the spiritual, which governs solely with grace and with the forgiveness of sins'. The spiritual kingdom, where Christ rules in the hearts of men, Luther asserted, we cannot see, 'because it consists only in faith

---

[49]   Melanchthon (1969), pp. 67–8.

and will continue until the last day'.[50] The political theology of the two kingdoms had been born.[51]

Luther liked to remind the believers of the fact that the temporal world is the kingdom ruled by Satan, the dominion of darkness from which we can be delivered only by the light of the Holy Spirit. The other spiritual world is the Kingdom of Christ, to which only God's grace can bring us. These two are bitterly opposed to one another, he wrote in *The Bondage of the Will* (1525), and the children of Adam and all of humanity are divided into two classes corresponding to the kingdoms.[52]

On the one hand, there are those belonging to the kingdom of God, 'all the true believers, who are in Christ and under Christ, for Christ is King and Lord in the kingdom of God'.[53] On the other hand, there are those who belong to the kingdom of the world. This is the majority of humankind. In this present life on earth, the masses are and will always be un-Christian and wicked. True Christians belong to the spiritual kingdom since they have turned from the carnal to the spiritual. They are saints, who have completed the process of conversion. But here on earth, fallible human beings cannot possibly see who is a saint and who is not. The spiritual kingdom is invisible. Therefore, in this earthly life, we have to accept that all live in the two kingdoms at the same time.

This split corresponded to two realms within the human being. Luther's entire account of Christian freedom was structured in terms of the twofold nature of the human being, spiritual and bodily. As he said, the opposition between these two spheres of human nature is commonly referred to as that between the soul and the flesh, or that between the inner and the outer man.[54] The soul alone is affected by the growth of faith; the flesh is intrinsically corrupt. In it, the inner man meets a contrary will 'which strives to serve the world and seeks its own advantage', and this will must be held in check and conformed to faith.[55] True Christians would eventually succeed in disciplining their flesh but they are few and

---

[50] Luther (1989), p. 138.
[51] For analysis, see Witte (2002), pp. 89–99.
[52] Luther (1989), p. 218.
[53] Luther (1989), p. 662.
[54] Luther (1989), p. 596.
[55] Luther (1989), p. 611.

far between. Therefore, the body should always be subject to the coercive laws of human authority.

In a chapter on Christian freedom in the *Institutes* (1559), Calvin drew the same distinction between the spiritual and the temporal jurisdiction. The former pertains the life of the soul; the latter the present life. The former resides in the inner mind; the latter regulates outward behaviour. 'The one we may call the spiritual kingdom, the other, the political kingdom.'[56] Luther's views expressed in *On Temporal Authority* (1523) built on the same foundation. Like all kingdoms and governments, he says, both of the kingdoms that divide human existence need their own laws and statutes. Christian freedom implies that human laws can never rule over the soul. Therefore, the laws of temporal authority extend only to life and property and external affairs on earth.[57] Human ordinances, Luther continued, are limited to the earthly life and the external dealings that men have with each other. This was the theory of the two kingdoms, which would play a central role throughout the Protestant world.

It said that God alone should rule in the spiritual sphere and, in matters concerning the salvation of the soul, only His Word should be taught. It is foolish to try and compel anyone to believe this or that, for God alone can know, judge, condemn, and change the souls of men. Faith is a free act. Human force has no role to play here.[58] An important theological justification for this freedom of the soul from human judgement was the belief that all humans are equally fallible and sinful. There is no privileged class to guide the believers to salvation. As fallible beings, we cannot possibly show others the way to heaven. This would be like a judge who blindly decides cases, which he can neither see nor hear.

In the temporal kingdom, on the contrary, human authority should not be questioned. The flesh has to be constrained by strict laws and severe punishment. If not, chaos will defeat order. People will pursue self-interest without being concerned about their fellow human beings in any way. They will kill, rob, and rape. In this earthly sphere, then, force *is* the legitimate instrument.

---

[56] Calvin (1960), vol. 1, p. 847. This basic doctrine of the two kingdoms returned in many of Calvin's works; see Vandrunen (2004).

[57] Luther (1989), p. 683.

[58] Luther (1989), pp. 680–8.

Importantly, the distinction between the two kingdoms did not entail some general separation of church and state. Luther and his followers viewed the temporal government as a divine order and Calvin suggested that church and state should assist each other in fulfilling their divine obligations.[59] Rather, the point was that secular authorities could not rule over the spiritual kingdom, which belonged exclusively to our Lord in heaven. Many activities of the church took place in the temporal sphere and here the secular authorities could very much assist the churches. The princes and magistrates were called on to punish any practice that went beyond the purely spiritual.

The Praxis of the Two Kingdoms

The theology of the two kingdoms would have enormous impact upon the development of Western political thought in centuries to come. It became the conceptual framework within which Protestant leaders and thinkers addressed many political issues confronting them. Not surprisingly, the location of the border between the two kingdoms was to become a principal issue in the clashes between different Christian groups.

In the free imperial city of Nürnberg, for instance, a debate took place that illustrated the issues at stake. During the second half of the 1520s, the major part of this city's population, including its clerics, laymen, and city council, had become advocates of the Protestant Reformation. However, when the city council began to impose a new orthodoxy and church order on the citizens, one of its members, Georg Frölich, objected in the name of religious freedom. He argued this freedom had been denied by the city council to the Anabaptist community. In 1530, this gave rise to a brief controversy on the question 'whether secular government has the right to wield the sword in matters of faith'.[60]

Frölich began by noting that there is no end to the executions and banishments for reasons of faith. Lutheran and Zwinglian governments refused to tolerate Anabaptists, while the 'papists' burn, hang, or banish Lutherans, Zwinglians, Anabaptists, and everyone else who is not of their faith.[61] It was

---

[59] Hamburger (2002), pp. 22–3.

[60] See Estes (1994).

[61] Estes (1994), p. 41.

obvious to Frölich that the Roman Catholic Church was inspired to persecution by its 'worthless' canon law. In contrast, the Reformation had shown that the New Testament made Christians free from all spiritual laws. It speaks of two kingdoms on earth: 'The spiritual kingdom is the kingdom of Christ in which Christ is king. Similarly, the secular realm also has its king, namely the emperor and other authorities. Just as each kingdom has its own distinct king, so each has its own distinct sceptre, goal, and end.'[62] The sceptre of the spiritual realm was the Word of God; the sceptre of the secular realm the sword.

This distinction showed that the secular government ought never to force any person to accept a particular faith. On the contrary, Christ had forbidden this in the Parable of the Tares,[63] where He revealed that the sword of the secular government should not be used to root heretics out of His kingdom (Matthew 13:24–30 [KJB]). The sum and substance of the matter, Frölich continued, was that a secular government must leave it entirely to Christ to determine and judge whether any teaching about faith is true or false. He needs no assistance from the temporal authority. This authority could use its sword or sceptre only in the secular realm, against external misdeeds such as harming the bodies or goods of other persons. The temporal sword could never succeed at forcing people to adhere to some faith. You could hang or drown them, but the choice to go to heaven or hell had to be left to them.[64]

In a period when the threat of rebellion was invoked as a reason for transgressing upon Christ's spiritual kingdom, Frölich insisted that the secular powers should respect the boundaries between the two realms of life. Thus, the distinction between the secular and the spiritual began to give shape to the political debates concerning religious toleration in this period. Importantly, Frölich's opponents in Nürnberg and elsewhere never

---

[62] Estes (1994), pp. 42–3.

[63] In the Parable of the Tares, Jesus likens the kingdom of heaven to a field where a man sowed good wheat seeds while his enemy sowed tares. When his servants want to remove the tares immediately, the man suggests that they should wait until harvest time, when the reapers will first gather and burn the tares and then gather the wheat and stack it in his barn. In the history of Christianity, this Parable has often been understood as an instruction to tolerate heretics here on earth: it is only at the time of the Last Judgement that heretics should be separated from true believers.

[64] Estes (1994), pp. 44–5.

questioned the notion of the two kingdoms. As one of them wrote, they all agreed that 'no human ordinance can possibly extend as far as heaven, over God, angels, souls, consciences, or anything on earth that no one can either see or hear, but solely to earth over the external dealings of men with one another which men can see, know, judge, condemn, or absolve'.[65]

However, these parties disagreed as to the nature of the separation between the spiritual and the temporal. The German theologian Johannes Brenz, for instance, argued it was indeed true that secular government should not punish faith, since faith was located in the hearts and consciences of men. But, he continued, one has to make a distinction 'between true or false faith on the one hand and the works and deeds of true or false faith on the other'.[66] Public behaviour based on faith clearly belonged to the temporal realm and its external matters. Therefore, the secular magistrate could wield the sword to curb false doctrine and worship among his subjects, whenever these entailed public crimes. One of the Nürnberg clerics agreed that 'teaching, preaching, the use of ceremonies, etc., are all external, and God's kingdom does not depend on them, even though they hinder or promote it'.[67] Hence, the government should control these aspects of life.

The disagreement in such controversies concerned *the location of the boundary* between the spiritual and the temporal. From one perspective, the spiritual sphere of freedom encompassed all matters related to faith. Therefore, groups such as the Anabaptists should always be left free by the secular authorities to believe and worship as they please. From the other perspective, all external manifestations of faith *belonged to the temporal sphere* and should therefore be disciplined by the secular authority and its coercive legal system. Such a standpoint could well entail punishment of the Anabaptist community whenever it practised its faith out in the open.[68]

---

[65] Estes (1994), p. 94.

[66] Estes (1994), p. 55.

[67] Estes (1994), p. 83.

[68] It is often suggested that the confrontation with seditious Anabaptists had Luther change his views about the two kingdoms drastically: he now backed the *Staatskirchentum* (state-churchdom). However, David Whitford (2004) cogently argues there was no such radical change in the Reformer's political thought. He continued to support the theology of the two kingdoms, but argued that the princes could punish the Anabaptists because these challenged secular authority.

This split of perspectives allows us to account for an internal tension within the Protestant Reformation. The theology of Christian freedom claimed that it was God's will that all believers should be free from human authority in the spiritual realm of religion. Importantly, it constituted a *normative* framework, which told any secular authority that it *ought not to* interfere in the religious realm or the spiritual kingdom. Each conscience *ought to be* left free from human interference. From this, it appeared to follow that religious toleration was the duty of all states and religious freedom the right of all men. Given the Reformation's own tendencies towards intolerance and persecution, how could it lie at the root of these principles of toleration and religious freedom?

The fact that early Reformers proclaimed Christian freedom as God's gift to humanity does not tell us much about its scope. Luther and Calvin insisted that this freedom was limited to the spiritual realm. Many types of blasphemy, heresy, and idolatry, they added, extended far beyond that realm and could not be tolerated. The distinction between private religious belief and the public practice and propagation of falsehood allowed for this. So, even though spiritual freedom was proclaimed as God's gift to humanity, this principle could be interpreted in various ways and its scope could shift in different directions.

*   *   *

The political theology of the two kingdoms formulated by the Reformers had a long theological history. The main point of the story told in this chapter has been to show how Christianity divided the world into two separate realms. Its conception of faith as a process of conversion to God was structured by the division between soul and body, between spirit and flesh, between the invisible and the visible. This corresponded to a partition of human social life into the spiritual and the temporal. As souls or spirits, human beings live in the eternal kingdom of heaven. As bodies, we live in the temporal kingdom of earth.

When monastic Christianity crafted conversion as *the* Christian way of life, this was conceptualized in terms of a turning away from the carnal to the spiritual realm. The process gave spiritual liberty to the priests of the Roman Catholic Church. This liberty, in turn, imparted them with spiritual authority and a higher position in the medieval hierarchy.

After the Papal Reform of the twelfth century, the process of conversion became the foundation to distinguish between the spiritual estate of clerics and the temporal estate of laymen.

All this changed dramatically once the Protestant Reformation unleashed its forces on the European continent. Every Christian was to go through the process of conversion, the Reformers insisted, and all believers were priests. Therefore, all possessed the precious treasure of Christian liberty. This transformed the distinction between the two spheres in a way that would affect Western political thought for centuries to come. The spiritual kingdom became the sphere of liberty or freedom. True religion demanded freedom of the soul from the idolatry of human works and laws. The sinful body, in contrast, was to remain subject to human secular authority and its coercive laws. As a consequence, the temporal kingdom turned into the realm of law and coercion.

The structural similarities between this political theology of the two kingdoms and the contemporary liberal model of religious toleration and the secular state are striking. Both divide human existence and society into two spheres, one of politics and another of religion. In the first sphere, human beings are subject to the laws of the secular authorities; the second is a sphere of freedom where the individual conscience can live according to its own religious beliefs and values. Both are also normative frameworks: they tell us that the political and the religious ought to be separated and that each human being ought to possess freedom of conscience. However, in themselves, such structural similarities cannot establish that the liberal model of secularism and religious toleration is a secular translation of the political theology of the two kingdoms. One could just as well point out the many differences between these two conceptual models to argue the opposite.

Yet, the fundamental problems faced by the liberal model's division of society into two separate spheres do indicate a connection. In the Protestant theology of Christian freedom and the two kingdoms, the distinction between the two spheres was relatively clear and coherent, because it could rely on clusters of other beliefs shared by Christian communities. Different clerics and rulers disagreed about the scope of the two kingdoms, but they all knew what they were referring to when they discussed these two, because they shared a common framework.

It was very clear that the opposition between the secular and the religious was an internal Christian distinction. It even made sense to speak of 'a Christian secular government'.[69] If the notion of the two kingdoms were to be extracted from this theological framework and reformulated in secular terms as though it concerned a neutral rational distinction, this would lead to intractable conceptual problems. One would no longer be able to refer to the shared theological background that lent sense and significance to this distinction. It would have to become a pre-theoretical given, never to be questioned. The following two chapters shall examine two questions: Did this indeed happen in the centuries following the Protestant Reformation? If it did, how did this secularization of political theology unfold itself?

[69] Frölich in Estes (1994), p. 53.

4. Liberty, Tyranny, and the Divine Order

Dare you for this adjure the civil sword
To force our consciences that Christ set free
And ride us with a Classic Hierarchy
New Presbyter is but Old Priest Writ Large.[1]

O n 27 October 1553, the Spanish physician Michael Servetus was burnt at the stake in Geneva. Even though Calvin had requested a less cruel death by decapitation, the city council insisted upon the pain and terror of the flames. The charges behind the execution were heresy and blasphemy: Servetus had denied such doctrines as the Trinity and Original Sin. This inspired the French Inquisition to execute the heretic in effigy months after the Geneva trial. As Servetus had been the victim of Catholic persecution for years, his execution by Protestant authorities gave rise to great controversy. To many, the event symbolized the utter betrayal of Christian freedom.

---

[1] Milton (1646).

According to the teachings of Christian freedom, neither church nor state could enforce laws in the spiritual realm. Yet, when the Reformers moved from dissent to establishment, they built churches that claimed authority over religious belief and divine worship. From the sixteenth century, Europe witnessed the formation of such 'confessional' churches with fixed doctrines and ecclesiastic discipline. This dynamic of 'confessionalization' gave rise to religious conflict on a scale not seen before in Europe.[2]

If the Reformation generated such conflict, how credible is the hypothesis that its theological framework produced the foundation of liberal toleration? To answer this question, we need to examine another dimension of post-Reformation Europe: in several regions, the formation of confessions gave rise to antithetical movements, which rejected the creeds and laws of confessional churches as human fabrications falsely superimposed onto divine revelation. These groups wished to realize the ideal of 'Christian freedom' and fight against 'spiritual tyranny'. This chapter will show how the normative model of religious toleration and the secular state emerged as a part of this anti-confessional movement.

The propelling force behind both the process of confessionalization and its antithesis was an internal dynamic of the Christian religion: the never-ending attempt to reform religious institutions and the community of believers so that they came closer and closer to embodying the order willed by God. This, I will call, 'the normative dynamic' of the Christian religion. The first section introduces a hypothesis about this dynamic that functions as the motor of Christian history and whose ultimate aim is to base the coexistence of Christian believers on the normative foundation of God's divine order.

The second section will take the case of the Dutch Republic to show how an internal tension at the heart of this normative dynamic gave shape to a conflict within the Reformation. On the one hand, confessionalization equated the divine order to a set of doctrines and rules of ecclesiastic discipline that defined the truly Christian community. Confessional churches had to aim to embody God's will in this sense. On the other hand, the anti-confessional movement viewed the divine order as a framework of Christian freedom, which allowed all believers to follow their own conscience and its representation of God's will.

---

[2] See Benedict (2000); Farr (2003); Ferry (1997); Headley, Hillerbrand, and Papalas (2004); Kolb (1996); Mentzer (1994); Nischan (1999); Po-Chia Hsia (1989); Reinhard (1983).

Finally, an analysis of the English toleration debates reveals how the emergence of liberal toleration strengthened the normative framework of anticlerical reform. This framework generated its own forms of intolerance by re-describing the Protestant confessional churches, Catholicism, and Judaism as the negations of its own norms. In the process, the principles of toleration, religious freedom, and the separation of politics and religion gradually turned into commonplaces of early modern European thought.

Doctrine, Discipline, and Divine Order

What makes an institution—any institution—into a *religious* institution? Following the logic of Balagangadhara's theory of religion, we can conjecture the following: a religious institution is one that reflects an explanatorily intelligible account of the cosmos. That is, much like the cosmos, such an institution would be an explanatorily intelligible entity: it should embody reasons or purposes, which allegedly caused it to come into being and propel it over time.

What does this mean in theological language? A religious institution is one that embodies the will of God. Believers see its nature and growth as expressions of God's purpose and try to find out the order and meaning He has instilled into the institution. Historically, we do know of institutions that took this form or, at least, were understood along these lines. Western Christendom approached the monastery and the Church as institutions that were simultaneously human and divine. The *Catechism of the Catholic Church*, for instance, says 'the Church is both the means and the goal of God's plan' and it approvingly cites the words of Clement of Alexandria: 'Just as God's will is creation and is called "the world," so his intention is the salvation of men, and it is called "the Church".'[3]

The Will of God on Earth

According to the Christian religion, the universe expresses God's will. Since He is perfect and omnipotent, His will must produce a world which cannot but be the best of all possible worlds. Translated into

---

[3] *Catechism of the Catholic Church*, § 760, § 778.

contemporary terminology, it is 'factual' and 'normative' at the same time. The factual and the normative, the 'is' and the 'ought', are united in God's will. However, human beings are unable to comprehend this unity because, in our limited understanding, the factual and the normative always fall apart.

It is impossible for the human intellect to make sense of the unity between 'is' and 'ought'.[4] Consequently, Christianity suggests, we can never fully understand either the Sovereign or His purpose on our own. Yet, this same religion also professes that God's purpose operates in human history in the form of divine providence, the act by which He orders all events in the universe so that the end for which it was created can be realized.[5] To understand historical events, then, one should decipher what God intends for human beings.

The predicament of grasping the unity of 'is' and 'ought' takes an acute form in religious institutions. Unlike secular human organizations, institutions like the monastery and the church were viewed as simultaneously divine and human. Since they should represent God's purpose on earth, they also had to exemplify the unity of fact and norm. However, human beings inevitably failed in expressing this unity. They noted the disjunction between 'ought' and 'is' in monastery and church: corruption prevailed; injustice existed; the frailty of the flesh could not be conquered.

This generated the normative dynamic that would shape the history of Western Christendom for centuries to come. From a human perspective, the factual and the normative always fell apart in these institutions. The factual came to be regarded as a testament of human sin; the normative took the form of moral ideals. This then led to new attempts to express the unity of fact and norm. Both monastery and church had to be reformed according to ever-stricter rules. Though populated by limited human beings, the Christian *ecclesia* (church) was expected to unite the factual and the normative. Every failure to do so generated new attempts,

---

[4] In modern moral philosophy, this difficulty takes the form of the 'is–ought' problem, which was first stated by David Hume: from factual premises, one can never infer a normative conclusion; consequently, there is an unbridgeable gap between 'is' and 'ought'. For analysis of this problem and some potential solutions, see Hudson (1969).

[5] Walker (1911).

which failed yet again, and so on. In this sense, God's purpose was not a concern of theologians alone. The strong sense of the unfolding of His purpose in human history generated a particular attitude towards social institutions in general.

Initially, this had started out as a normative stance towards the Church, which found its theological justification in the work of Saint Augustine. According to him, the saeculum—the secular world that would last until the second coming of Christ—was a 'corpus permixtum', a mixture of saints and sinners. The sinners are enslaved to the flesh and to man; the saints follow God and the spirit. Whereas the former make up the earthly city, the latter form the heavenly city of God, 'the one guided and fashioned by love of self, the other by love of God'.[6] In the church on earth, the *civitas Dei* (the city of God) is embedded in the *civitas terrena* (the earthly city). Still, the heavenly city reflects the perfect state of the human community desired by God.

Therefore, genuine Christians should always pursue this ideal. It is what the church strives to be. In the best of all possible worlds, this ideal would encompass humanity; in our actual world, this goal cannot be attained until the end of times. As Robert Markus argues, Augustine presented the heavenly city as an eschatological orientation: 'The cities of men are judged by reference to the City of God. Of that City the monastery was a dim anticipation, a shadowy representation, in so far as it was capable of representation on earth.' No human community on earth could come close to the celestial City. Therefore, this City 'is not a model, but an anchor, a direction, the fixed point at the far end of the Church's unending pilgrimage'.[7] In Augustine's words, 'These two cities are entangled together in this world, and intermixed until the last judgement effect their separation.'[8] This separation would purge the communion of saints from sinners. The City of God, then, is what the church *ought to be* but *never can be* here on earth. It is the community where fact and norm shall eventually coincide.

The basic hypothesis of this section is that this stance towards the Christian ecclesia or community of believers generated a core dynamic

---

[6] Augustine (2000), p. 13.
[7] Markus (1990), p. 168.
[8] Augustine (2000), p. 35; see also Markus (1988), p. 62.

propelling the historical development of post-Reformation Europe. The dominant experience that the Church (or the Christian community more generally) had to embody the divine order set in motion a process of confessionalization. In this process, the confessional churches construed themselves in terms of the disjunction between fact and norm. Time and again, falsity ought to be rooted out by reconfirming true doctrine and sin should be restrained by embracing church discipline. Each confessional church—Lutheran, Calvinist, and Roman-Catholic— identified the divine order with its own particular system of doctrine and discipline. The consequence was the partition of European society into distinct confessions.

In the Lutheran tradition, the confessional church took the form of a *Staatskirchentum*: religious and secular authorities were unified in the state. As vice-regents of God, political rulers ought to hand down the true knowledge of God, incorrupt religion, the pure gospel, and rightly organized churches.[9] In the Calvinist world, ecclesiastic councils called 'consistories' took up these tasks.[10] Both belief and behaviour had to be controlled, from doctrinal deviancy to the sexual conduct of church members. The confessional church came to be viewed as the means to realize and preserve divine order in society.

The Fixation of Doctrine

The first half of the sixteenth century had been a time of religious confusion. Many believers failed to see clear lines of demarcation between Catholicism and the different streams within the Reformation. Both churchgoers and clerics were confused by the many disagreements about true doctrine.[11] Eventually, the dynamic of confessionalization brought an end to this confusion.

Lutherans and Calvinists established clerical authorities dictating articles of faith and rules of conduct to the laity. Believers had to endorse confessions of faith and memorize catechisms. Each confessional church

---

[9] Melanchthon, *De Ecclesiae Autoritate* (1539), cited in Keen (1996), pp. 9–10.

[10] Kingdon (1972), p. 4.

[11] Po-Chia Hsia (1989), pp. 40–1; Abray (1985), p. 25.

claimed to possess the truth and conceived of others in terms of false-hood. Each thought itself universal—the *confessio catholica*—the exclusive voice of the one revealed truth.[12] Given the disagreements in interpreting Scripture, each church also saw the need to document its version of revealed truth and distinguish this from that of its rivals. In Robert Kolb's words: 'Confessing the faith requires rejection of everything that contradicts and threatens the faith.' Therefore, the churches needed both 'positive assertions of what God has told His people' and negative statements that 'demarcate God's truth from human perversion and error'.[13]

This generated a flood of confessions of faith and other credal documents in sixteenth- and seventeenth-century Europe. To name but a few: the *Augsburg Confession*, *Formula of Concord*, and *Book of Concord* of the Lutherans; the *Second Helvetic Confession*, *Heidelberg Catechism*, and *Canons of the Synod of Dort* of the Calvinists; the *Decrees and Canons of the Council of Trent* of the Roman-Catholics; and the *Thirty-Nine Articles* of the Anglicans. Once such doctrinal boundaries were in place, the churches began to engage in pamphlet wars about true doctrine.[14]

Lay members also had to become aware of what distinguished them as 'true Christians' from 'heretics'. Thus, educational systems emphasized the teaching of confessional doctrine through catechisms and other material.[15] Sermons had to reinforce articles of faith and clarify lines of demarcation. In order to prevent the devil's lies from invading God's truth, the clergy demanded from the laity a public confession of faith and rejection of all forms of heresy.[16]

One way of confessing true faith was to highlight practices that reflected distinct teachings, such as the Lutheran Elevation of the Host and the Calvinist breaking of the bread in communion. Thus, the Reformation established a tight link between beliefs and practices: more than ever, ceremonies counted as external signs that marked the true Christian and expressed his religious beliefs.[17] Early Christianity had already generated

[12] Zeeden (1985), p. 67; see also Schilling (1992), p. 229.
[13] Kolb (1991), pp. 15–18.
[14] Benedict (2002), p. 505; Schilling (1992), p. 229.
[15] Po-Chia Hsia (1989), p. 113; Schilling (1992), p. 232.
[16] Ferry (1997), p. 1143, p. 1164; Nischan (1997), p. 201.
[17] Nischan (1984); Nischan (1997), pp. 202–15; Nischan (1999).

an attitude where practice was viewed as the embodiment of belief.[18] Confessionalization now reinforced this attitude, for the representation of doctrines in practices allowed one to distinguish the confessions from each other. By manifesting its orthodox doctrines in distinct practices, the true church sought to separate itself from its false counterparts.

To account for this fixation of doctrine, we need to turn back to the basic hypothesis of this section. As a religious institution, each confessional church aims to embody God's will, which He has revealed in His Word. To find out what God intends, one needs a correct understanding of His Word, in so far as this is possible for human beings. This entails having a correct interpretation of the Bible.

Three major dimensions are involved here. The first concerns the truth claim of religion. Since there can be only one sovereign Creator, there cannot be several competing purposes and accounts of His divine purpose. Therefore, the correct interpretation of His revelation gains the greatest significance: the body of doctrine that systematizes this interpretation also conveys God's will. And since His will is not limited to any one group of people, but covers all of humanity, this particular set of doctrines cannot but claim all-encompassing truth. Hence, each confessional church claimed to be the one confessio catholica, which represented truth for all. In this sense, the fixation of doctrine during the post-Reformation period reflects the moment of proselytization of the double dynamic of religion, which emphasizes the particularity of a religion and its message.

Second, since the church as a community of believers seeks to embody God's will, all of its members should be aware of the correct interpretation of His revelation. But this cannot possibly be transmitted or taught as a complete reading of all chapters and verses of Scripture. To spread this correct interpretation among the believers and thus give them the necessary but always flawed account of God's will, one cannot but sum it up in a body of doctrines. The resulting creeds, catechisms, and confessions of faith serve as summaries of the correct account of God's will and as heuristic devices for correctly interpreting His Word.

Third, each confession also repeatedly discovered that its believers were ignorant of true doctrine. They turned out to make false claims about God's revelation of His will and thus corrupted the church. In other

---

[18] See Balagangadhara (2005a), Chapter 2.

words, even when it came to belief, the factual and the normative fell apart in each confessional church: its members did not know what they ought to know. This led to incessant attempts to spread true doctrine among the believers in the form of catechisms, creeds, and demands that these should be explicitly endorsed by all. It also generated a recurring concern for securing the doctrinal boundaries of each confession ever more clearly and strictly.

After all, anything beyond these boundaries opposed God's will and was of evil origin: a ploy of Satan to seduce sinful human beings. Hence, each confessional church always had to keep fighting against the influx of falsity and the corruption of doctrine in the community of believers. Nothing less was at stake 'than the antithesis between Christ's church and the devil's church, which corresponds to the opposition between pure doctrine and the devil's doctrine'.[19]

The War on Sin

The fixation of doctrine was not the only step necessary to the ongoing attempt to build confessional churches that exemplified God's will. In fact, the greatest threat to introducing and retaining divine order in any human community was neither theological confusion nor internal dissent. It was the sin of idolatry.

The threefold distinction between the truly religious, the idolatrous, and the indifferent had been fundamental to Christianity from its beginnings in the Roman Empire. This distinction had allowed Christians to decide in which practices of pagan society they could participate and which practices were sinful and therefore off limits. It divided social practices into three realms: those obligatory (true worship), permitted (secular or indifferent practices), and prohibited (idolatry and sin).[20] Protestant authorities now began to perform much the same kind of operation on medieval society: they wished to reform a variety of practices and customs, because these were rejected as instances of idolatry and sin to be avoided at all cost by Christians.

---

[19] Gensichen (1967), p. 57.

[20] Markus (1990) and (2006). It is well illustrated by Tertullian's *De Idololatria* (1987), 11.6–8, pp. 43–5 and 16.1–2, p. 55.

Reformed consistories reproved those who consulted 'magicians' to cure ailing relatives and played at 'divination'.[21] Dancing was associated with 'idolatrous' Catholic customs such as votive festivals. Not only was Carnival suspect, so were donning costumes and masks, playing music and cards, and holding banquets. Pastors disapproved of folk customs related to the cycles of nature. They also opposed the celebration of festivals, including Christmas, for the laity had to stop clinging to 'the old superstition of observing feast days'. From France to Scotland, such practices were denounced as celebrations of idolaters.[22]

This obsession with the sin of idolatry also emerged in Lutheran jurisdictions. The popular *Teufelbuch* (devil-book) genre of the late sixteenth century conceived of all kinds of acts, emotions, and attitudes as indirect worship of the devil.[23] People who worried about money or food were called idolaters of 'the Worry Devil'; others were said to be victims of the 'Hellish Spirit of Sadness' or the 'Melancholy Devil'.[24] Carnival was described as a pagan festival preserved by the medieval church to promote its own invented festivals.[25]

The principal means for eradicating idolatry and sin were the laws of church discipline. The word 'discipline' was omnipresent in the writings and sermons of confessional spokesmen. Elaborate bodies of ecclesiastic discipline emerged. Systems of parish or household visitations by pastors, magistrates, and elders examined lay compliance to church law. Punishment of violations was harsh, ranging from reprimands and fines to public humiliation and excommunication. Clerical authorities excommunicated church members for acts as diverse as being present at a dance and public urinating without turning one's back.[26] Churches designed intricate protocols for the punishment of recalcitrant members so as to ensure their moral reform.[27] This resulted in clerical intrusion into the lives of ordinary

---

[21] Mentzer (1987), p. 94.

[22] Mentzer (1996), Graham (1996).

[23] Nischan (1999), p. 4.

[24] Kolb (1982), p. 74, p. 79, pp. 81–2.

[25] Nischan (1999), p. 8.

[26] Benedict (2002), pp. 102–3; Chareyre (1994), p. 88; Karant-Nunn (1994) and (1997); Mentzer (1994).

[27] Kingdon (1972), p. 10; Parker (2001), p. 229.

Christians never seen before: 'Almost no one—rich or poor, female or male, literate or illiterate—escaped the watchful gaze of the pastors and elders.'[28]

Ironically, in order to eradicate the idolatry of human laws, Protestant churches instated laws that encroached deeply onto the life of the believer. But the clerics disarmed this irony: the new laws truly derived from God's Word, they said, while the old were human fabrications. If ecclesiastic discipline was closely followed, the church could move closer to divine order. Disciplinary laws would also ensure that communities lived in harmony during the never-ending journey to realize God's purpose for humanity.[29]

This dimension of confessionalization reveals how the monasticization of daily life began to transform Christian communities across early modern Europe. They turned into 'secular' monastic structures, which discarded the spatial limitations and spiritual isolation of a monastery. Reformers translated the monastic norm of an ascetic, spiritual, and frugal life into disciplinary systems. All conduct deviating from church laws was considered sinful. The disciplining of sexuality, pleasure, and human emotion was so strict that its laws could not but be violated. Much like monastic rules, these laws meant to create awareness of human iniquity and call the believer to contrition and conversion.[30] Through its disciplinary system, each confession strove to bridge the unbridgeable gulf between the church *as it was* and the church *as it ought to be*. Day by day, the community of believers had to be purged from sin more fully and draw nearer to the Creator's divine order.[31]

Freedom from the Precepts of Men

Resistance against the confessional churches soon materialized. Dissenters rejected the confessional project and its rigid doctrine, discipline, and

---

[28] Mentzer (2000), p. 7; see also Graham (1996); McIntosh (2004); Mentzer (2004); Monter (1976); G. Parker (1994); Roodenburg (1990).

[29] For example, see Calvin's statements on discipline as the sinews of the church in his *Institutes of the Christian Religion*, vol. 2, 1229–30; also see Bucer (1969) and the claims of the Polish Reformer John a Lasco, cited in Benedict (2002), p. 72.

[30] Schilling (1987).

[31] See Bucer (1969), p. 225 and John Knox, cited in Parker (1994), p. 159.

polemics. In many parts of Europe, 'Christians without a church' challenged the foundations of clerical authority. They endorsed a variety of theological positions but held in common the forceful rejection of confessionalism and the aspiration to found the community of believers in the doctrine of Christian freedom.[32]

The first of these voices appeared in the German and Swiss territories. Silent dissenters like the Lutheran pastor Valentin Weigel and outspoken rebels like the humanist Sebastian Castellio charged the churches with the sin of placing human precepts above the Word of God and persecuting anyone who refused to give in.[33] Protestant churches, they argued, were no better than papal tyranny.

In the Dutch Republic, the Reformed Church became the target of similar criticism. From the 1580s to the Synod of Dordrecht in 1618, this nation became the arena of a battle between strict Calvinists and anticlerical Christians, 'a local manifestation of a much broader struggle between the champions and opponents of confessionalism'.[34] The Dutch case is of particular interest, for this country 'has been depicted and praised again and again as an isle of toleration'.[35] The conditions that allowed for the practice of tolerance have been studied extensively.[36] Yet, the question remains: What role did *normative principles* of religious toleration and liberty of conscience play in the Dutch Reformation?

Human Expedient or Divine Gift?

In the 1570s, an interesting early debate concerning the toleration of 'heretics' took place in the United Provinces. At its root lay the Pacification of Ghent (1576), a treaty among the northern and southern provinces of the Netherlands, whereby they agreed to join forces against the 'Spanish

---

[32]   Kolakowski (1987); see also Po-Chia Hsia (1989), p. 170.

[33]   Bainton (1935); Castellio (1971); Karant-Nunn (1994); Weeks (2000).

[34]   Kaplan (1995), p. 5. See also his (1994). For illustrations from France, see Abray (1985).

[35]   Mout (1997), p. 37.

[36]   Berkvens-Stevelinck, Israel, and Meyjes (1997); Kaplan (2007); Kooi (2000); Po-Chia Hsia and van Nierop (2002).

oppressor'. Whereas the Pacification confirmed the status of Catholicism as the official religion of other States, it granted freedom to the Calvinists of Holland and Zeeland.[37]

A pamphlet communicating 'the correct understanding of the Pacification' interpreted the policy of the Dutch States as a token of their recognition of liberty of conscience.[38] Speaking for the Calvinists, the author argued that they had been restored in full liberty, both of material goods and of conscience. This second liberty included interior worship of God in the heart and exterior worship through confessions of faith and ceremonial practices. Everyone could now satisfy his conscience, practise religion freely, and serve God as he thinks he should. 'This liberty', the author concluded, 'belongs to us according to natural law'.[39] These thoughts had deep roots in the faith of their author.

Catholic theologians interpreted the toleration granted by the Pacification differently. The University of Louvain, a centre of orthodox theology, had examined the problem. Its conclusion was that one could tolerate heretical opinions without approving of them, if this allowed one to obtain a greater good or avoid a greater evil. In a text dated 1578, Louvain theologian Jean de Lens summed up the justification for the toleration policy. Considering the present state of affairs, his colleagues judged that one might tolerate for some time the evil existing in Holland and Zeeland. But they never admitted the frivolous notion of liberty as 'the gift of God', of which the heretics made use. 'Otherwise, they would not merely have to accept for some time the status quo in Holland and Zeeland, but approve liberty of conscience at all times in favour of the heretics of all provinces.'[40]

The contrast could not be starker. The Catholic perspective viewed toleration as a temporary expedient forced upon the authorities by current circumstances. This notion of *tolerantia* had been part of medieval canon law, where it determined how ecclesiastical authorities should deal with Judaism and sins like prostitution. Jewish rites were considered an evil that had to be tolerated; the major evil thus prevented was forcible

---

[37] Anonymous (1578).
[38] Anonymous (1579).
[39] Anonymous (1579), pp. 63–4.
[40] Jean de Lens, cited in Lecler (1955), vol. 2, p. 198.

conversion.[41] Similarly, toleration of prostitution prevented the prolif-eration of adultery and rape. Molanus, another theologian and rector of Louvain University, wrote that toleration of heretical opinions may be advisable in certain circumstances, but should never be regarded as a virtuous thing in an absolute sense.[42] In contrast, the Reformed author did consider toleration as an absolute value, since its foundation lay in the freedom gifted by God to humanity.

The point here is *not* that Protestants advocated genuine principles of toleration, while Catholics only grudgingly accepted accommodation of heretics. Drawing on ancient rhetoric, humanist thinkers like Erasmus of Rotterdam and the *politiques* of sixteenth-century France had developed prudential conceptions of tolerance.[43] In contrast, Protestant thinkers like the above pamphleteer presented a *normative* model of toleration and freedom of conscience, which soon began to overshadow such potentially valuable alternatives as the one standard to be followed everywhere.

The Commandments of Men

'Christian liberty' became disputed ground during the Dutch Reformation. The Revolt against Spain had symbolized a rejection of the Inquisition and its attempt to impose religious uniformity. But those expecting religious freedom to reign supreme were disappointed: the Reformed Church began to build its own ecclesiastic structures and imposed church laws and confessions of faith. In a rerun of the early Reformation, anticlerical Christians now called upon the principles of spiritual liberty and blamed the Reformed for failing to realize these. They noted the disjunction between 'is' and 'ought' in the church and once again argued for bridging this gap by aiming to embody the norms of Christian freedom through the individual process of conversion. The point was central to the work of two polemicists of the late-sixteenth-century Dutch Republic.

[41] Bejczy (1997).

[42] Johannes Molanus, cited in Lecler (1955), vol. 2, p. 203.

[43] Remer (1996), pp. 41–51; Vanheeswijck (2008). For the *politiques*, a group of powerful men in sixteenth-century France who put the welfare of the state above the unity of religion, see Butterfield (1977), p. 573. Political expedi-ency was equally popular among authors who defended some form of scepticism towards Christian dogmatics. See Tuck (1988), p. 35 and Levine (1999), pp. 3–5.

Dirck Volckertsz Coornhert, a former secretary of the town of Haarlem, had been imprisoned by the Spanish and fled the Netherlands. He returned in 1572 and became a secretary of the States of Holland at the time of the Dutch Revolt. During the next fifteen years, his polemical writings would get him into trouble several times. Another spokesman of anti-confessional sentiment, Caspar Coolhaes, had converted to Lutheranism in the 1560s. After a spell of hedge-preaching in Holland, he fled to Germany. In 1574, he was called back to Leiden to become a preacher of Reformed religion. However, he soon clashed with the clergy and was excommunicated in 1582.[44]

Both men shared the concern that the Reformed Church's confessions and catechisms were human additions to God's revelation. Had not Jesus said, 'In vain do they worship me, teaching as doctrines the commandments of men' (Mark 7:7, Matthew 15:9 [English Standard Version])? One of Coornhert's pamphlets examined the Dutch catechism 'in order to understand whether it emerged from Scripture or from human ingenuity'.[45] The clergy compelled schools to use this catechism as the principal source of religious education. To challenge this, Coornhert intended to prove that it deviated from apostolic teachings and contained additions to Scripture. The clergy, he said, wanted to become rulers over the faith of others.

Similarly, Coolhaes warned the Calvinist clerics that the addition of doctrines to Scripture was a service to Satan, who harmed the church by deceiving these clerics into the illusion that they possessed more power than God had given them. This was most obvious in the fabrication of articles of faith. 'Antichrist omits from and adds to God's word', he wrote, introduces 'alien teachings' and 'establishes rules and laws that entangle the conscience and destroy Christian freedom'.[46] Such additions attributed to humanity the capacity that was God's alone: to save us from sin.

---

[44] Kooi (2000), pp. 91–7.

[45] Coornhert (1582a). See also his (1589). Most of Coornhert's works are collected in a rare three-volume edition by Jacob Aertsz Colom: *Wercken* (Amsterdam, 1630). All translations from Dutch are my own.

[46] Coolhaes, 'Christelycke Vermaninghe' (1584), in Rogge (1856–8), vol. 2, p. 7, pp. 30–1.

As Coolhaes explained elsewhere, good works could not help procure salvation; only the work of the Spirit generates faith in us.[47] Only thus can we come to salvation: 'As long as a man has not yet been in the school of the Spirit, he is the old man and does not know God and Christ; and even if he has knowledge, this is a carnal and literal, rather than a truthful and lively knowledge.' When bound to human precepts, the Spirit's work in the soul is obstructed.[48] According to Coolhaes, the Reformed Church had become an obstacle to spiritual conversion; it prevented true reform of the soul.

Such charges forced the clergy to explain the importance of confessions and catechisms. The first, they said, reminded believers of the correct interpretation of God's revelation, while catechisms served to teach children this set of beliefs. The texts also defined the doctrinal limits that distinguished the true church from heresy and brought unity through the clarity of the *fundamenta*.[49] In the later clash between Remonstrants and Contraremonstrants, the latter continued to defend catechisms and confessions as 'the pith and marrow' of Scripture.[50] A Remonstrant leader retorted: 'When the catechism and the confession are the marrow of Scripture, what then is the purpose of Scripture itself? What end do the bones serve, when the marrow has been removed, but to be thrown onto the dunghill?'[51]

Tyranny Strikes Again

Dutch anticlerical Christians condemned the Protestant churches and the papal hierarchy as forms of religious tyranny. Coolhaes wrote that the

---

[47] Rogge (1856–8), vol. 1, pp. 161–2.

[48] Rogge (1856–8), vol. 2, p. 11, pp. 14–15.

[49] These issues surfaced in a debate regarding the catechism of Gouda, composed as an alternative to the official Reformed catechism. See the dialogue in Donteclock (1608).

[50] Arnoldi Vander Linde (1629), Van Drielenburch (1616).

[51] Johannes Uytenbogaert in Van Drielenburch (1616), pp. 8–9. See also Rogge (1856–8), pp. 180–1. The theologian Jacobus Arminius, the intellectual guide of the Remonstrants, had similar objections to confessions and catechisms. See Arminius (1956), pp. 193–275. See also Brandt (1677), p. 58.

Calvinists were sliding into the yoke of papal idolatry by putting human laws higher than God. With its system of canon law, the Catholic hierarchy had imposed more laws on the free church of the New Testament than had existed even among the Jews. The Dutch Reformed Church has made the same mistake in recent times. Thus, it divided the baptized into pieces, separate confessions, all of which shout: 'Look, here is CHRIST! This is God's church! One has to believe in this manner! Anyone who does not believe thus cannot attain salvation! He is unworthy of the Lord's table! He is a heretic, freethinker, libertine, unbeliever, disrupter of ecclesiastic peace!'[52]

Across the Dutch Republic, opponents of the Calvinists spoke of the 'new Genevan popes' and cried out: 'Better the Spanish Inquisition than Genevan discipline.'[53] Coornhert joined the choir. During a heated conflict with the consistory, the Leiden magistracy had asked him to compose a justification of its own position.[54] In this justification, he accused the clergy of adopting another ploy from the Pope's handbook, namely, arrogating the power to ordain temporal authorities and calling on them to persecute heretics. Coornhert requested the magistrates to rescue liberty of conscience from these wolves.[55] But magistrates could also constitute a threat. In another pamphlet, Coornhert castigated the authorities of Holland for their desire to 'appropriate the rule over the spiritual kingdom of God, where the Lord Christ alone and no worldly government may rule.'[56]

Coornhert's main text regarding freedom of conscience, the *Synodus vander Conscientien Vryheidt* (1582), had the form of a synod among representatives of different denominations. One of its sessions juxtaposed two options: Should one allow liberty of conscience? Or should political authorities permit only the exercise of that religion which they consider true? Gamaliel, the character representing Coornhert's viewpoints, replied that religion works in the heart of men and lies beyond the scope of human authority. Therefore, the conscience ought not to be forced in any way and

---

[52] Rogge (1856–8), vol. 2, p. 8.
[53] Kaplan (1995), p. 105.
[54] Kooi (2000), pp. 55–89.
[55] Coornhert (1597).
[56] Coornhert (1579).

belongs to the discretion of God alone. 'All of which makes me believe that all coercion of conscience, even if it only concerned prohibition of a practice, which one or another party considers necessary to salvation, is by no means Godly nor decent ... For faith is to stand apart and free from all subjection of men.'[57]

In a diatribe against the neo-stoic humanist Justus Lipsius, Coornhert again explained why secular authorities should stay away from religion. In his *Politicorum Libri Sex* (1589), Lipsius had argued that unity of religion should be maintained in any polity. Magistrates should persecute groups openly heretic, while silent or secret heretics should be left free. Coornhert pointed out that Lipsius mixed 'the government of Godly and human matters' and 'attributes them to the earthly Prince, as though the latter can command both'. This was deceptive, since the 'visible king' and his temporal laws rule only the 'bodies and possessions' but not 'the visible subjects' invisible souls'. [58] The prince should not interfere where he is as much subject as his subjects. Lipsius' ungodly advice would bring about 'the papacy, a horrible bloodshed of many thousands of innocent men.'[59]

This rejection of the Reformed Church constituted another step in the attempt to realize the divine order on earth. Once the Reformation had identified freedom in the religious realm as the will of God, this became the norm that true Christians should pursue. Dissenters invoked this norm to reject the confessional churches as bad imitations of Catholic idolatry. The normative framework behind the Reformation critique of the papal hierarchy now gave shape to the anticlerical rejection of Calvinist and Lutheran churches. Thus, the principle of religious freedom seeped into the common sense of early modern Europe.

Strikingly, the dialectic interplay between proselytization and secularization returned in this dynamic. Eventually, Christian groups inspired by anti-confessional stances, such as the Remonstrants and the Mennonites, felt the need to formulate confessions of faith to demarcate their doctrinal boundaries.[60] The justification was that they lived in an age which let errors dominate, ignored the major articles of faith, refused to distinguish

---

[57] Coornhert (1582b), fol. xxii–xxiii.
[58] Coornhert and Lipsius (1590), p. 61.
[59] Coornhert and Lipsius (1590), pp. 16–19, pp. 57–8, p. 109.
[60] Zijlstra (2002).

indifferent doctrines from those necessary, and bound 'the consciences of men ... to human fabrications'. Therefore, good teachers were compelled to give a clear explanation of divine revelation to the populace. Ironically, these anti-confessional groups now produced the same arguments for their confessions as the strict Calvinists.[61]

A Reformation Ever Reforming

The Antichrist was a central character in the writings of English advocates of toleration. Even though the intellectual world of this age brought forth crucial scientific discoveries, local toleration debates were also animated by anxiety about Satan and his vicar. Surprisingly, allegations of satanic inspiration were often more strident in texts in favour of toleration, also marked by the shrill tone of their anticlerical arguments.

The English Reformation had a pattern different from its German, Swiss, and Dutch counterparts. However, the never-ending attempt to have the church embody the norms of the divine order remained its propelling force. Originally, the Anglicans accused the Church of imposing idolatry upon the English people: the priesthood had misguided the monarch and usurped secular power. Soon, the Puritans called for a further Reformation and pointed out that Anglicans had failed in achieving Christian liberty. Henry VIII had cast the church 'into a mould half Popish halfe Protestant', as Roger Williams put it.[62] An observer told his fellow church members: 'We are for a Popery of our own, a Yoke of our own making that we would have the slavish Laity to wear.'[63]

Once the Presbyterian Church had been established, internal dissenters like the Baptists, Quakers, and radical Puritans challenged this on the grounds that it was not as God desired it to be. Instead, it was another tyranny over the minds of men. After migrating to the new world, radical Puritans built congregations in early America, only to see these attacked by dissenters in similar ways. The normative model of toleration consolidated as a part of this dynamic of 'further Reformation' or the ongoing pursuit to bridge the gap between the factual and the normative.

---

[61] Episcopius and Uytenbogaert (1621), pp. 7–9.

[62] Williams (1644), p. 64.

[63] Anonymous (1688a), pp. 16–17.

Religious Toleration and Anticlerical Diatribe

In England, the earliest substantive pleas for a general liberty of conscience flowed from the pens of members of the first Baptist church in London. In 1611, Thomas Helwys had led this group from their refuge in Holland back to the homeland. Scarcely had they settled down when Helwys and another Baptist, Leonard Busher, published tracts against 'religious tyranny'. They objected to the King's power over religion and argued that Christ had ordained the same means of faith for king and subject.[64]

The advocacy of toleration in the English Reformation shared three elements with the anti-confessional dynamic in other parts of Europe. First, the aversion towards clerical 'tyranny' was rooted in the belief that the two realms of the world should not be blended. Tyranny was the result of confusing the temporal with the spiritual, which made a travesty of religion. Seventeenth-century advocates of toleration emphasized the point repeatedly: false religion created a cocktail of politics and religion. Thus, the true spiritual order was lost and 'a Carnal, Worldly, Politick, Ecclesiastical Church-State' was erected in its stead.[65]

Again the English debates revolved around the boundaries of the sphere of religion and conscience and the consequent scope of religious freedom. For some, the limits of toleration and liberty should be fixed by the laws of the Old Testament and thus exclude all forms of false religion; others insisted that the coming of the Gospel had freed humanity from these laws and that it was not up to the magistrate to punish idolaters and heretics.[66] Again, the frame of reference for determining the scope of religion and its liberty lay in one's preferred interpretation of the Word of God.

The second element common to early modern toleration discourse across Europe was the offensive against 'the priests of the devil'. These assaults on clerics of all stripes and colours had their roots in the conviction that individual believers ought to be free to subject their souls to God's will.[67] The advocacy of toleration always retained this connection

---

[64] Helwys (1612); Busher (1966), pp. 18–19.

[65] The phrase is from Gordon (1675), pp. 7–9, pp. 11–13. The point is also made by Croope (1656), pp. 9–10; Milton (1659), pp. 37–8; Williams (1644), pp. 79–80.

[66] Woodhouse (1992), pp. 125–61.

[67] Busher (1966), pp. 19–20, pp. 34–5.

to anti-catholic and anticlerical discourse. Early modern tracts were filled with attacks against priests, presbyters, and other prelates: 'Where Romish Tyrannie hath the upper hand, Darkness of minde, and superstition stand.'[68]

A third common element was the claim that the blending of religion with politics caused division and conflict. By the end of the seventeenth century, a consensus had emerged that persecution and religious strife were rooted not in religion *but in the human corruption of religion.* Worldly interests brought coercion, conflict, and confusion in religious matters. By contrast, 'if every Man were left to himself, to follow what Religion he pleases', the latitudinarian Edward Synge stated, 'it is very probable that most Men, having no Worldly Interest to serve by this or that Religion, would in time, be brought to agree in all the great and necessary Truths of Religion; which are plain and evident to every sober and inquisitive Person'.[69]

The idea that religious discord was the product of human cunning was widespread in early modern Europe.[70] It was part of a classical Christian story about the degeneration of religion: corrupt leaders had invented new doctrines, presented as revelations from God. Inspired by worldly ambition, they commanded their followers to defend these fabrications under the guise of religion and the promise of salvation. This caused conflict between different confessions, since each of these swore by its own set of human doctrines. The road to peace was obvious: ending the human exploitation of religion by returning to divine revelation.

Universal Toleration and Its Negation

Often, the scope of toleration remained narrow. Neither 'atheism' nor 'popery' and 'idolatry' were considered suitable objects of toleration. To

---

[68] The quote is from Richardson (1966), pp. 235–85, pp. 279–82. See also Anonymous (1652); Croope (1656), pp. 3–4; Dell (1646); J.V.C.O. (1663), p. 38, p. 45f.; Gordon (1675), pp. 10–13; Overton (1645), p. 1, p. 14; Wolseley (1668).

[69] Synge (1698), p. 6, pp. 100–1.

[70] Some examples: Corbet (1668), p. 10; Sturgion (1966), p. 333; Taylor (1648); Walwyn (1647), p. 4.

many, it was equally anathema to tolerate the 'tyranny' of Protestant churches. Take the case of John Milton, an avid supporter of toleration. He wrote that 'poperie and idolatrie ... may not plead to be tolerated' and 'that a magistrate can hardly err in prohibiting and quite removing at least the publick and scandalous use therof'. Protestant churches that enforced some religion, he added, 'deserve as little to be tolerated themselves, being no less guiltie of poperie in the most popish point'.[71]

Yet, in seventeenth-century England, several thinkers argued for granting liberty of conscience to *all*, including Catholics, pagans, Jews, and Muslims.[72] As early as 1612, Thomas Helwys had said that 'mens religion to God is betwixt God and themselves ... Let them be heretikes, Turcks, Jewes, or whatsoever it apperteynes not to the earthly power to punish them in the least measure'.[73] These thinkers—Leonard Busher, Roger Williams, William Penn, Henry Robinson, William Walwyn, and others—extended the scope of toleration to 'false religion' and 'heresy'.

This step was not inspired by any growing indifference towards the worship of God. All these men were pious Christians who wished to obey His will. Indeed, they considered many forms of religion as flagrant violations of God's will, including those they were willing to tolerate. In their eyes, Catholics remained heretics; Judaism and Islam amounted to deficient worship; and pagans were devil worshippers. Still, these thinkers argued for a general freedom for all such practices. What inspired them to extend toleration to *all* forms of religion?

Compare the works of two well known thinkers of this period, Roger Williams and John Milton. Both challenged the justification of persecution based on the model of the national church of Israel. Some Puritans had invoked an old tradition to justify the persecution of stubborn heretics. They conceived of the Christian community as a people living under a covenant with God, analogous to the Old Testament nation of Israel, which became the model for the truly Christian nation.[74] Much like the kings of Israel, secular rulers of Reformed nations were to be the keepers of the Two Tables of the covenant. And the authority to enforce the First

---

71 Milton (1659), pp. 35–6.
72 Carlin (1996), Coffey (1998).
73 Helwys (1612), p. 69.
74 See Stanford Reid (1988).

Table included persecution of heretics and idolaters. Williams rejected such claims in his *Bloudy Tenent of Persecution* (1644), which argued for the toleration of all forms of worship. Fifteen years later, Milton adopted a parallel line of argument in his *Treatise of Civil Power in Ecclesiastical Causes* (1659) but explicitly barred 'papists' and 'pagans' from the scope of toleration.

Roger Williams was a man of many experiences. Besides causing controversy in the Massachusetts Bay Colony and founding Rhode Island, he had spent years among Native Americans studying their language, religion, and customs. In the report of this study, he repeatedly articulated his horror towards the local idolatry. 'The Priest' of native religion, he said, did many peculiar things while performing ceremonies. This had been related to him by native informants, Williams admitted, 'for after once being in their Houses and beholding what their Worship was, I durst never bee an eye witness, Spectatour, or looker on, least I should have been partaker of Sathans Inventions and Worships.'[75] In spite of this aversion towards idolatry, Williams stated the following proposition in the table of contents of the *Bloudy Tenent*:

> It is the will and command of God, that since the coming of his Sonne the Lord Iesus a permission of the most Paganish, Jewish, Turkish or Antichristian consciences and worships, bee granted to all men in all Nations and Countries: and they are onely to bee fought against with that Sword which is only (in Soule matters) able to conquer, to wit, the Sword of Gods Spirit, the Word of God.

Even though idolatry desecrated the will of God, it ought to be tolerated, for it was as much His will that no conscience should be coerced.

In a dialogue, Williams had the characters 'Truth' and 'Peace' defend the general thesis that, after the coming of Christ, the Lord wished to grant freedom to all forms of worship in this world. This thesis was founded in the belief that Christian conversion requires the free work of the Spirit, which cannot be shackled by the sword of human coercion. Here, only one sword could help, namely the 'soul-piercing', 'soul-saving' Word of God.[76] In an image borrowed from the Parable of the Tares,

---

[75] Williams (1643), pp. 119–20.
[76] Williams (1643), pp. 64–5, pp. 79–80.

Williams described the church and the civil state as two separate gardens. The garden of the spiritual church was *distinct* and *independent* of that of the civil state. Therefore, 'a false Religion and Worship will not hurt the Civill State, in case the worshippers breake no civill Law'.[77] In Christ, the spiritual church of God had been separated from the carnal world.

Milton agreed that civil magistrates could not use the sword of coercion in matters of religion for it had no power in this realm. He stressed that no body of men could 'be the infallible judges or determiners in matters of religion' for consciences other than their own. And, he added: 'That Christ is the only lawgiver of his church and that it is here meant in religious matters, no well grounded Christian will deny'.[78] His argumentation was very close to that of Williams: Christian magistrates should not imitate the kings of Israel, since religion under the gospel is fundamentally different from religion under the law. The old covenant can no longer be invoked to persecute heretics and idolaters, for the new covenant is written upon the heart of every believer.[79]

In the eyes of these authors, the Roman Church did not stand alone as a negation of spiritual freedom, but was accompanied by the Hebrew religion: because of its elaborate body of sacred laws, this religion became another instance of 'spiritual tyranny'. The law of the first covenant had lost its validity, they argued, while the second covenant was one of grace and freedom. Thus, unlike the kings of Israel, secular authorities of today could not possess the authority to enforce religion. From this perspective, 'jewry' joined 'popery' as another prototypical negation of the norms of Christian freedom.

The shared theology explains the parallels of Milton and Williams, but also makes the rift between their conclusions all the more puzzling. How could this framework entail universal toleration in one case, while excluding 'popery' and 'idolatry' in the other? Milton's answer was clear: neither Catholicism nor paganism ought to be tolerated because they were political entities supported by a foreign civil power *rather than religions*. They did not belong to the spiritual realm. The consciences of 'papists' and 'idolaters' could not be free, because they had lost that liberty through

---

[77] Williams (1643), p. 103.
[78] Milton (1659), pp. 5–6, p. 10.
[79] Williams (1643), pp. 37–8, 47–8.

their own subjection to human laws. Under this description, Catholicism and paganism were threats to the civil order and harmful to the temporal interests of society.[80]

Generally, the normative framework behind the principles of Christian freedom lent coherence to the claims for universal toleration: Christian liberty was the will of God; anything going against it was not. If 'Meekness, Mildness, Unity, Peace, and Concord, are the Vertues that embellish Christian Jurisdiction', the founding father of Pennsylvania, William Penn, wrote, 'Cruelty, Rigor, Persecution and Violence, must be the marks of Antichristian Tyranny'.[81] Clerical coercion of religion was wrong because it 'is contrary to the purpose of God in the Order of the Creation, who made and ordain'd all Man-kind free from Bondage, and never advanc'd him over all the Works of his Creation, to be a contemptible Slave to the Will of his fellow Creature, even in things Temporal; much less in matters Spiritual and relating to Eternity'.[82] God's purpose was to free humanity from religious oppression by providing equal freedom to all consciences. When a faction of priests imposed a particular form of religion on the believers, it defied the divine will, and this sin was a disruption of the order that the Lord had laid in His creation.

*   *   *

Some early modern thinkers viewed liberty of conscience as a divine gift to humanity. Therefore they could consistently argue that the duty of a true Christian was to tolerate heresy and idolatry. God's will was the normative premise that transformed toleration into a moral obligation. Thus, Christian liberty became the focus of a never-ending effort to realize God's will on earth. It functioned as the central aim of one side of the normative dynamic that propelled the historical development of the Protestant Reformation. Many were now convinced that certain norms reflected the divine order: humans had no right to interfere in each other's forms of worship, they ought not to bind others to their own fallible understanding of religion, and the civil magistrate must steer clear of religion.

[80] Milton (1659), pp. 35–6; italics added.
[81] Penn (1687), p. 5. See also Penn (1685) and (1971).
[82] Penn (1687), pp. 10–11.

This chapter has argued that the tension between the confessional and anti-confessional movements in early modern Europe resulted from two distinct ways of imagining God's will for humanity. The confessional party identified the divine order with a particular confessional system of doctrine and discipline enforced by clerical authorities. The anti-confessional groups equated God's will with the universality of toleration and liberty of conscience. This entailed a rejection of all clerical institutions and church laws, which supposedly disrupted the fabric of religion.

This clash reflected two dimensions of the Reformation's monasticization of daily life. On one hand, confessionalization stressed the transformation of the community of believers into a 'secular monastery'. Each community had to be brought under strict norms of belief and behaviour, which aimed to purify it of sin and bring the believers to contrition. On the other hand, anti-confessionalism emphasized individual faith modelled on the monastic process of conversion: each soul ought to be free to undergo this process; the work of the Spirit could not be constrained by human authority. Here, the individual was expected to internalize the norms of belief and behaviour. Obedience to these norms was now monitored internally, rather than by any external authority: the conscience not only had to make each believer aware of his violations of moral norms, but should also punish him for these sins.

Out of this clash a normative model of religious toleration emerged, which stated that all forms of religion should be freed from political authority and human laws. Its advocates systematically described certain institutions in society as the negations of this model and its norms. This produced scornful descriptions of the confessional churches and the papacy as prototypes of religious tyranny, corrupt institutions that divided the body of Christ and imposed their own doctrines and laws on all believers. Thus, this form of toleration generated its own forms of intolerance: because communities had to coexist within this normative model, any 'deviant' community or tradition could be transformed into the negation of its norms. Originally, 'popery' and 'jewry' played this unenviable role; later the confessional churches joined in. Today, the same template is applied to Islam, which has now become the religion that seeks to unite politics and religion and refuses to conform to the liberal model.

In generic terms, confessional Europe was conceptualized as a clash of communities, each endorsing competing systems of beliefs and values. The normative model of toleration came with *this inbuilt conception of religious conflict.* It viewed all conflicts between 'religious' communities as variations on a general scheme: a conflict of beliefs and values considered absolute truth and enforced by clerical authorities. This conception would shape the dominant discourse for centuries to come and compel diversity to take a particular form. To fit into the liberal model of toleration, each tradition in society needs to take the form of a religious community defined by a set of beliefs and values. This model continues to steer many nation-states of contemporary Europe and North America: the liberal secular state ought to refrain from interfering in religion and it should be tolerant of the different religious communities in society and impartial towards their purported competing beliefs and values.

5. The Enlightenment and the Secular

In an eighteenth-century pamphlet written by a Jesuit author, a French lady asked her parish priest to clarify the idea of toleration. For some time now, she observed, all kinds of people have been discussing this idea, 'the noble and the populace, the ignorant and the learned, the soldier and the philosopher'. However, the lady added, the term remained as obscure to her as ever.[1] This indicates how widespread the idea of toleration had become across Europe. Never before had this notion been discussed so widely as in the learned journals and coffee houses of this age.[2]

This was much to the dislike of the Church, which refused to accept toleration as a normative value. The pamphlet's priest told the inquisitive lady that civil tolerance was an evil to be endured to avoid greater evils, such as 'revolts, civil wars, and the ruin of religion'.[3] In contrast,

---

[1] De Doyar (1782), p. 3.
[2] Adams (1991); Schillings (1997).
[3] De Doyar (1782), p. 76

the Enlightenment philosophers presented toleration as an essential moral principle. In his *Dictionnaire philosophique* (1764), Voltaire called toleration 'the prerogative of humanity' and 'the first law of nature'.[4] The antagonism between *curé* and *philosophe* could not be stronger. Whereas the priest claimed that toleration was 'the favourite dogma of the philosophers', who were really indifferent or even intolerant towards religion,[5] the philosopher asserted that persecution had always been inspired by 'jealous priests, who armed the prejudices of the magistrates and the politic manoeuvres of the ministers'.[6]

Did the Enlightenment succeed at cutting loose the normative model of toleration from its theological moorings? Textbook stories claim that this era emancipated European minds from the tutelage of religious doctrine. The rise of toleration is taken to reflect this dramatic break between Western modernity and its Christian past. But how can one prove that the Enlightenment liberated liberal toleration from its ties to Christian theology? To do so, one should demonstrate that thinkers in this period developed a normative conception of toleration independent from religious premises and ideas. This conception cannot rely on any theological notions but should be accessible to all humans with the relevant cognitive capacities, regardless of religious background.

This chapter will examine whether this kind of conceptual break indeed occurred during the Enlightenment. In the first section, the stage belongs to John Locke, whose *Letter Concerning Toleration* (1689) is regarded as one of the prototypical formulations of liberal toleration. The second section looks at toleration theorists of the French Enlightenment from Pierre Bayle to Denis Diderot. Throughout, the question remains the same: did these thinkers succeed at formulating *secular* theories of toleration and religious freedom?

The Soul of John Locke

The legacy of John Locke has been the subject of a major debate in the past decades. One group of authors characterizes him as a chief architect of secular liberalism. Michael Zuckert argues that Locke 'is a decidedly

---

[4] Voltaire (1998), p. 188.
[5] De Doyar (1782), p. 6, p. 24.
[6] Voltaire (1998), p. 188.

modern philosopher' and that liberal democracy is 'a system clearly descended from Lockean liberalism'.[7] Similarly, many authors endorse the continuing significance of Locke's political thought and locate the proto-typical model of liberal toleration in his writings.[8]

Another group of authors questions the relevance of Locke's political theory to secular liberal democracy. This camp suggests that his thought is so deeply rooted in the religious views of his day that it loses its intelligibility outside this context. In a classic study, John Dunn points out 'the intimate dependence of an extremely high proportion of Locke's arguments for their very intelligibility, let alone plausibility, on a series of theological commitments'.[9] John Marshall and Richard Ashcraft agree that 'Locke's theology' was 'the central axiom of his political theory'.[10]

More recently, Jeremy Waldron has demonstrated that Locke's conception of equality depends on theological premises. 'The theological content cannot simply be bracketed off as a curiosity', he says, for it 'shapes and informs the account through and through'. Without this background, this conception is 'simply unintelligible' and therefore 'Lockean equality is not fit to be taught as a secular doctrine; it is a conception of equality that makes no sense except in the light of a particular account of the relation between man and God'.[11] Again, other authors agree that the foundations of Locke's political theory lie in his religious beliefs and context.[12]

Yet, generations of eminent scholars have discussed Locke as though his core ideas are independent from theological premises. The continuities between his notions of toleration, equality, and rights and those of today are striking. His texts have been interpreted in ways that make them

---

[7] Zuckert (2002), p. 1, p. 20.

[8] Bou-Habib (2003), pp. 623–5; Creppell (1996), pp. 231–2; Forster (2005), p. 21; Grant (1987), pp. 198–205; Tuckness (2002), pp. 288–98; Vernon (2013), pp. 215–30; Wilhelm (1999), pp. 145–66.

[9] Dunn (1969), p. xi.

[10] Marshall (1994), p. xviii. See Ashcraft (1996), p. 208.

[11] Waldron (2002), p. 82.

[12] Harris (1994a) and (1994b); Kelly (1991); Parker (2004); Schwartzmann (2005); Stanton (2006).

accessible apparently without presupposing any Christian beliefs. Still, advocates of the thesis that Locke's political thought depends on theological foundations have also demonstrated in detail that one cannot grasp many of his claims without an underlying Protestant framework.

Why is this issue important? If Locke's theory depends on theological premises, it cannot be understood as secular political theory. This generates a set of problems with regard to the status of liberal toleration. First, it means that one can make sense of Lockean toleration *only* within the framework of Christian doctrine. Why, then, has it been understood by so many as a prototype of secular liberalism?

Second, perhaps the liberal model of toleration is not related to Locke's thought in any significant way. Then why have so many liberal theorists made the mistake of regarding him as their philosophical ancestor? If they are misguided, one should account for the persistent illusion that Lockean toleration shares its basic structure with the modern liberal model. Even if one discards these views as false consciousness, one should save the phenomena by explaining the nature of the illusion.

Third, perhaps liberal toleration is sustained by the same conceptual scheme as Locke's model. Then the implication would be that—unless given a separate secular foundation—the modern notion also depends on theological premises. The significance of liberal toleration would then be limited to Christian societies or those who share the same intuitive and common-sense beliefs. This would entail that neither western theories of toleration nor their theorists have become secular. In the non-Western societies, the liberal model of toleration would also fail to make sense and thus it could hardly be a norm for all plural societies.

Waldron notes the problem with regards to the notion of equality: 'It may seem to us now that we can make do with a purely secular notion of human equality; but as a matter of ethical history, that notion has been shaped and fashioned on the basis of religion. That is where all the hard work was done.' Maybe, he writes, 'the notion of humans as one another's equals will begin to fall apart, under pressure, without the presence of the religious conception that shaped it'.[13] Could the same be true for the liberal model of toleration?

---

[13] Waldron (2002), pp. 242–3.

Locke and the Two Spheres

In the *Letter Concerning Toleration* (1689), Locke intends to 'distinguish exactly the business of civil government from that of religion, and to settle the just bonds that lie between the one and the other'.[14] He divides social life into two spheres: the sphere of civil interests and that of religious pursuits. Civil interests pertain to the liberty and health of the body, and to the possession of outward things such as money, lands, and furniture. To secure these, humanity is compelled to enter into society and 'the commonwealth' comes into being.

This commonwealth is 'a society of men constituted only for the procuring, preserving, and advancing [of] their own civil interests'. It has nothing to do with the religious pursuits of its members. Therefore, 'the jurisdiction of the magistrate reaches only to these civil concernments' and it 'neither can nor ought in any manner to be extended to the soul and its pursuit of salvation'.[15] By 'magistrate', Locke understands 'the supreme legislative power of any society, not considering the form of government or number of persons wherein it is placed'.[16] His claim is that any such power is restricted to the civil interests of its subjects.

If Locke's model of toleration requires such a twofold division, then it may also confront the puzzle of the two spheres: how does he distinguish the sphere of religion from that of civil interests? Admittedly, Locke says, 'a good life' involves religion and piety, but it 'concerns also the civil government'.[17] Moral actions fall under the jurisdictions of both magistrate and conscience. This creates the danger of one encroaching upon the other. Therefore, it is of vital import to distinguish between these two realms. First, Locke characterizes the spiritual realm of religion: 'Every man has an immortal soul, capable of eternal happiness or misery; whose happiness depending upon his believing and doing those things in life, which are necessary to the obtaining of God's favour, and are prescribed by God to that end' and 'the care of each man's salvation belongs only to himself'.[18]

---

[14] Locke (2003), p. 218.
[15] Locke (2003), p. 218.
[16] Locke (1997a), p. 11.
[17] Locke (2003), p. 241.
[18] Locke (2003), p. 241.

The realm of religion is that of immortal souls striving for salvation by worshipping God. It is *the other world*, whose obligations override everything *of this world*.

In this realm, 'all force and compulsion are to be forborn'.[19] In that of civil interests, however, force and compulsion are necessary:

> But besides their souls, which are immortal, men have also their temporal lives here upon earth; the state whereof being frail and fleeting, and the duration uncertain, they have need of several outward conveniencies to the support thereof, which are to be procured by pains and industry ... But the pravity of mankind being such, that they had rather injuriously prey upon the fruits of other men's labours than take pains to provide for themselves; the necessity of preserving men in the possession of what honest industry has already acquired, and also of preserving their liberty and strength, whereby they may acquire what they farther want, obliges men to enter into society with one another; that by mutual assistance and joint force, they may secure unto each other their properties, in the things that contribute to the comfort and happiness of this life ...[20]

This realm corresponds to the temporal lives that human beings live on earth, where they need material goods to survive. Through the 'original compact', they enter into civil society and entrust the power to protect these interests to the civil magistrate.

The reason for entering into civil society also determines the boundaries of its legislative power: it ought to be directed only towards 'the temporal good and outward prosperity of the society', and 'it is also evident what liberty remains to men in reference to their eternal salvation, and that is, that every one should do what he in his conscience is persuaded to be acceptable to the Almighty, on whose good pleasure and acceptance depends his eternal happiness'.[21] Locke's text leaves no doubt: religion is the spiritual realm of the soul, free from human authority and laws; the commonwealth is the temporal realm of the body subject to the civil powers.

'There is a twofold society', Locke stated in an earlier note, 'of which almost all men in the world are members, and that from the twofold

---

[19] Locke (2003), p. 242.
[20] Locke (2003), p. 242.
[21] Locke (2003), pp. 242–3.

concernment they have to attain a twofold happiness; viz. that of this world and that of the other: and hence there arises these two following societies, viz. religious and civil.'[22] On the basis of this distinction, he explained his view of toleration, which he would develop more fully in later writings.[23] This theological division between civil and religious society, between this world and the other, between body and soul, is necessary to retain the basic intelligibility of his theory.

The conceptual schemes of Locke's theory are virtually identical to those of the theology of Christian liberty. Luther and Calvin claimed that God's promise of grace in Christ makes religion free from human laws, but this freedom is confined to the realm of the soul. The body would always remain sinful and therefore ought to be subject to the laws of the temporal power. God dispensed a fraction of His sovereignty to the princes so that they may restrain human depravity. Neither prince nor priest, however, had the authority to infringe upon the relationship between God and an individual soul.

In Locke's theory, the sovereignty of civil government is justified in terms of a social contract, but its justification of political coercion is very similar. As he puts it, 'the pravity of mankind being such, that they had rather injuriously prey upon the fruits of other men's labours than take pains to provide for themselves', men are obliged to enter into society and bestow coercive power on civil authorities.[24] This is another way of saying that carnal man is sinful and should be restrained by laws. The soul is liberated through the liberty and power of faith. And so it is in Locke's theory of toleration: the temporal life of our bodies in civil society is subject to the sovereign of the original compact; the religious life of our souls becomes a sovereign sphere in and of itself.

Locke's theory transforms common ideas from Protestant political theology into topoi of toleration. Consequently, his toleration theory looks like a secularized replica of the model of Christian liberty and the two kingdoms. This model has been secularized in the sense that part of its theological content is discarded, while retaining its basic conceptual patterns as topoi. In Locke's *Letter*, the theology is

---

[22] Locke (1997b), p. 216.
[23] Locke (1997c), (1690), and (1692).
[24] Locke (2003), p. 242.

still explicit. Many have shown how his arguments for toleration are theological.[25] His conception of the church as 'a voluntary society of men, joining themselves together to their own accord, in order to the public worshipping of God' also presupposes the autonomy of the believer's soul in his relation to God.[26]

The theology behind Locke's theory derives from his interpretation of Scripture, calling upon the familiar contrast between the Old and the New Testament: in the Jewish commonwealth, idolaters were to be rooted out, because the laws 'established there concerning the worship of one invisible Deity, were the civil laws of that people, and a part of their political government, in which God himself was the legislator'. But, Locke added, 'There is absolutely no such thing, under the Gospel, as a Christian commonwealth.'[27] In other words, God's revelation demonstrated that a distinctly *Christian* civil society *could never exist*. In contrast, a Judaic civil society did exist, because it was constituted by laws revealed by God to the nation of Israel. The coming of Christ had superseded this model. Thus, according to Locke, a commonwealth under the Gospel is characterized by its separation of civil from religious affairs. To put it paradoxically, and somewhat anachronistically, from this perspective, religion and politics are unified *precisely when* they are separated.

Its theological framework prevents this model of toleration from including religions that fail to live up to its separation of civil and religious society. As Locke wrote: 'That church can have no right to be tolerated by the magistrate, which is constituted upon such a bottom, that all those who enter into it, do thereby, *ipso facto*, deliver themselves up to the protection and service of another prince.'[28] This excludes Catholicism, so long as it demands obedience to the papal hierarchy in civil society. Atheism, another threat to civil society, was also excluded. This is the case because the outer limits of Locke's toleration model are fixed by the theology of Christian freedom and its notion of true religion.

---

[25] Dees (1997); Dunn (1991); Waldron (1988) and (2002).
[26] Locke (2003), pp. 220–6.
[27] Locke (2003), p. 239.
[28] Locke (2003), p. 245.

The Model of American Liberalism

Locke's model would prove a perfect fit for eighteenth-century America. Eventually, it would translate into the constitutional principles of religious freedom and the separation of church and state. Did this principle emancipate liberal toleration from its theological framework? At first sight, this appears to be the case: God is not even mentioned in the American Constitution.

Historically, the separation principle was defended by two groups: 'liberal Protestants' like the Baptists, Quakers, and others, and 'Enlightenment rationalists' or 'secularists' such as Thomas Jefferson and James Madison. The first explicitly invoked the theological framework of Christian liberty.[29] When the colonies gained independence in 1776, this framework was translated into legal and political forms. The diversity of denominations in most states guaranteed that the right to worship God according to the dictates of the conscience would be protected by law.[30] Legal documents declared that all would be free to fulfil 'the duty which we owe to our Creator'.[31] These formulas were meaningful because they presupposed a common understanding of *what religion is*: the duty and right of all to worship their Creator in such manner as they see fit.

Scholars argue that the separation of church and state had religious premises for this group, while it was a secular principle for Enlightenment freethinkers.[32] Did the theological framework really disappear in the political thought of American founders like Jefferson? It is difficult to give a straightforward answer, because he did not develop any clear theory. His thoughts on this matter must be reconstructed from a few paragraphs in his writings. Nonetheless, these statements shaped the American tradition of separation of church and state.

---

[29] In his study of the influence of Locke's political thought on the American Revolution, Steven Dworetz shows how the common theological background of Christian liberty allowed the preachers of various Protestant confessions in the colonies to shape the American thought on religion and its liberty. Dworetz (1990), p. 137, p. 177.

[30] Beneke (2006).

[31] Perry (1952), p. 312, p. 329, p. 349.

[32] Jacoby (2004), pp. 1–65; McLoughlin (1991), pp. 249–69.

Take the famous *Act for Establishing Religious Freedom* (1786). One cannot overstate its significance, claims Susan Jacoby, 'for, much to the dismay of religious conservatives, it would become the template for the secularist provisions of the federal Constitution'.[33] Prima facie, this does not break with the earlier theological model. In fact, the justification of the Virginia Act reads like a digest of Christian liberty. It talks about 'the Almighty God who hath created the mind free' and emphasizes that temporal punishments related to religion are 'a departure from the plan of the Holy Author of our religion'.[34] This is theology if anything is. Naturally, one could argue that these claims are 'a rhetorical flourish, not a legal requirement'.[35] Can the theology indeed be dismissed as rhetoric?

From the Virginia Act, it is but a small step to the establishment clause in the first article of the *First Ten Amendments to the Constitution* of 15 December 1791. Jefferson's understanding of the establishment clause as 'a wall of separation' appeared in a letter to the Danbury Baptist Association (1 January 1802):

> Believing with you that religion is a matter which lies solely between man and his God, that he owes account to none other for his faith or his worship, that the legislative powers of government reach actions only, and not opinions, I contemplate with sovereign reverence that act of the whole American people which declared that their legislature should 'make no law respecting an establishment of religion, or prohibiting the free exercise thereof', thus building a wall of separation between Church and State.[36]

This metaphor is crucial: the wall of separation has achieved an 'almost canonical status' in the interpretation of the establishment clause and the American judiciary has made it 'a virtual rule of constitutional law'.[37] Strikingly, two out of three reasons in this passage are explicit religious doctrines. Religion is a matter between each individual and his or her God and others ought not to intrude upon this relationship. In his *Notes on the State of Virginia* (1787), Jefferson said that many still believe that

---

[33] Jacoby (2004), p. 19.
[34] Jefferson (1955), pp. 223–5.
[35] Jacoby (2004), p. 24.
[36] Jefferson (1903), pp. 281–2.
[37] Davis (2003), pp. 7–8; see also Gaustad (1998).

the operations of the mind are subject to legal coercion, but rulers can only govern the domains which we submit to their power: 'The rights of conscience we never submitted, we could not submit. We are answerable for them to our God.'[38]

Nevertheless, some of Jefferson's arguments appear secular. What remains of his case if we discard all explicitly theological elements? If we take away God from his account in the Virginia bill and his *Notes*, here is what remains: (*a*) Our civil rights are distinct and independent of our religious opinions. (*b*) Religious opinions are harmless to civil society and therefore civil government ought to leave these free: 'The legitimate powers of government extend to such acts only as are injurious to others. But it does me no injury for my neighbour to say there are twenty gods, or no god. It neither picks my pocket nor breaks my leg.' (*c*) Legislators are fallible men and therefore should not rule over the faith of others: 'subject opinion to coercion: whom will you make your inquisitors? Fallible men; men governed by bad passions, by private as well as public reasons.'[39]

The first principle presupposes the separation of civil and religious society. When one disagrees that religion ought to be separated from civil political society, one also fails to see why civil rights should be independent of religious opinions. Only the harm and fallibility principles then remain. What happens when these are applied to early modern Western societies, including Jefferson's America? Many churches, magistrates, and citizens were convinced that God would inflict catastrophes on any Christian society allowing heresy, blasphemy, or false religion. Radical Protestants and Deists insisted that God would never interfere in civil society in this way.

Any magistrate implementing these two principles would face a conflict. According to the fallibility principle, he would have to acknowledge that both opinions about God and His wrath were held by fallible humans and should not be imposed on others. The harm principle, however, would lead to incompatible results accordingly as the magistrate held one of the two beliefs. If he believed that God would never interfere in earthly life, he could indeed insist that 'it does me no injury for my neighbour to say there are twenty gods, or no god'.[40] But if he held the other belief,

[38] Jefferson (1955), p. 159.
[39] Jefferson (1955), pp. 159–61.
[40] Jefferson (1955), pp. 159–61.

civil society would be strongly affected by toleration, according to him. The two principles conflict: in order that the harm principle may lead to toleration, the belief about God's non-interference in temporal society needs to be imposed on all citizens.

In Jefferson's account, this inconsistency does not arise, because the principles are based on the belief that religion is strictly an individual matter between each believer and God. Hence, such claims as 'Almighty God hath created the mind free', 'religion is a matter which lies solely between man and his God', and that we are answerable to God alone for the rights of conscience are *not* rhetorical flourishes. They provide the theological framework necessary to make sense of Jefferson's separation of church and state. This framework can either be explicitly present; or it takes the form of topoi embedded in common sense.

The conceptual problems arise precisely because principles are extracted from a conceptual framework without heeding its theological constraints. This framework claims that religion is the relation between the individual believer and God. In Locke's theory, both the consideration of human fallibility and the principle that all religions ought to be tolerated so long as they do not harm civil society are limited by this theological view of religion. One thing is certain: God's wrath will not destroy societies allowing heresy and idolatry, since religion is the spiritual relationship between God and the soul, distinct and independent from temporal society. In other words, Lockean toleration is consistent within this theological framework, but after secularizing its principles into independent normative tenets, intractable conceptual problems arise.

The Secularization of Christian Freedom

'John Locke is the essential philosopher-advocate of liberal freedom and government—and of the state of mind designed to protect and spread them.'[41] Why have generations read Locke as the father of secular liberal democracy? What explains the structural similarities between his model of toleration and the modern liberal model?

The following hypothesis addresses these questions: the modern liberal conception of toleration emerged from the secularization of Christian

---

[41] Faulkner (2003), p. 320.

freedom and its separation of the two kingdoms. That is, the patterns that recurred across the different versions of this theology were transformed into topoi of western political thought. We read Locke as though his Christianity is but a religious layer that provided colour to the liberal structure of his political thought. He is the father of modern liberal-ism first and a Protestant thinker second. We are wrong. His political thought is Christian to the core. We are right to identify the basic scheme of liberal toleration in Locke's *Letter*. But this does not demonstrate that his thought is secular political theory; it indicates that modern liberal thought conceals religious structures behind secular garb.

The steps from Locke to Jefferson and beyond are not those of a ratio-nal Enlightenment extending its secular values to humanity, but those of an internal religious dynamic of secularization spreading Christian principles in secular guise. The liberal model of toleration is constrained by the conceptual schemes it inherited from its theological background. The puzzle of the two spheres illustrates this. In the theology of Christian liberty, the division of society into a sphere of political coercion and one of religious freedom does not cause any conceptual problems. It is founded in Christian anthropology: each individual consists of a soul and a body; and human life and society consist of spiritual and temporal realms accordingly. Human authorities can rule over the latter alone, for God is the only spiritual Lord. In Locke's defence of toleration in the *Letter*, these theological elements are still present. They are necessary to make sense of his account, for it is impossible to identify any of the two domains without reference to these background beliefs.

Once we take the step to the modern liberal thought on tolera-tion, however, the division of society into political and religious realms becomes a pre-theoretical starting point. No need is felt to clarify it; it is simply presupposed. The consequence is opacity: one does not know how to identify either the private domain of religious liberty or its public counterpart. This problem emerges because the liberal notion of tolera-tion builds on theological schemes rid of their saliently Christian features.

In the seventeenth-century debates about toleration among Christians, there was agreement on the principles of Christian liberty, but the boundaries of religion and the implications of these principles were contested. Some claimed that religious liberty referred only to freedom of belief; others argued that it also encompassed the freedom to express and practice beliefs. These debates took place against the background of a shared framework about the nature and characteristics of religion. For instance, the participants agreed that men should worship God and strive for the salvation of their souls or that the eternal spiritual world existed and sin had to be resisted. Such a minimal consensus, necessary to render the positions intelligible, is precisely what is missing in the contemporary debates.

This gives us further insight into the relationship between the dynamic of secularization and liberal political theory. Tropes or recurring patterns from Protestant political theology are retained, while their propositional content is rejected. These patterns are transformed into topoi interpreted and formulated in various ways. Importantly, such topoi operate as clusters: in order to make sense, they rely on a series of related theological concepts and metaphysical beliefs about humanity. Even though the clusters are subject to a range of interpretations, these are constrained by certain limits, namely those of the conceptual framework inherited from generic Christian theology.

The secularization of Christian liberty produces a series of normative principles as axioms of liberal political thought: for instance, the right to religious freedom and the separation of state and religion. Both make perfect sense when embedded in Protestant doctrine, as they are in the writings of Locke. The norm that individuals ought to be free in the spiritual realm is sustained by a set of beliefs about true faith as the work of God in the soul. The necessity of separating state and religion becomes equally obvious when this understanding of religion is present in the background.

These norms had such an obvious character to Locke because they were 'willed by God'. When extracted from this theological framework, they seem to retain their self-evident character: all reasonable thinking on the problem of diversity in a democratic society should take the right to religious liberty and the separation of church and state as its starting points.[42] Yet, political theorists feel the need to provide normative justifications for these principles of religious liberty.

---

[42] As Gordon Schochet puts it: 'The guiding presumptions—widely shared in the West—are that religion is generally a matter of personal conscience and that religious practices that do not threaten the stability or security of the state ought not to be interfered with.' Schochet (2003), p. 165.

This is a consequence of the secularization of norms based on a specific *religious* account of religion and its freedom. One can no longer invoke the theological conception of human existence to justify the principles of liberal toleration. One feels the need to provide a secular justification; but one lacks the conceptual resources to do so. That is, no scientific or secular theory is available to identify the realm of 'religion' across different societies or to explain what it means for 'worship' to be free.

The Conscience of the Philosophers

The classic understanding of the Enlightenment as the liberation of Western political thinking from the clutches of Christian doctrine stands diametrically opposed to the hypothesis presented in the previous section. In one case, secularization is viewed as the gradual decline of the hold of religion on Western political thought. In the other, the secularization of political thought amounts to the transformation of tropes from Christian-theological thinking into the topoi of modern Western culture. These topoi are clusters of commonplace ideas that help develop 'secular' theories concerning human existence. But did secularization take this form among all political thinkers of the Enlightenment? Perhaps there were thinkers other than Locke and Jefferson who did succeed at secularizing the liberal thinking about toleration without retaining any theological sediment.

The Rights of the Erring Conscience

The most avid advocates of toleration in the eighteenth century were the French Enlightenment philosophers. The groundwork for the debates had been laid in the late seventeenth century by the famous 'philosophe de Rotterdam', Pierre Bayle. Until the 1960s, Bayle was read as a crypto-atheist who cloaked his radical ideas in terms of Protestant theology. Later historians argued that he was a Calvinist whose theories rested on a foundation of Reformed theology.[43] Recently, Jonathan Israel suggests that the judgement 'that Bayle was genuinely the sincere Calvinist as he professed to be' is a 'rather eccentric' and 'in any case highly implausible

---

[43] Labrousse (1963–4), Rex (1965), Sandberg (1964).

claim'. Bayle's theory, he adds, was in fact 'an entirely secular conception of toleration and individual freedom'.[44]

Israel's claim is part of a larger distinction between a moderate mainstream Enlightenment, rooted in religion, and a radical Enlightenment, which supposedly emancipated Western thinking from religious dogma. In this classification, Locke belonged to the mainstream branch, whereas Bayle was a member of the radical Enlightenment. Israel claims one is wrong to discern a convergence between Locke's and Bayle's theories of toleration, for 'the two theories are actually totally different and incompatible, the first Protestant, theological, and limited, the latter entirely non-theological and universal'.[45] If Israel is right, then Bayle's theory should instantiate a fundamental conceptual break between the Enlightenment philosophy of toleration and the Protestant theology of Christian freedom.

As a Huguenot, Bayle had taken refuge in the Netherlands to escape persecution in Louis XIV's France. The revocation of the Edict of Nantes had withdrawn the rights granted by Henry IV in 1598 to 'those of the Reformed Religion, to live and dwell in all the Cities and places of this our Kingdom and Countreys under our obedience, without being inquired after, vexed, molested, or compelled to do any thing in Religion, contrary to their Conscience'.[46] Under the new policy, Huguenots were harassed systematically to return to Catholicism. Bayle examined the justifications for this policy of religious persecution in his *Philosophical Commentary* (1686), a commentary on Christ's words in the Gospel of Luke: 'Go out to the highways and hedges and compel people to come in, that my house may be filled' (Luke 14:23 [ESV]).

My concern is not that of identifying Bayle's religious convictions. Rather, the focus is on his theory of toleration and its purported independence from Christian ideas. Some of Bayle's arguments could certainly be called 'secular'. He drew upon the peaceful diversity of 'sects' and philosophical schools among the ancient Greeks and Romans in

---

[44] Israel (2004), pp. 3–5; see also his (2001), pp. 335–6, and (2006), pp. 145–54.

[45] Israel (2006), p. 146.

[46] Henry IV of France, 'The Edict of Nantes', 1 January 1598, cited in Forst (2013), p. 27.

order to refute the claim that toleration inevitably brings about disorder in society.[47] Yet, we are not looking for secular arguments but for *a conception of toleration entirely non-theological*, as Israel puts it. Prudential arguments for toleration had long been popular, but the basic normative principles remained theological: religion ought always to be free from human authority, because God alone could rule over our souls and judge our consciences. What needs to be settled, then, is the extent to which Bayle's conception of toleration is indeed independent from such theological ideas.

The core of Bayle's theory revolved around 'the rights of the erring conscience'. He argued that a conscience deceived by false religion should have the same rights as one following true religion. This principle extended freedom to the misguided conscience. Thus, toleration should encompass not only Muslims and Jews but 'heretics' and 'idolaters' also. How had Bayle come to this view?

Bayle asserts that this principle followed from a number of other principles, acknowledged by 'all the World'. First, the intention to disobey God is a sin. Second, the will to disobey the fixed and final judgement of one's conscience is equivalent to the will to disobey God. Whatever the conscience declares, it declares as God's will. It is one and the same thing to say 'my conscience judges a particular action to be good or bad' or 'my conscience judges this particular action to be pleasing or displeasing to God'. From the previous two, the third principle is derived: whatever is done against the dictate of conscience is sin. The fourth emphasizes that the worst kind of sin is that committed while being aware of its sinful nature. And any act against the judgement of conscience is a sin of this kind.[48]

Bayle's fifth principle is more complex: an act that is good if done according to the directions of conscience, would become worse, if done against the instruction of conscience, than another act done according to the instruction of conscience, which would be incontestably wrong if conscience had not commanded it. For instance, if one's conscience told one not to give alms to a beggar and one still insisted on doing so, this act would be worse than scolding the same beggar if this was the instruction

---

of one's conscience. In other words, conscience is the ultimate tribunal of the morality of one's actions:

> From all these Principles I may reasonably conclude, that the first and most indispensable of all our Obligations, is that of never acting against the Instincts of Conscience; and that every Action done against the Lights of Conscience is essentially evil ... There is therefore an eternal and immutable Law, obliging Man, upon pain of incurring the Guilt of the most heinous mortal Sin that can be committed, never to do any thing in violation and in despite of Conscience.[49]

To go against what one believes to be God's will is contempt of God, even if one's understanding is deceived. Therefore, all religions should be tolerated, because (so Bayle assumed) their followers think theirs is the true revelation of God's will. To compel them to reject their religion is equivalent to compelling them to sin, since it entails violating the conscience.[50]

How had Bayle come to the conviction that the principles from which he derived the rights of the erring conscience were acknowledged by the entire world? His *Commentary* proposes that God engraved the common principles of reason on the human soul. Both 'reason' and 'conscience', in his view, are the natural light implanted by God into our souls with the purpose of conveying His will. Bayle believes that the Almighty had printed on Adam's mind the eternal law so that Adam knew he should obey his Maker—not so much because of an outward prohibition, but because of the inward light guiding his conscience. After the Fall, this inner light had become more important because Adam experienced that two forces could direct him. Now it was necessary to have a rule to judge by, because of the fear to confuse between God's revelation and the devil's enticements 'disguis'd under the fairest Appearances.'[51]

It should be clear that Bayle did not build a secular theory of conscience and its freedom. His account of the rights of the erring conscience was founded in the classical theology of freedom developed during the two preceding centuries. 'Conscience of right and wrong' was not some secular moral criterion internalized by an individual for Bayle. The Lord had

---

[49] Bayle (2005), p. 227.
[50] Bayle (2005), pp. 225–7.
[51] Bayle (2005), pp. 70–1.

imprinted it onto the soul to abet the believer in distinguishing between the divine will and the devious intentions of Satan.

Similarly, the granting of rights to the erroneous conscience is not founded in some secular notion of reciprocity or equity. Bayle's ultimate concern was different: the conscience can be deceived by the devil, but fallible humans lack the capacity to know when their consciences convey God's will and when they are misled. No human can judge the conscience of another. Only God has perfect knowledge of His will and of His creatures' consciences. Therefore, each individual's conscience is the definitive tribunal for the judgement of his or her acts: whatever it prescribes, it prescribes as God's will. From all this, it follows that an erroneous conscience has the same rights as the right conscience.

The Yoke of 'Popery'

Bayle's understanding of religion was very close to that of Locke and earlier advocates of toleration. The essence of religion consists of an inward disposition of the soul towards God. Therefore, external acts of religion are approved by God only in proportion to the internal acts of the mind from which they proceed. 'It's evident then', Bayle pointed out, 'that the only reasonable way of inspiring Religion, is by producing in the Soul certain Judgments with relation to God, and certain Motions of the Will'. Threats, fines, banishment, torturing, and any other form of compulsion cannot form in the soul the judgements and motions of the will that constitute the essence of religion. Motions of the will brought about by compulsion have no relation to God but only to the persecutors. Those compelled fear their persecutors and act accordingly; this does not contribute to the reverence, love, and fear due to the Supreme Being.

Like so many Protestant thinkers, Bayle argued that compulsion generated the worst sin, namely hypocrisy towards God. Insomuch as outward signs of religion exist without corresponding interior states of the soul, they are acts of hypocrisy and falsehood. This made it all too obvious to him that it was contrary to good sense, to the light of nature, and to the common principles of reason, to exercise violence upon the conscience in order to impose any religion.[52]

[52] Bayle (2005), pp. 76–7.

Of course, there are limits to liberty. Bayle's rights of the erring conscience did not entail that the sovereign should always tolerate all religions. If the principles of a 'sect' harmed the public good, threats and temporal punishment could be used for reasons of state. Secular authorities may first try to convert the sect's members away from their harmful principles by friendly conferences, books, and instructions. If these had no effect, however, the authorities could very justly force them to settle elsewhere.[53] In other words, toleration was confined to the spiritual realm and did not extend to doctrines with harmful impact on state and society. So long as followers of a religion preach submission to the magistrate, pay taxes, and acknowledge that no man should be disturbed in the possession of his right and peaceable enjoyment of his goods, there is no ground for persecuting them simply because they refuse to entertain some belief or form of worship.[54]

Much like 'the commonwealth' in Locke's theory, Bayle's realm of the public good corresponds to what had been called 'the temporal kingdom' in political theology. Where it concerned such matters as enjoyment of property, bodily welfare, and reputation in society, civil authority should not be questioned. But so long as the principles and practices of a religious group do not violate the laws of this domain, they ought to be left completely free. In religion, the inalienable rights of the conscience prevented the magistrate from imposing any law.

The basic structure of Bayle's theory of toleration does not differ fundamentally from its predecessors in the Dutch Republic and elsewhere. In several texts, he simultaneously defends the absolute power of kings over their subjects and the unconditional freedom of conscience that kings should grant even to known heretics.[55] This he could do because of the strict division between the outward realm of the body and the inward realm of conscience, which he had inherited from political theology. Hence, the following conclusion simply has no grounds: 'In contrast to Locke's theological toleration, toleration in Bayle rests exclusively on the principles of equity and secular i.e. non-theologically explicated or rooted morality ...'[56]

---

[53] Bayle (2005), p. 114.
[54] Bayle (2005), pp. 188–9.
[55] Simonutti (1996), pp. 543–4.
[56] Israel (2004), p. 7.

The theological constraints shared by Locke and Bayle give rise to another common feature: Catholicism is a problematic candidate for toleration. In the preface to the English translation of his *Commentary*, Bayle makes no secret of his aversion towards 'the Papists'. 'The very Papists in this Country are the first to cry out', he writes, 'that nothing is more unjust than vexing Men on the score of Conscience.'[57] But this sounds ridiculous, perfidious, and insincere: not long before English Catholics had persecuted anyone who refused to attend mass and, if in power, they would do the same.

The difficulty is that Catholicism fails to respect the basic norm of Bayle's theory: the separation of the conscience from human authority. According to Catholic tradition, the conscience is subject to the Church's authority. Therefore, Bayle believes, Catholics always have the tendency to try and usurp the magistrate's authority in order to coerce consciences. Doctrines about the papacy's supreme authority directly threaten the sovereign's authority. Such doctrines, Bayle declares, are not worthy of toleration. Therefore, all states that had shaken off 'the Yoke of Popery' should make the most severe laws against its readmission. Where 'papists' still lived, they should be kept in chains like so many lions and leopards. But the state should neither disturb the private exercise of religion of Catholic subjects, nor should it prevent them from raising their children in their faith. From this perspective, no coercion of religion is involved, for the penal laws imposed on Catholics had purely temporal reasons.[58]

From the Catholic perspective, however, this did involve coercion of religion. Bayle's model forced their religion to remain within certain limits: individuals were allowed to believe in the truth of Catholicism, but no Church could be permitted that exercised authority over the believers in the secular world. These were not the limitations of a neutral political framework. Rather, as was the case in Locke's account, they derived from the theological framework behind Bayle's model of toleration. Even where both thinkers invoked 'secular' raison d'état, their reasons were based in a deeply normative *and* theological view of religion.

An extraordinary shift had taken place in the theorizing of Bayle, Locke, and other early Enlightenment thinkers. In medieval Christianity,

---

[57] Bayle (2005), pp. 38–9.
[58] Bayle (2005), pp. 190–2.

liberty had been a function of submission to the Sovereign: one became free in so far as one turned to God and submitted one's own will to His will. As the clergy went through conversion, it gained spiritual authority over the laity, including kings and emperors. In Protestant doctrine, the result of each believer's conversion to God was a spiritual freedom that put limits on the coercive powers of secular authorities. At the same time, submission to secular authority was a precondition of this freedom. In the realm of the flesh, believers should always obey its coercive laws; any form of religion preventing this could not be tolerated.

In Bayle and Locke's political theories, liberty of conscience likewise presupposed submission to secular authority. Religion could be free only in so far as it did not encroach upon the sovereignty of the emerging nation state. No religion could claim for itself coercive powers or demand subjection to any extraterritorial authority. The self-evidence of this standpoint in the modern world cannot hide its theological roots. Its consequence was the rejection of Catholicism as an expression of *false* religion, which could not, in its current form, be tolerated according to 'secular' raison d'état, precisely because it failed to separate religion from politics.[59]

This step resulted from the secularization of the normative dynamic behind the historical development of the Protestant Reformation. In its explicitly religious form, this dynamic was propelled by the ever-recurring gap between the norm of God's will and the fact of human failure to live up to this norm. It involved descriptions of the religious institutions of Catholicism, Judaism, and confessional Protestantism as negations of the norms of Christian freedom. In the moment of secularization, these norms were transformed into principles of the public order and reason of the modern nation state. However, the disjunction between norm and fact remained: the Roman-Catholic Church and other institutions continued to be described as negations of the normative model of liberal toleration, which had to adapt themselves to this model or disappear.

---

[59] In today's liberal discourse, Islam has come to replace Catholicism as the prototypical religion that has not yet learnt the art of separation and supposedly encroaches upon the realm that belongs exclusively to the state. See Shakman Hurd (2007).

Generally, the structural similarities between the toleration theories of Locke and Bayle are as striking as are their common theological moorings. Contra Israel, Bayle's theory is not 'entirely non-theological and universal'; it is as much 'Protestant, theological, and limited' as is Locke's. These theories indirectly imposed Protestant theological structures onto all groups in society. In this sense, the dominance of liberal toleration unto this day indicates that the European wars of religion had a victor after all: in important ways, the Protestant Reformation fashioned the political structures of the modern West and the Church adapted itself to these structures.

Topoi of Toleration

Originally, the principles of toleration had drawn their power from a framework of beliefs about God, the soul and its conversion, and faith as the work of the Holy Spirit. To understand divine revelation, it was said, human beings need the illumination of the Spirit. But how do we know when our understanding is enlightened by His presence. Who is to judge? One man ought not to impose his own beliefs on another, because all humans were equally fallible as opposed to our infallible Creator. As the Puritan John Saltmarsh put it in *Smoke in the Temple* (1646), we should not assume any power of infallibility over each other, 'for there lies as much on one side for compulsions as on another, respectively to one another, for another's evidence is as dark to me as mine to him, and mine to him as his to me, till the Lord enlighten us both for discerning alike'.[60]

Likewise, Enlightenment philosophers often argued as follows: all human beings are weak and prone to make mistakes; therefore, they ought to tolerate each other's errors. Voltaire wrote that toleration is the prerogative of humanity: 'We are all steeped in weaknesses and errors: let us forgive one another's follies, it is the first law of nature.' Similarly, the entry 'Tolérance' in the *Encyclopédie* of Diderot and d'Alembert—'one of the most prominent texts of the period on the subject'[61]—said that toleration was the virtue of any weak being that had to live together with

---

[60] Saltmarsh (1992), pp. 181–2.
[61] Tomaselli (2000), p. 88.

other similar beings. In spite of intelligence, humanity was burdened with errors and passions. Hence, without toleration, life on earth would be continuously disrupted by discord.[62]

At face value, the significance and coherence of these claims are unclear. First, if humans are always fallible, this also goes for those who propose fallibility as a justification of toleration. But then this argument becomes self-defeating: we can never know infallibly that all humans are equally fallible and prone to error; therefore we ought not to impose our belief about human fallibility on others in the form of a principle of toleration. Second, in what sense does the fact that humans commit errors make us weak beings? Why should this tendency to err lead to strife? As human beings, we learn only from our errors, so this can hardly be an expression of weakness, unless of course humanity is contrasted to some infallible Being.

The substance of this argument becomes clear when one imagines the behaviour of a group that imposes its religion on others because some men are not considered as prone to error as others. This group thinks it possesses a truth binding on all and therefore persecutes others. In fact, this rehashes the story of anticlerical theology: inspired by the devil, clerics believed they had an infallible and coercive authority to impose spiritual laws on the believers.

Protestant advocates of Christian liberty had emphasized that all were equally fallible in their knowledge of God's will. This was true, for God had revealed it to be so. No human institution had the authority to bind others to its understanding of religion. In this sense, fallibility in religious matters was a ground for toleration. In the Enlightenment version, the point remained the same: given our epistemic limitations, we are never certain about the truth and therefore ought not to impose our beliefs on others. The argument about the weakness of erring beings is a 'secular' translation of a theological justification for toleration. In this sense, Christian religious ideas constitute *the conditions of intelligibility* of the Enlightenment philosophy of toleration.

The eighteenth-century philosopher's arguments for toleration were often fragmentary. In contrast to Locke's *Letter* or Bayle's *Commentary*, for instance, Voltaire's chief essay on the topic, the *Traité de la Tolérance*

---

[62] Romilly (1986), p. 335.

(1763), did not lay out any coherent theory. This difference in style also illustrates a different stance: Voltaire found it self-evident that toleration is a moral obligation. He limited himself to exclamations about the irrationality of intolerance, persecution, and fanaticism: 'Philosophy, the sister of religion, has disarmed the hands that superstition had so long stained with blood; and the human mind awakening from its intoxication, is amazed at the excesses into which fanaticism has led it.' Similarly: 'Toleration, in fine, never led to civil war; intolerance has covered the earth with carnage. Choose, then, between these rivals—between the mother who would have her son slain and the mother who yields, provided his life be spared.'[63]

Such remarks were powerful only because centuries of theological debate had prepared the ground. Like his predecessors, Voltaire suggested that it was not religion, but its *abuse* when wrongly conceived, which inspired intolerance.[64] In his *Philosophical Dictionary* (1764), he affirmed that the chief obstacle to the rise of toleration was the human exploitation of religion as a means to power. 'Dissension is the great evil of mankind', he wrote, 'and toleration its only remedy.' Everyone knew this. Yet powerful men and jealous priests had opposed it because they abused religion in order to advance their selfish interests. Similarly, the motto of the *philosophes*, attributed to Denis Diderot, is hardly a paragon of toleration: 'Men will never be free until the last king is strangled with the entrails of the last priest.' The advocacy of toleration continued to go hand in hand with the anticlerical diatribes of the Reformation.

In the absence of this background, it would be difficult to make sense of moral arguments for toleration that are themselves violently intolerant. In fact, the philosophes' claims were often impossible to tell apart from the theology of Protestant dissenters. In his *Traité*, Voltaire wrote: 'One does not need great art and skilful eloquence to prove that Christians ought to tolerate each other—nay, even to regard all men as brothers ... Assuredly; are we not all children of the same father, creatures of the same God?' Or: 'Must each individual usurp the rights of the Deity, and decide, before he does, the eternal lot of all men?' Such religious doctrines could now be raised as rhetorical questions.

---

[63] Voltaire (1994), p. 161, p. 165, p. 169.

[64] Voltaire (1994), pp. 160–1.

Some historians argue that Voltaire was part of the mainstream religious Enlightenment, but place Diderot in the secular camp of the radical Enlightenment.[65] Still, irrespective of his personal atheism, Diderot also reproduced the norms of Protestant dissent. Consider his entry 'Intolérance' in the *Encyclopédie*:

> It is impious to seek to impose laws upon conscience, the universal principle of our actions. Conscience must be enlightened and not constrained. Men who fall into error in good faith should be pitied, never punished. Neither men of good faith nor men of bad faith should be subject to torment; judgement over them must be left to God.[66]

Soon, the need would no longer be felt to refer to the belief that God alone could judge the human conscience; it became axiomatic that each individual's conscience ought to be free. Diderot pointed out that it could not be truly Christian to persecute one's fellow humans, because the spiritual kingdom was not of this world: 'When you hate your brother, and preach hatred to your neighbour, is it the spirit of God which inspires you? Christ has said: My kingdom is not of this world, and you, his disciples, wish to tyrannise over this world!' Finally, he stressed that salvation of the soul was an individual matter: 'Bring about your own salvation. Pray for mine, and recognise that everything you allow yourself beyond that is an appalling injustice in the eyes of God and men.'[67]

The hold of the topoi of Christian freedom on eighteenth-century French political thought becomes even clearer in the work of the 'anti-Enlightenment' thinker Jean-Jacques Rousseau. In the chapter on civil religion of *Du contrat social* (1762), Rousseau discussed the limits of the authority conferred by the social contract onto the sovereign:

> The right which the social pact gives to the sovereign over its subjects does not ... go beyond the limits of public utility. Subjects, then, owe no account of their opinions to the sovereign except so far as those opinions are of importance to the community. Now it is very important for the State that every citizen should have a religion which may make him delight in his

---

[65] Israel (2004), pp. 814–24.
[66] Diderot (1992), pp. 29–30.
[67] Diderot (1992), p. 30.

duties; but the dogmas of this religion concern neither the State nor its members, except so far as they affect morality and the duties which he who professes it is bound to perform toward others. Each may have, in addition, such opinions as he pleases, without its being the business of the sovereign to know them; for, as he has no jurisdiction in the other world, the destiny of his subjects in the life to come, whatever it may be, is not his affair, provided they are good citizens in this life.[68]

This generates a central question: Which opinions affect morality and are therefore of importance to the community? Which do not? To the average eighteenth-century Catholic, obedience to the papacy and its bulls was of the greatest importance to the community and greatly affected the duties one ought to perform towards others. After all, the salvation of the community of believers depended on such beliefs and salvation constituted the paramount interest of the Church. Calvinists and Deists, however, held completely different answers to the same question. Who had the authority to arbitrate between these opinions? Prima facie, the sovereign could not, since he was not allowed to interfere in, *or even know*, the opinions of his subjects concerning the other world.

To Rousseau and many of his predecessors, it was obvious that the sovereign had no jurisdiction in the other world and no authority over the religious opinions of his subjects, so long as they were good citizens in this world. However, whenever a conflict came into being between the subjects' life in this world *as good citizens* and their religious life *as devout men*, their religion should be banned. This was consistent with Rousseau's theory of the general will, which no longer allowed any institution but the state to claim sovereignty in this world. Only the state could embody the general will. Given the social contract, men-as-citizens also had to represent this general will *in their capacity as members of the state*. This conflicted with religious organizations that claimed to represent 'the general will' for believers in this earthly life. These encroached upon the realm of the state and prevented the devout from being good citizens. Therefore, such religions should be banned.

Unsurprisingly, Rousseau identified a flawed type of religion that could not be tolerated, namely, 'the religion of the priest', which 'giving to men two sets of laws, two leaders, two fatherlands, imposes on them contradictory

[68]   Rousseau (2002), p. 252.

duties, and prevents them from being simultaneously devout men and citizens. Catholicism belonged to this type, along with the religion of 'the Lamas' and the Japanese. This kind of religion was 'so evidently bad that it would be a waste of time to stop and prove this'.[69]

Why was this type of religion so evidently bad? Members of a state could be devout men, but only if this allowed them to be citizens devoted to the general will at the same time. The 'religion of the priest' prevented them from doing so because it tied the devout to another sovereign. In this sense, Catholicism and similar religions would inevitably clash with the general will: they generated a conflict between *homme* (man) and *citoyen* (citizen). The Roman-Catholic hierarchy had to give up the claim that it possessed sovereignty here on earth and represented the general will (God's will) and the general interest of the community of believers (salvation).[70]

In other words, Rousseau's political theory reproduced the constraints put on Catholicism by Protestant political theology but did so in terms of the general will. Reformers argued that the Church could not be a religious or divine institution, for it could not embody God's will on earth but was merely a human political institution. This point derived from the axiom that no human could have authority over another's religion. The ruler's sovereignty was limited to this temporal world. Rousseau's point was virtually identical: no religious institution could claim that it represented God's general will on earth. Only the sovereign nation state could represent the general will and possess the resultant authority. Any religion that infringed on this monopoly was self-evidently bad for it compelled the devout to subjection to another sovereign than the state and thus made them bad citizens. Such religions had to be banned by the state.

The Emergence of *Laïcité*

Did the philosophes appeal to theology because they addressed an audience still largely Christian? They explicitly denied the truth of Christian

---

[69] Rousseau (2002), pp. 249–50.

[70] See Riley (1986) for an argument that shows how the theological idea of God's will to save all men was transformed into 'the citizen's "general will" to place the common good above his "particular" will as a private self'.

doctrines and interpreted terms like 'God', 'conscience', and 'religion' differently than most theologians, this much is clear. How could their principles of toleration then be said to depend on a theological framework?

Whatever beliefs or disbeliefs they expressed, the Enlightenment philosophers continued to defend principles developed within the confines of a specific theological framework during the previous centuries. In the meantime, *no alternative secular theories* had materialized concerning the phenomena of religion and conscience. *No new framework* had come up to answer questions like the following: What is the nature and structure of the conscience? Why should human fallibility prevent us from imposing our beliefs upon others? How is the realm of religion identified and distinguished from that of politics across societies? The only framework available for interpreting and answering such questions remained the background theology of Christian freedom, no matter how vaguely formulated. Its principles, such as the separation of the two kingdoms and the autonomy of each conscience, had become topoi of Enlightenment philosophy.

However, the French Enlightenment interpreted these topoi in a way that diverged significantly from the earlier interpretations by Dutch and English Protestant thinkers. The problem situation in France was very different from that of the Dutch Republic or England. The latter countries had to accommodate a multiplicity of Protestant groups, Catholics, and Jews in the same society. A particular model of religious toleration and freedom brought the solution: the state ought not to interfere in the religion of its subjects and should allow each community to live by its religious beliefs and values. In contrast, the problem in France was the dominance of the Catholic Church and its grip on politics and education. The Enlightenment thinkers wished to bring an end to this, as Voltaire's motto '*écrasez l'infâme*' indicated ('crush the infamous'—'the infamous' referring to the tyranny of the Church).

The philosophes reproduced the Protestant critique of Catholicism but transformed this into a general critique of organized religion, which according to them was dogmatic, superstitious, and dominated by a duplicitous power-hungry clergy. Instead of arguing that the state should refrain from interfering in religion and tolerate all forms of religion (except those that harmed the public order), they developed a different principle: given these harmful properties, the Church and all other forms of organized religion ought to be banned from politics, education, and the public sphere.

This principle emerged from the convergence of two factors: the secularization of anticlerical theology into a general critique of religion and the concern to break the hold of the Church on society. Gradually, it gave rise to the anti-religious model of laïcité of the French Republic. This model strives to ban all manifestations of organized religion from the public sphere. However, because it draws upon the same topoi inherited from anticlerical theology, it can often be combined with the earlier-mentioned model of religious toleration and freedom. The different secular states of contemporary Europe are constituted by the interplay between these two models. We see in them the alternation between concerns about state interference in religion, religious freedom, and toleration on the one hand, and concerns about banning all expressions of religion from the public sphere on the other hand.

* * *

Enlightenment thinkers crafted the formulas about religion and politics that remain self-evident to the liberals of our times. From Locke and Bayle to Jefferson and Diderot, these principles never cast off the conceptual baggage inherited from Christianity. They revolved around topoi: clusters of secularized theological ideas that could be articulated, interpreted, combined, and permutated in different ways. Consequently, theory formation concerning these ideas remained within the cognitive limits set by the theological foundations upon which it was built.

That is to say, the liberal model of secularism and toleration operates under certain conditions of intelligibility. In order to retain its sense and significance, it requires the background presence of a series of secularized theological notions: religion is a universal domain of all societies; human beings have a conscience; religion and politics are two distinct spheres of human social existence; and many other beliefs. The moment of secularization of Christianity's double dynamic of universalization transferred these clusters of ideas from explicitly theological settings to the common-sense reasoning of Western societies and from there to liberal political theory.

In the absence of this background, the liberal model faces fundamental problems that threaten its intelligibility and accessibility. These problems arise from trying to provide secular foundations for the model of Christian freedom and its two kingdoms. Showing in 'secular' language that such claims of Christianity are true is about as plausible as explaining the notion of 'Christ' without bringing in beliefs about Original Sin and God's promise to humanity. In other words, Christian theology constitutes the basic conditions of intelligibility for normative liberal theories of toleration and secularism. Where it is not available, these theories threaten to become unintelligible.

This may seem like a bold claim. But then such a hypothesis is also vulnerable because its cognitive value can be tested: it should possess the ability to predict new facts and its consequences should prove to be true. This is what distinguishes it from a random collection of historical facts or ad hoc account about the rise of modern liberalism. The remaining chapters turn to this task of testing the hypothesis: Does the liberal model indeed bring about unanticipated and intractable problems, when it enters cultural contexts where its conditions of intelligibility are missing?

6. Religious Toleration in British India

I s it impossible to be faithful to our highest obligations, while at the same time we exhibit perfect toleration towards all systems of religious belief besides our own?'[1] So wrote an author reflecting on the role of Christian statesmen in British India in 1859. By the late eighteenth century, the principle of tolerating 'idolatry' and 'heresy' had travelled to the colonies. In India, the colonial government confronted the issue of tolerating practices deemed idolatrous and immoral. This generated a thorny question: was the policy of religious toleration reconcilable with the duties of Christian believers?

The British believed that Hindu religion and the caste system constituted 'religious tyranny'. Drawing on anticlerical theology, both missionaries and orientalists agreed that Brahmin priests had cloaked their human fabrications as divine revelation and manipulated ignorant believers to satisfy their worldly desires. Yet, much to the dismay of the missionaries, the orientalists argued that the government ought to tolerate the religious

[1] Laclear (1859), p. 56.

practices of the Hindus. At the dawn of the Raj, religious toleration and impartial rule became guiding principles of colonial policymaking.

This belief in the moral value of toleration generates a problem. Most British colonials in this period were Protestant believers of some kind. They held different beliefs but all viewed the Bible as the revelation of God's will, believed that His will should be obeyed by all human creatures, and claimed that one's duties as a Christian included persuading others to convert to God. Minimally, this implied that one should prevent violations of God's will when in a position to do so. The British also agreed that many Hindu practices violated divine and natural law. From this, it seemed to follow that wherever the authorities could do so, they ought to prevent the practice of 'false religion'. Given the restrictions on forced conversion, they could perhaps not eradicate Hindu beliefs but they certainly ought to prevent these from being practiced. Yet, colonial administrators not only argued that Hindu practices should be tolerated, but also integrated Hindu law into colonial jurisdiction.

This chapter looks closer into this issue. The first section examines the British policy of tolerating controversial practices like sati or 'widow-burning'. Colonial officials looked for scriptural sanctions for these practices in order to justify the policy of religious toleration. This approach was constituted by the normative framework of Christian freedom. The second section shows how this framework did not leave the Indian traditions untouched. Under the impact of the toleration policy, these traditions were fundamentally restructured according to a specific model of religion. This transformation gave rise not only to the Hindu reform movements of the nineteenth century but also to a strand of 'fundamentalism' that played a major role in the emergence of Hindu nationalism.

The Liberty of Hindu Tyranny

When the East India Company became a governing power in Bengal, critical policy decisions had to be made. What should be the stance of colonial rulers towards indigenous beliefs and practices? In 1793, it was decided that the laws of Quran and 'Shaster' would be preserved in civil and religious usages.[2] Time and again, officials stated 'that it is a fundamental

---

[2] See Kaye (1859), pp. 366–96. The 'Shaster' was the general name given by the British to the supposed scriptures of 'heathen religion' in India.

principle of the British government, to allow the most complete toleration in matters of religion, to all classes of its native subjects'.[3] British rule aimed to establish a liberal state in India, which over the years repeatedly reaffirmed 'its ancient policy of perfect neutrality in matters affecting the religion of the people of India'.[4]

The first Governor General of Bengal, Warren Hastings, introduced toleration as the official policy of British rule. This entailed that officials would tolerate, study, and even endorse practices and laws of the Hindu population. The dominant explanations of this situation run along two lines: on one hand, the debates about the toleration policy reflected the concern that the population would unite and defeat the British if the latter failed to accept indigenous customs.[5] On the other hand, this is often connected to the power–knowledge nexus in the colonial state: the British desired to know Hindu laws and scriptures and protected the same so as to secure colonial power and its economic benefits.[6] In other words, today's dominant explanations of the British toleration policy present political expediency as its decisive motive.

The explanation often takes the following form. When the East India Company became a governing power, two major decisions were made: to exclude settlement of British civilians, so as to avoid antagonizing the natives and creating a troublesome settler power; and to continue government protection of Indian religions and ban evangelization by Christian missionaries. With these measures, it is said, the British intended to conciliate the prejudices of the natives and prevent rebellion.

[3] From a letter to the register of the *nizamat adalat* (provincial court), dated 5 December 1812, signed by G. Dowdeswell, Chief Secretary to the Bengal government, *British Parliamentary Papers* (*BPP*) 1821, vol. 18, p. 31.

[4] The quote is from a despatch by Lord Ellenborough endorsed by Lord Stanley in the House of Commons on 30 July 1858, in Stock (1899), pp. 251–2. From its beginning, the colonial state was explicitly viewed in terms of religious toleration. From 1857, colonial officials and missionaries described the state's principle and policy as 'religious neutrality'. See Farquhar (1915), p. 11; Kaye (1859); Laclear (1859); Stock (1899), p. 157, pp. 235–80; Tupper (1893), pp. 311–12.

[5] Hastings (1968), pp. 1–8; Munro (1968), pp. 121–34; Teignmouth (1968), pp. 9–20.

[6] Cohn (1996), pp. 57–75; Dirks (2006), pp. 209–24; Irschick (1994); Mani (1998); Zastoupil and Moir (1999), pp. 1–72.

In doing so, the Company took on the role played by earlier Muslim and Hindu rulers.[7]

A 1793 regulation framed by Lord Cornwallis and Sir George Barlow stated that 'the regulations which may be adopted for the internal government of the country will be calculated to preserve ... the laws of the Shastre and the Koran in matters to which they have been invariably applied', and also 'to protect them in the free exercise of their religion'.[8] The domestic sphere was specifically put off limits. An Act of Parliament declared that 'in order that due regard may be had to the civil and religious usages of the natives, be it enacted that the rights and authorities of fathers of families and masters of families, according as the same may be exercised by the Gentoo or Mahomedan law, shall be preserved to them within their families respectively'.[9] Several scholars note that British rulers, in creating Hindu and Muslim family law, were following the English circumstance where marriage and inheritance came under Anglican Church law.[10]

There are two problems with this explanation. First, it does not answer the question raised here, which is not about explaining why tolerance was of prudential value to the East India Company. Sources show that such arguments played a role. The first two orientalists who compiled Hindu legal codes, Nathaniel Halhed and William Jones, invoked the many benefits of allowing the subjects to live by the laws 'which they have been taught to believe sacred'.[11] Hastings shared these notions of expediency. But my question is different: Why did toleration become an unconditional moral obligation for the colonial state? Here, arguments from expediency do not help, for these had existed centuries before toleration assumed the status of a moral principle.

Second, the explanation begs the question. The British looked for justifications for Indian practices in 'sacred texts'. In fact, they searched feverishly for scriptural sanctions for practices that their own religion condemned. They did not just follow earlier Muslim rulers, but tried to identify Hindu scriptures, codify these, and build laws around them. In

---

[7]   See Carson (2001), pp. 45–70; Dirks (2006), pp. 209–24, p. 298. For an overview of the historical developments, see Kaye (1859), pp. 366–96.

[8]   Kaye (1859), pp. 374–5.

[9]   Kaye (1859), p. 375.

[10]   Derrett (1968), pp. 233–7; Lariviere (1989), pp. 757–69.

[11]   W. Jones (2000), p. xvi. See also Halhed (2000), p. xi.

other words, scriptural foundations played a normative role in justifying toleration. By appealing to Hindu texts the British provided a moral justification for the laws they enacted. Why resort to such justifications unless one felt that the toleration policy required normative foundations?

Sacred Law or Civil Crime?

Take the colonial policy with respect to practices like sati or self-immolation of widows. By the end of the eighteenth century, most colonials thought of sati as the most detestable precept of the system of 'Hindu sacred law'. Nevertheless, until Lord William Bentinck, Governor-General of India, decided to abolish it in 1829, the colonial government tolerated the practice.

The question whether or not sati was a religious practice was central to colonial discourse. Was it a civil custom or Hindu sacred law? In the second half of the eighteenth century, Halhed had ridiculed Alexander Dow, author of an early dissertation on the Hindus, for denying that sati was a religious duty of Hindu widows.[12] The collectors and magistrates in Bengal soon raised the same issue. From 1789 onwards, they noted that the 'rites and superstitions of the Hindoo religion should be allowed with the most unqualified tolerance', but asked for special instructions regarding 'a practice at which human nature shudders'.[13]

The *nizamat adalat* or provincial court was requested by the government 'to ascertain ... by means of a reference to the pundits', how far the practice of sati was 'founded in the religious opinions of the Hindoos'.[14] All agreed that the practice, 'horrid and revolting even as a voluntary one, should be prohibited and entirely abolished'.[15] Still, in 1812, the government noted that the pundits had concluded that sati was part of Hindu law:

[12] Halhed (2000), pp. xlvi–xlvii, pp. lxx–lxxi. Dow (1970), p. 116.

[13] Letter from the Collector of Shahabad (M.H. Brooke), to Charles Earl Cornwallis, Governor General in Council, Fort William, in *BPP* (1821), vol. 18, p. 22. See pp. 22–24 for other examples.

[14] 'Extract Bengal Judicial Consultations, 7th February 1805', in *BPP* (1821), vol. 18, p. 24.

[15] 'Extract Bengal Judicial Consultations, 5th December 1812', in *BPP* (1821), vol. 18, p. 27.

The practice, generally speaking, being thus recognized and encouraged by the doctrines of the Hindoo religion, it appears evident that the course which the British government should follow, according to the principle of religious toleration already noticed, is to allow the practice in those cases in which it is countenanced by their religion; and to prevent it in others in which it is by the same authority prohibited.[16]

The government discourse was unambiguous: where local customs deviated from 'the Shaster', the latter had precedence. Even though awareness existed of regional variations, the colonial state did not systematically try to find out whether local Hindus really considered sati central to their customs. Some magistrates did do so on their own initiative. The official stance, however, revolved around the issue of scriptural sanctions: pundits were asked whether in 'case of ... a widow's burning herself with the corpse of her deceased husband, *are any and what rules prescribed by the Shasters* for the manner in which the rite is to be performed ...?'[17]

Similar questions were raised about other practices. A Bengal case concerned a Muslim who had buried alive his leprous mother-in-law, after she had requested him to burn her. The court stated that while this Muslim should be convicted, in the case of a Hindu indicted for a similar offence, the judgement of the pundits showed 'that the prisoner was justified by the ordinances of the Hindoo faith in assisting at the suicide of a leper'. As a judge had remarked in an earlier case: 'I am assured, that in the case of Hindoos it is countenanced and enjoined by their religion.'[18] Pundits quoted the 'Brahma Poorana' to show that the act was indeed 'sanctioned by the Shaster'.[19] Consequently, the state ought to allow it among Hindus.

[16] 'To the Register of the Nizamut Adawlut', (5th December 1812, signed by G. Dowdeswell, Chief Secretary to Government), in *BPP* (1821), vol. 18, p. 31.

[17] 'Translation of certain Questions proposed to the Hindoo Law Officers of the Sudder Dewanny Adawlut, regarding the burning of Widows, &c. and their Replies in conformity with the authorities current in Bengal and Benares', in *BPP* (1821), vol. 18, p. 115, italics added.

[18] 'Extract from the Report of the Criminal Cases adjudged by the Court of Nizamut Adawlut, in the year 1810', in *BPP* (1821), vol. 18, pp. 25–6.

[19] 'Extract from the Report of the Criminal Cases adjudged by the Court of Nizamut Adawlut, in the year 1810', in *BPP* (1821), vol. 18, pp. 25–6.

Perhaps the most shocking custom was that of 'offering human sacrifice to the Ganges, where they are devoured by the sharks'. A similar debate ensued here. It was decided that the practice should be allowed among the aged and infirm, since it was considered by Hindus 'instrumental to their happiness in a future state of existence' and 'sanctioned by express tenets in their most sacred books'. Where it concerned children, however, officials found that the custom 'stands not either on the prescriptive laws of antiquity, or on any tenet of the Shanscrit'. Consequently, an 1802 law declared any person who assisted in forcing 'any individual to be a victim of this superstition' guilty of murder.[20] Of female infanticide, it was similarly concluded that it has 'not the sanction of any religion, or of any law' and could therefore be eradicated.[21]

However, in the case of a widow, who was 'at her own request, buried alive with her deceased husband', the judgement was different:

> It appearing from the answer of the pundits ... that the practice in question is authorized by the Shasters, I am directed to communicate to you the opinion of the court that no prosecution should be instituted against the persons who may have been concerned in the interment of the woman ...; provided however, of course, that those persons are of the Hindoo persuasion, and not otherwise.[22]

The decision was negative for women of the 'joogee cast who have buried themselves alive with their husbands', because 'from the answer of the pundit of this court on the subject', it appeared that this sacrifice 'is not tolerated by the Shaster'.[23] In such cases the customs of native subjects were not respected, even if abolition of a practice might cause unrest. This indicates how prudence fails to explain the toleration policy, since this would entail allowing any practice established since 'time immemorial'

---

[20] Anonymous (1804), pp. 29–30.

[21] 'Minute of Mr. G. L. Prendergast', in *BPP* (1821), vol. 18, pp. 246–7. See Malcolm (1833), p. 32.

[22] *BPP* (1821), vol. 18, pp. 38–9.

[23] 'Letter from Searman Bird, senior judge and J. Rattray, 2nd judge at Dacca to M. H. Turnbull, esq. Register to the Nizamut Adawlut, Fort William, dated 19th August 1816', in *BPP* (1821), vol. 18, p. 101.

among the natives. Rather, the search for scriptural sanctions indicates the aim to give moral foundations to this policy.[24]

Though prudential considerations had a role to play, the early nine-teenth-century sati debate was replete with normative reasoning. Officials who opposed allowing sati shared two major concerns with the advocates of toleration: the scriptural foundation of the practice and the voluntary nature of the act. The acting superintendent of police of the Lower Provinces, Walter Ewer, desired to undermine one of these justifications for toleration, when he wrote that 'there are many reasons for thinking that such an event, as a voluntary suttee, very rarely occurs' and 'that the widow is scarcely ever a free agent at the performance of a suttee'. Instead, he suggested, the widow was the victim of 'the surrounding crowd of hungry brahmins and interested relations'. Since sati was not a voluntary act but a priestly imposition, Ewer suggested, the religious liberty of Hindu widows was not at stake. Hence, it was immoral to tolerate this cruel practice. Next, Ewer turned to the question of scriptural sanction. Even though some texts recommend it, he pointed out, Manu and other authorities of great respectability do not and the act 'is nowhere enjoined by any of the Shasters'. Besides, the practice 'may be almost called local' and could hardly be part of the Hindu religion and its sacred law.[25]

Most replies to Ewer's letters left no doubt as to the official adherence to the 'fundamental' and 'invariable principle of the British government to protect the whole of its subjects in the free exercise of their religion, and in the performance of their religious ceremonies'.[26] Those who agreed with Ewer simply tried to amplify his attack against the normative arguments

---

[24] See Mani (1998), p. 15 for a typical explanation of the toleration of sati as a pragmatic measure. Major (2006) acknowledges the importance of the *moral principle* of toleration in the colonial debate.

[25] Letter from W. Ewer, Acting Superintendent of Police in the Lower Provinces to W.B. Bayley, esq. Secretary to Government in the Judicial Department, (Calcutta, 18th November 1818), in *BPP* (1821), vol. 18, pp. 227–9.

[26] 'A Regulation for maintaining an observance of the Restrictions pre-scribed by the Shaster in the burning of Hindoo Widows on the Funeral Piles of their Husbands, or otherwise', in *BPP* (1821), vol. 18, p. 126. See pp. 232–40 for the replies to Ewer.

for tolerating sati.[27] Later, the official debate in the Bombay Presidency invoked more or less the same set of arguments pro and contra toleration. So did the disputes in popular journals and pamphlets.

In 1822, sati became the subject of a lively polemic in the *Asiatic Journal*. One letter denied the scriptural sanctions and claimed that 'almost all of the poor females who are insidiously immolated to promote the views of priestcraft and self-interest, are *previously stupified and intoxicated by drugs*, and *do not* offer themselves a willing sacrifice'.[28] Abolition was the only just measure to deal with the practice, the author argued, as had been the case for infanticide and child sacrifice. Another letter questioned the legitimacy of the comparison and restated the reasons for toleration:

> [I]t is solely because the burning of widows has its foundation, whether erroneously or not, in the religion of the country, that the British laws do not and *ought not to interfere*. Infanticide, however, practised in India, has no sanction from any one of its systems of religion, but, on the contrary, is abhorred and repudiated by them all. It is simply a civil act, and is, therefore, cognizable by simply civil or temporal laws; but the burning of widows is a spiritual and religious act (however detestable), and therefore only out of the reach of that code of criminal law which the British nation has permitted itself to impose upon India.[29]

Still, the normative grounds for tolerating sati gradually crumbled. In 1823, the Court of Directors of the East India Company wrote from London to the Bengal Judicial Department that they were 'averse ... to the practice of making British courts expounders and vindicators of the Hindoo religion, when it leads to acts which, not less as legislators than as Christians, we abominate'.[30]

The pressure for abolishing sati grew stronger by the year. As the moral justifications lost their weight, arguments from expediency began

---

[27] See the letter from E. Molony, acting magistrate at Zillah Burdwan, to W. Ewer, esq. Acting Superintendent of Police, Lower Provinces, Fort William (Zillah Burdwan, 14th December 1818), in *BPP* (1821), vol. 18, p. 235.

[28] MacDonald (1822), pp. 220–6.

[29] Kendall (1822), pp. 446–56; italics added.

[30] Letter from the Court of Directors to the Bengal Judicial Department, Lower Provinces, (London, 17th June 1823), in *BPP* (1824), vol. 24, p. 45.

to dominate: government interference would induce alienation, disorder, and rebellion. But opponents easily countered this point: the government had violated a central tenet of Hindu religion like the sanctity of Brahmins (by allowing the death penalty) and this had not created any disorder. The same went for the laws against child sacrifice and other customs. Besides, it was said, the practice was local rather than universal and limited to specific groups.[31] Eventually, Lord Bentinck abolished sati in 1829. By that time, some Bengalis had adopted the normative language of toleration: a petition objected that this measure infringed upon a sacred duty of Hindu widows and was 'an unjust and intolerant dictation in matters of conscience'.[32]

The Search for Scriptural Sanctions

Why did the British attempt to locate 'ancient religious texts' and to seek justification or condemnation for controversial practices there? This question cannot be answered by claiming that 'the project of the colonial state ... sought to develop an exact science of ruling, which was, in turn, dependent on precise knowledges' and 'a uniformly applicable law'.[33] Other governments in India had neither needed such a uniformly applicable law nor looked for it in Hindu 'sacred texts'. To add that this had to do with 'the conception of textuality'[34] of the Europeans shifts the question: whence this conception which compelled them to identify moral laws in Hindu texts?

The argument that the British were familiar with the significance of ecclesiastical law and scriptural interpretation in England, though true, fails as an answer. What were they familiar with? Among other things, they held the idea of the 'ancient lawgiver' who revealed the rules followed by a religious community. In Manu, the British thought they had found such a 'lawgiver'—the Hindu equivalent of what Moses was

---

[31] See *BPP* (1825), vol. 24, 13, pp. 20–6 and (1826–7), vol. 20, 4, pp. 28–30. See also Anonymous (1856), p. 649.

[32] 'The Petition of the orthodox Hindu community of Calcutta against the Suttee Regulation', in Majumdar (1988), pp. 156–63.

[33] Mani (1998), pp. 36–9.

[34] Mani (1998), pp. 36–7.

to the Jews.[35] In his text, they tried to discern the fundamental moral laws that Hindus ought to obey. They also codified it, because the basic obligations of Hindu religion had to be identified.

In short, the British argued that, if certain practices belonged to the religious laws of the Hindus, the colonial state had a moral obligation to tolerate them. Irrespective of individual motives, the formulation of colonial policies appealed to these laws. Throughout the nineteenth century, sources from British India confirmed this normative view of toleration. In 1814, an official government document stated that the transfer of power from native to European agency had rendered it incumbent upon the colonials, 'from motives of policy *as well as from a principle of justice*, to consult the feelings, and even yield to the prejudices, of the natives, whenever it can be done with safety to our dominions.'[36] In 1846, the editors of an Anglo-Marathi missionary periodical argued as follows: 'The toleration of the various systems of religion by the British Government in this country is ... not merely good policy; it is the course which every Christian Government is in duty bound to pursue.'[37] In 1859, a historical narrative of colonial rule stated: 'What was held to be the duty of the Government was the practice of general toleration towards all the religions professed by the people under their rule, permitting every man, without restraint and without interference, to worship his God, true or false, in his own way.'[38]

How could Christians insist that it was a *moral duty* to tolerate religious practices that constituted 'violations' of God's law? Any answer should be able to explain as to why the colonial state was convinced that it ought to

---

[35] The Europeans had looked for such an ancient lawgiver long before they learned about and translated the *Manusmrti*. At first, they believed to have found him in 'Bremaw' or Brahma. See Lord (1630), pp. 40–5, where it is described how the 'Banians' believed that God communicated religion (or His law) to the world by a book delivered to Bremaw, which was named 'the Shaster'. A few of many citations on Manu as the ancient lawgiver: *BPP* (1823), vol. 17, p. 103; W. Jones (2000), pp. iii–iv, p. xvi; Kaye (1898), p. 22; MacDonald (1822), p. 222; Peggs (1830), p. 79.

[36] 'Court of Directors' Public Department dispatch to the governor-general in council of Fort William in Bengal, dated 3 June 1814', in Zastoupil and Moir (1999), pp. 93–7, p. 94; italics mine.

[37] 'Toleration of False Religions', *The Dnyanodaya*, 15 December 1846.

[38] Kaye (1859), p. 367, p. 375.

tolerate practices whenever these had foundations in Hindu religion. For the reasons stated above, prudential arguments fail to account for this.

In March 1821, the Baptist missionary publication *Friend of India* published a paper acknowledging the European roots of the controversy, which suggested that 'female immolation' was 'a practice cognizable by the civil power, though sheltered beneath the mantle of religion'. It turned to John Locke's letters concerning toleration to argue that the moment 'a purely religious rite ... infringes on the laws of society, its character is changed, and is transformed into a civil crime'. Locke had written that the magistrate 'ought not to forbid the preaching or professing of any speculative opinions in any church, because they have no manner of relation to the civil rights of the subject; for it does not belong unto the magistrate to make use of his sword in punishing every thing indifferently which he takes to be his sin against God'. Did this allow child sacrifice in a religious assembly? No, Locke said, for such 'things are not lawful in the ordinary course of life, nor in any private house, and therefore neither are they so in the worship of God'.[39] This distinction between religious and civil practices was self-evident to Locke. So was the claim that the former ought to be allowed freely, while the latter ought to be punished if unlawful.

The framework underlying Locke's theory clarifies why it was so important to know whether the 'sacred laws of the Hindu religion' sanctioned sati and other practices. According to this Christian religious framework, all human souls have equal access to God and live to obey Him. Nevertheless, the devil and his priests corrupt this sense by imposing their fabrications as divinely revealed commandments upon innocent believers. In order to understand such people and go about with them, one should find out what they believe to be God's will for humanity. Which specific set of laws did the Hindus mistake for God's revelation?

This was the obsession of early colonial scholars. Thus, Halhed stated that the Hindu's 'allegiance to his own supposed revelations of the Divine Will' is as firm as that of the Christian and that the Hindu scriptures were

---

[39] See 'Extract' from a Paper 'On Female Immolation,' published in the Quarterly Series of the 'Friend of India', for March 1821', *BPP* (1824), vol. 23, pp. 20–1. Both the argument and the quotes from Locke were also adopted in a speech (presented to the Courts of Proprietors of East India Stock) in Poynder (1827), pp. 14–16.

seen 'as the immediate Revelations of the Almighty'.[40] Jones believed that, in 'the Ordinances of Menu', he had found the original sacred laws of the Hindus, supposedly revealed by God to Manu. It 'must be remembered', he said, 'that those laws are actually revered, as the word of the Most High' by the Hindus.[41] Charles Grant agreed: 'The Hindoo law stands upon the same authority as the Hindoo religion; both are parts of one system, which they believe to have been divinely revealed. That law is regarded by them therefore with a superstitious veneration, which institutions avowedly of human origin do not produce.'[42] James Mill in his *History of British India* (1820) confirmed the same: 'From the opinion of the Hindus that the Divine Being dictated all their laws, they acknowledge nothing as law but what is found in some one or other of their sacred books.'[43] Therefore, it was of utmost significance to find out whether sati or any other practice belonged to Hindu religion and its scriptures. If it did, Hindus would consider it a duty prescribed by God.

Why ought sati to be tolerated if this was the case? This is where Christian liberty and its model of the two kingdoms come in again. According to this framework, human authority could rule over the secular realm only—that is, the body and its material interests. In the religious realm, God alone could know, judge, and rule. Abstracting from pruden-tial considerations, this theological background defined the limits of the *normative* attitudes of British colonials, as it also had in the toleration debates of Protestant Europe.

Both evangelicals and orientalists conceived of paganism as the equiva-lent of 'popish idolatry': it could not but be a religious tyranny that usurped God's authority. As the evangelical Grant put it, commenting on the 'Hindu law' of Manu's Code: 'Nothing is more plain, than that this whole fabric is the work of a crafty and imperious priesthood, who feigned a divine revelation and appointment, to invest their own order, in perpetuity, with the most absolute empire over the civil state of the Hindoos, as well as over their minds.'[44] William Jones, the rationalist Christian and gifted orientalist, called the same work 'a system of despotism and

---

[40] Halhed (2000), pp. xiii–xv.
[41] W. Jones (2000), p. xvi.
[42] C. Grant (1970), p. 34.
[43] J. Mill (1820), p. 244.
[44] C. Grant (1970), pp. 34–5.

priestcraft'.[45] According to the British, Hindu religion revolved around cunning priests, who imposed a corrupt body of rites and rules on the believers as though these were necessary to salvation.

Yet, the normative stances towards 'false religion' ranged between two limits. On one hand, the view that Christian liberty was God's will for humanity could be interpreted 'minimally': it granted freedom of conscience to Protestants but did not include the toleration of heresy and idolatry. This stance rejected false religion as spiritual tyranny. Hindu religion blended the religious and political spheres; its priests assumed the authority of divine revelation and ruled over innocent souls. The task was to save the latter from the yoke of tyranny and grant them Christian spiritual liberty.

On the other hand, one's attitude could draw on a 'maximal' principle including the toleration of idolatry and heresy. In the words of *Dnyanodaya*, an Anglo-Marathi missionary periodical commenting on religious toleration in British India:

> So long as men do not interfere with the rights and privileges of others, they are responsible for their religious opinions and their modes of worship, not to the civil Government, but to the Majesty on high. The Government that interferes with the religious opinions of its subjects may justly be charged with tyranny. Instead of protecting them in the enjoyment of their natural rights, it becomes an oppressor. Such a course, whether it be regarded as good or bad policy, would certainly be most anti-christian and unjust.[46]

According to this view, it is God's will that every individual should be free to follow what he or she believes to be His command. Among its justifications was the belief that no one could know God's will with certainty. Therefore, one ought never to bind any other conscience to one's own interpretation of divine revelation.

Separation of State and Religion

From the late 1830s, another debate crystallized regarding the relation between the colonial government and the practices it called 'the religious

---

[45] W. Jones (2000), p. xv.
[46] 'Toleration of False Religions', *The Dnyanodaya*, 15 December 1846.

ceremonies of the natives'. The British had maintained some of the connections that Indian kings traditionally had to the practices and festivals
of their subjects. They imposed a pilgrim tax and administered temples
and other religious institutions, including management of funds and revenues. This set off a controversy leading to a stricter separation between
state and religion.

A dispatch from London dated 8 August 1839 expressed the 'anxious
desire' of the Court of Directors of the East India Company to abolish
the pilgrim tax and discontinue the government's management of religious institutions. These had to be resigned into the hands of the natives.
The directors further desired 'that you will make such arrangements as
may appear to you to be necessary for relieving all our servants, whether
Christians, Mahomedans, or Hindoos, from the compulsory performance
of any acts which you may consider to be justly liable to objections on the
ground of religious scruples'.[47] The concern was identical to that behind
the policy of religious toleration. No religious believer should ever be
compelled to participate in a practice going against whatever his religion
commanded.

In 1841, another dispatch added that officers of the colonial government could not participate in practices like 'the decoration of idols and
images, or the presentation of offering to them'. Managing 'the Temple
of Juggernauth' was considered particularly disturbing, given the horrors
of allowing a temple cart to crush devotees under its wheels: 'If we are
not to expect the interposition of Government to abolish practices which
every humane mind condemns, we are entitled to demand that at least its
patronage and support may be withdrawn from the iniquitous system.'[48]
Official documents began to circulate on the subject of the separation of
the Christian Authorities in India from the management of Lands and

[47] 'Copy of a Despatch, dated 8th August 1839, relating to the Withdrawal
of Interference with the Religious Ceremonies of the Natives of India', *BPP*
(1839), vol. 39 (Idolatry [India]).

[48] 'Letter from the Court of Directors of the East India Company to the
Governor-General of India in Council; dated 4th April 1843, No. 6', in 'Copy of
a Legislative Dispatch from the Court of Directors of the East India Company
to the Governor-General of India in Council, relative to the Superintendence of
Native Religious Institutions', *BPP* (1844), vol. 36.

Revenues connected with Mahomedan and Hindoo Worship'. All departments were informed of 'the discontinuance of any interference on the part of the Government or its officers with the management of the religious institutions of the natives'.[49]

Some officials loathed the policy of temple management, which had them contribute funds to the support of a religion they knew to be false: 'We are bound to tolerate all religions, but not I conceive to support any but our own'.[50] Others disagreed: the *lex non scripta* (unwritten law) of the Indian people, one official argued, expected the government to control these institutions, which would now be transferred to persons who shall not be actuated 'by pure and disinterested motives' in the performance of their duty.[51] Another official reminded the Court of Directors that the security of the British Empire in India depended upon continuing to maintain the religious institutions of the people and their endowments. Only persons ignorant of the consequences could argue the opposite:

> And as it is manifest that we cannot wean (our Indian subjects), but slowly and gradually, from their ancient superstitions, we cannot be too cautious how we offend their prejudices, or make them suspect that we design to deprive their religion of the toleration and protection which we are understood to have guaranteed to it, and which every government is bound to afford to the religion of its subjects. It is their confidence in this protection that has hitherto kept the Brahmins faithful subjects of the British Government, and has secured the fidelity and attachment of the native army, composed chiefly of Hindoos.[52]

Still, the orders were clear and officials put an end to the support they had given to traditional practices and festivals. This policy of stricter separation between state and religion was inspired by concerns about the connection

---

[49] *BPP* (1845), vol. 34, pp. 1–109.

[50] 'From the Collector and Magistrate of Currachee (Captain H.W. Preedy) to the Secretary to Government of Scinde, dated Currachee, 28 November 1843', in *BPP* (1845), vol. 34, p. 29.

[51] 'From C. H. Hallett, Esq. Collector of Chellumbrun, South Arcot, to the Secretary to the Board of Revenue, Fort St. George; dated 10 May 1842', *BPP* (1845), vol. 34, p. 43.

[52] 'Minute by the Honourable T.H. Maddock; dated 8 July 1844', in *BPP* (1845), vol. 34, pp. 102–3.

between a Christian government and the false religion of its subjects. Rather than follow the example of earlier kings, Christian principles demanded that the government should keep away from native religious practices.

In 1857, a decisive event took place that would determine the policies of the colonial state for the next nine decades: 'The Great Mutiny' of 1857. The historical details are unimportant to the current argument. All one needs to know is that the mutiny of Indian troops in North India threatened the British hold over these territories and its causes were attributed to insufficient respect for 'the religious prejudices of the natives' (the rebellion appeared to have started when Indian soldiers were ordered to bite open paper rifle cartridges covered in animal fat). Consequently, the Queen and her advisers decided that she should now take upon herself the government of the Indian territories, which had so far been administered by the Company. In a proclamation to the princes, chiefs, and people of British India, dated 1 November 1858, she upheld the religious toleration and neutrality of the colonial state:

> Firmly relying Ourselves on the truth of Christianity, and acknowledging with gratitude the solace of Religion, We disclaim alike the Right and the Desire to impose our Convictions on any of Our Subjects. We declare it to be Our Royal Will and Pleasure that none be in any wise favored, none molested or disquieted by reason of their Religious Faith or Observances; but that all shall alike enjoy the equal and impartial protection of the Law: and We do strictly charge and enjoin all those who may be in authority under Us, that they abstain from all interference with the Religious Belief or Worship of any of Our Subjects, on pain of Our highest Displeasure.[53]

In 1908, King Edward VII, Emperor of India, celebrated the fiftieth anniversary of his mother's charter with another proclamation which affirmed that no subject had been 'favoured, molested, or disquieted, by reason of his religious belief or worship'. All had enjoyed equal protection of the law, 'administered without disrespect to creed or caste, or to usage and ideas rooted in your civilisation'.[54]

[53] *Copies of the Proclamation of the King, Emperor of India, to the Princes and Peoples of India, of the 2nd day of November 1908, and the Proclamation of the late Queen Victoria of the 1st day of November 1858, to the Princes, Chiefs, and People of India* (London: India Office, 13 November 1908), p. 2.

[54] *Copies of the Proclamation of the King*, p. 4.

Evidently, these reaffirmations of religious toleration were rooted in concerns about causing another rebellion. Irrespective of such prudential concerns, however, the conceptual form taken by this policy continued to follow the religious framework of liberal toleration. This demonstrates how principled considerations had now subordinated the prudential modes of tolerating different religions. Even though the British did fret about the practical consequences of denying religious freedom to their colonial subjects, the official foundation of their policy was very different: it consisted of the normative model of religious toleration that resulted from the secularization of the political theology of Christian freedom.

The Reform of Hindu Religion

The colonial toleration policy did not leave indigenous traditions in India untouched. Traditionally, the many *dharmaśastra* treatises had not been rules of law, but described customs of different groups and localities and contained a variety of reflections, sayings, and maxims for settling disputes. The British did not allow these traditions to continue to play the same role in society as before. Instead, they began to reform and codify them into a systematic, uniform, and consistent body of sacred law. For several decades, the early colonial government attempted to extract from Sanskrit treatises one set of rules that could be applied to all Hindus as civil law and to appoint Brahmin pundits as priestly interpreters of this body of law.[55]

Hindu Law and False Religion

The policy to retain 'the laws of the Shaster' soon created problems for the administration of justice in British India, since it was unclear what exactly this supposed sacred law of the Hindus consisted of. This problem manifested itself in two ways.

First, as argued in the previous section, the toleration policy compelled colonial officials to determine which practices were truly religious and hence had to be tolerated. At this first level, Protestant notions of false religion operated implicitly. Even though the colonial government and

---

[55]   Bhattacharyya-Panda (2008); Cohn (1996), pp. 57–75; Derrett (1968); Lariviere (1989); Nelson (1877) and (1881); Shah (2010).

its courts of law approached the Hindu traditions as religion tout court, without adding predicates of falsity, they nevertheless smuggled in the theological distinction between true religion as the revelation of God and false religion as human additions to religion. In fact, the Christian distinction between the religious, the secular, and the idolatrous was introduced as though it concerned a distinction *internal to* Hindu religion. Some practices were accepted as truly religious, while others were rejected as illegitimate additions to religion.

The boundary was drawn along the lines of the Protestant division between the essentials commanded by God in Scripture and indifferent things falsely superimposed as religion. In its original theological form, this division denounced idolatry for presenting human laws and works as means to the justification of the soul, while Christ alone was 'the Lamb of God who takes away the sin of the world' (John 1:29 [ESV]). Consider the Roman-Catholic Mass and its celebration of the Eucharist: Lutheran and Calvinist creeds rejected it as idolatry, because human works were presented as spiritual and necessary to salvation.[56] More generally, forcing human commands upon the believers would weaken the article of Christian freedom and pave the way for idolatry: 'Through it human commands will ultimately increase and will be regarded as service to God equal to that which God has commanded; even worse, they will even be given precedence over what he has commanded.'[57] In other words, human works and laws became idolatrous when regarded as religious. Then they became human fabrications added to God's revelation—'teachings of demons' decorated with the name of God (1 Tim. 4:1 [ESV]).[58] In its secularized form, this division between pure religion and human additions was viewed as a general characteristic of all religions, including Hinduism. Since the task of locating this boundary was displaced to the 'scriptures' and 'priests' of 'Hindu religion', the colonial legal system effectively transplanted this conceptual structure *into* the Hindu traditions.

[56] See the Smalcald Articles, Part II, Article 2 in Kolb and Wengert (2000), pp. 301–5 and 'Chapter 27: Of Rites, Ceremonies and Things Indifferent' of the Second Helvetic Confession, in Pelikan and Hotchkiss (2003), pp. 521–2.

[57] From the 'Formula of Concord, Solid Declaration, Article X: Ecclesiastical Practices', in Kolb and Wengert (2000), p. 638.

[58] Luther (1999), vol. 21, p. 251.

At a more general level, the question emerged as to what rules should guide judicial decisions in Hindu law. 'There is hardly any question arising out of Hindoo law, that may not be either affirmed or denied, under the sanction of texts, which are held to be equal in point of authority', so concluded a man of great experience, Sir Francis Macnaghten, Supreme Court Judge at Fort William in Calcutta (present-day Kolkata).[59] In a work distributed to all Bengal courts, he admitted that the plethora of contradictions, unintelligible passages, and conflicting authorities were extremely problematic:

> I may be asked, if I myself, have not shown that the contradictions amount to a nullity of the *Hindoo* law? I admit that there is much in the books, which is quite unintelligible; I admit, in many instances, where authors can be understood, that they neutralize the authority of each other. Still I say, their own is the only law to be administered to them. It is our duty to select such parts of the code, as may be most beneficial to the people. These will be confirmed into use, by their undeviating application to cases, which may call for decision in our Courts of Justice; *we may command consistency, at least; we may hope, in time, to cleanse the system of its aggregated corruptions, and to defecate the impurity of ages.*[60]

By creating such a consistent system, one could avoid the partiality of native lawyers: 'We shall then by a series of adjudications give consistency to the law, and leave the rights of a people unmolested.'[61]

Sir William Jones had come to very similar conclusions in a 1788 letter to the Marquis Cornwallis, where he explained that the judges could not 'give judgement only from the opinions of the native lawyers and scholars', who deceived them by quoting half-sentences from a single obscure text 'as express authority, though perhaps, in the very book from which it was selected, it might be differently explained, or introduced only for the purpose of being exploded'. Jones called for a digest of Hindu law after the

---

[59] MacNaghten (1824), p. iii.

[60] MacNaghten (1824), p. vi; italics added. See also Sir Archibald Galloway's concern about the lack of clarity in Hindu law in his (1825), p. 240: 'The Hindoo law, as a body of jurisprudence, has no intrinsic value; and instead of having been universally and uniformly administered throughout India, what there is of it is different in almost every soubah [province].'

[61] MacNaghten (1824), pp. xi–xii.

model of Justinian's Pandects, which would be consulted by the courts as a fixed standard of justice, free from impositions and fabrications of native lawyers.[62]

The same predicament surfaced in the Bombay Presidency. In a Minute dated 22 July 1823, Governor Elphinstone described the 'Dhurm Shaster' as 'a collection of ancient treatises neither clear nor consistent in themselves, and now buried under a heap of more modern commentaries', whose content no one really knew. It had been replaced by customs 'modified by the convenience of the different castes or communities and no longer deriving authority from any written text'. The uncertainty of all decisions was obvious, since judges had to rely upon pundits who could come to any decision by quoting from 'a variety of books' with the same book having 'a variety of decisions on the same question'. There were only two potential remedies: either creating a new code founded on general principles or compiling 'a complete and consistent code from the mass of written laws and the fragments of tradition, determining on general principles of jurisprudence those points where the Hindoo books and traditions present only conflicting authorities ...' [63] Given the attachment of the natives to their institutions, the second was the only viable option. The incredible variety and intricacy of customs and 'caste rules' surfaced when administrators collected these in different parts of India.[64] Yet, the conviction remained that all this derived from the degeneration of an original Hindu code.

This was embedded in a general image of Hindu religion as an originally pure doctrinal core, similar to Christian theism, which had been corrupted by human additions. In the words of one author: 'The genuine principles of the Hindû religion inculcate the most sublime notions; though its rites are debased with idolatry and superstition.'[65] To make disappear all contradictions and antinomies from Indian religion, so a French orientalist recommended, one had to travel back to the point

---

[62] W. Jones (1970), pp. 795–6.

[63] Elphinstone in Steele (1868), preface.

[64] See Steele (1868) and the notes on Harry Borradaile's work in 'Bombay: Correspondence relative to the employment of Mr. Borradaile in the compilation and translation of certain works, 29 June 1829', in *Board's Collections 53185, 1832–1833, vol. 1339*, British Library Reference: IOR/F/4/1339.

[65] Anonymous (1800), pp. 3–4.

where each sect had departed and examine the original principle, express it in its purity, and then expose the aberrations that ruined it.[66] Indeed this approach was applied to Hindu law, which 'in its pure and original state, does not furnish many instances of uncertainty or confusion. The speculations of commentators have done much to unsettle it, and the venality of Pundits has done more'.[67] Now it was a matter of bringing back the pure Hindu code.

Again, the same crucial shift occurred here. Missionaries and other critics denounced Hindu law as the fabrication of Brahmin priests, feigning divine revelation in order to prescribe it as God's law and thus transform believers into 'only *Machines*, which are mov'd by their *Priests*'.[68] In this sense, Hindu law exemplified 'false religion': it imposed human inventions as though necessary to salvation and human laws as God's will. In the missionaries' eyes, this necessitated a wholesale rejection of this 'heathen religion' and conversion to the true God, that is, their particular version of Christianity.

While the colonial government did not approach Hindu law in the same way, it retained this theological distinction between true and false at a fundamental level. The British never prohibited false religion or idolatry, but did conceive of 'religion' in general—and 'Hindu religion' in particu-lar—in terms of the Protestant-Christian model of a set of scriptural rules reflecting the revealed will of God. But Hindu traditions and dharmaśāstra treatises did not behave like such a consistent set. When colonial officials and scholars tried to extract a consistent code, they rejected many aspects of these traditions as human accretions, impositions of native lawyers, or fabrications of priests. In other words, the process of codification was structured by Protestant topoi about false religion and its degeneration.[69]

Consequently, the normative framework behind the colonial legal system compelled Hindu traditions to *internalize* the Christian division between the religious, the secular, and the falsely religious. The conceptual realm of false religion and idolatry had been secularized in the sense that

---

[66] Lacroix de Marlès (1828), vol. I, pp. 16–7.

[67] Macnaughten (1829), p. iv.

[68] The phrase is from La Crequinière (1705), p. 136; see also C. Grant (1970), pp. 34–5.

[69] The same theology had inspired demands for legal rationalization and codification in England. See Likhovski (1999) and Yelle (2005).

it became an implicit criterion presented as internal to Hindu religion. All aspects of Indian traditions that did not fit into the codified model of Hindu law were rejected as illegitimate human additions to true 'Hindu religion' or denounced as ceremonies and rites that had no role to play in genuine 'Hindu law'. Thus, these aspects were relegated to a hidden realm of false religion.

Topoi concerning false religion would continue to shape legal reasoning about Hinduism in postcolonial India. From the 1950s, the theological distinction between genuine religion and superstitious accretions played a crucial role in the development of the doctrine of 'essential practices'. Supreme Court judges began to reform 'Hindu religion' along the lines of theological ideas they had inherited from the colonial jurists. One eminent judge, P.B. Gajendragadkar, said the following about the relation between the constitutional article on religious freedom and certain traditional practices:

> [I]n order that the practices in question should be treated as a part of religion they must be regarded by the said religion as its essential and integral part; otherwise even purely secular practices which are not an essential or an integral part of religion are apt to be clothed with a religious form and may make a claim for being treated as religious practices within the meaning of Art. 26. Similarly, *even practices though religious may have sprung from merely superstitious beliefs and may in that sense be extraneous and unessential accretions to religion itself.*[70]

Drawing on such ill-understood topoi, inherited from the theological division between true religion and idolatry, judges appropriated the authority to determine which practices of the Indian traditions were essentially religious and which were secular or superstitious, and could, therefore, be regulated, reformed, or removed by the state and its legal system.

Transforming Tradition into Religion

Colonial toleration had introduced a coercive mechanism to found practices in scriptures and doctrines. The government informed its Indian subjects that practices would be allowed only if these had doctrinal

[70] *The Durgah Committee, Ajmer vs Syed Hussain Ali and Others* on 17 March, 1961; 1961 AIR 1402, 1962 SCR (1) 383; italics mine.

foundations. Hence, not only the pundits in the courts but also Hindus in society set out on a mission to find scriptural sanctions for a variety of practices. This turned into a strategy to defend the validity of ancestral traditions. Paradoxically, liberal principles of toleration forced the colonized to transform their traditions into a religion mapped onto the model of biblical religion.

This transformation altered the pattern of dissent and agreement within the Hindu traditions. Its impact is clearest in the writings of the reformer Raja Rammohun Roy and his opponents. A rich Brahmin with a Persian and Arabic education, Roy has been glorified as the father of the modern Indian Renaissance.[71] In fact, he took crucial conceptual steps towards the creation of Hindu fundamentalism by accepting the view that traditional practices ought to be founded in scriptures.[72]

Roy intended to revive 'Hinduism' by transforming it into a religion along the biblical model. He spoke of the Vedas as though they were Scripture, of the Shastras as though they were church law, and of Manu as though he was Moses, the lawgiver of a people. He wished to demonstrate that truth was to be found in Vedic religion, rather than in its rivals Islam or Christianity.[73] Convinced that the whole body of Hindu theology, law, and literature was contained in the Vedas, Roy denounced rituals as idolatrous fabrications and tried to convince his countrymen of the true meaning of their sacred books.[74] He did all this 'for the purpose of diffusing Hindu scriptural knowledge among the adherents of that religion'.[75] These scriptures, he thought, acknowledged that only the true God ought to be worshipped, but self-interested Brahmin priests had led believers into 'the temple of idolatry'.[76] Now, the aim was to reform Hindu practices according to scriptural sanctions.

When the government decided to tolerate sati, Roy produced tract after tract arguing that it had no scriptural foundation, since neither the

[71] Ahmed (1965), Sen (1993).

[72] Roy (1982), p. 113.

[73] Rammohun Roy started *The Brahmunical Magazine or The Missionary and the Brahmun, being a vindication of the Hindoo Religion against the attacks of Christian missionaries* in 1821 and produced a series of issues, all of which defended the truth of Hinduism against Christian arguments.

[74] Roy (1982), p. 3.

[75] Roy (1982), p. 45.

[76] Roy (1982), p. 69, p. 21.

Vedas nor Manu recognized it.[77] This inspired some conservative Hindus of Calcutta to argue that he was wrong: scriptural foundations did exist for sati.[78] Thus, this reformer transmitted the religious model that sought to justify Hindu practices in terms of textual doctrines. While the liberal colonial state had initiated the genesis of this model of 'Hindu religion' among its pundits, a thinker like Roy disseminated it among the public.

From this debate emerged a group that claimed to represent 'the orthodox Hindu community of Calcutta'. In its petition against the abolition of sati, this group argued that 'the Hindoo religion is founded, like all religions, on usage as well as precept, and one when immemorial is held equally sacred with the other'. Therefore, 'the sacrifice of self-immolation called suttee, which is not merely a sacred duty but a high privilege to her who sincerely believes in the doctrines of their religion', ought not to be interfered with. The group combined a typical Indian attitude towards practices as age-old ancestral traditions with the tendency to provide them with doctrinal foundations.[79]

In this way, colonial toleration had instigated a restructuring of Hindu traditions, which soon acquired institutional shape. In 1830, the group appealed to 'the orthodox Hindus' about the necessity of establishing a Dharma Sabha, which would 'devise means for protecting our religion and our excellent customs and usages'.[80] This association met in the summer of 1830 to protest against the abolition of sati. Accordingly, as Roy opposed it, the Dharma Sabha was even more convinced that local traditions needed protection against 'their opponents who wish the overthrow of religion'.[81]

---

[77] See 'Translation of a Conference between an Advocate for, and an Opponent of, the Practice of Burning Widows Alive', 'A Second Conference between an Advocate for, and an Opponent of, the Practice of Burning Widows Alive', 'Abstract of the Arguments regarding the Burning of Widows, considered as a Religious Rite', and 'Address to Lord William Bentinck', in Roy (1982).

[78] Majumdar (1988), pp. 97–156.

[79] 'The Petition of the orthodox Hindu community of Calcutta against the Suttee regulation (January 14, 1830)', in Majumdar (1988), pp. 156–63.

[80] 'An appeal to the orthodox Hindus on the necessity of establishing the Dhurma Subha (February 6, 1830)', in Majumdar (1988), pp. 163–5.

[81] From a lamentation on the rejection of the sati appeal in the *Samachar Chandrika*, the journal of the Dharma Sabha, in Majumdar (1988), pp. 205–7.

Hindu Reform and Religious Fundamentalism

The colonial intervention had triggered the rise of Hindu reform movements. In their turn, these movements provoked traditional Hindus to organize themselves and defend conservative interpretations of the 'teachings of Hindu religion' sanctioning existing practices. Orthodox Hindu associations opposed the reform movement but accepted its model of religion. This fuelled the conviction in India that Hinduism, Islam, and Christianity were rival religions with competing truth claims. Both reform movements and orthodox associations intended to defend Hinduism against the assault of Christian missionaries. They were also hostile to Indian Muslims, viewed as representatives of an aggressive religion that had earlier attempted to destroy their traditions.

The chief agency of reform in the nineteenth century was the Arya Samaj. In his autobiography, its founder Swami Dayanand Saraswati recounts how he came to the conviction that Hindu traditions were in need of reform. After an orthodox Sanskrit education, he had left home dissatisfied. On his wanderings through North India, he witnessed all kinds of traditions, many of which appalled him. Everywhere, he saw 'profound ignorance or ridiculous superstition' and temples 'full of idols and priests'.[82]

The movement established by Dayanand further disseminated the normative Protestant understanding of religion. A teacher had convinced him that religious truth lay in the Vedas and Shastras. Earlier, these texts had been important only to some strands within the Hindu traditions. Some colonial authors were already aware of this problem. Walter Ewer stated in 1818 that 'it is well known that not one man in a thousand knows anything of the contents of the Shasters'.[83] Or as Sir John Strachey put it:

> If a religion be a creed with certain distinctive tenets, the Hinduism of the mass of people is not a religion at all. Their religion is in no way represented by the sacred books of Sanskrit literature. The sanctity of the Vedas is an accepted article of faith among Hindus who have heard of their existence, but they have nothing to do with the existing popular beliefs. The Puranas,

---

[82] Dayanand Saraswati (1978), p. 39.
[83] *BPP* (1821), vol. 18, p. 229.

and other comparatively late works, which Elphinstone says may be called the scriptures of modern Hinduism, have no practical connection with the religion of the great majority of the population.[84]

After the colonial state identified some texts as *the* Hindu scriptures and legal codes, however, reformers began to preach the same as gospel truth. Dayanand regarded them 'as infallible and as authority by their very nature'. In fact, 'they are self-authoritative and do not stand in need of any other book to uphold their authority'.[85] The Vedas and Shastras embodied religious truth. Like Roy, he insisted that the texts revealed a monotheistic Hinduism, similar and superior to Christianity and Islam.

Dayanand composed the foundational text of the Arya Samaj, the *Sathyarth Prakash* or *Light of Truth* (1875) along the lines of catechisms. It claimed to contain the one correct interpretation of Vedas and Shastras, whereas all *purana*s and other traditional stories were denounced as 'forged books'. The true confession of faith followed:

> We believe that the *Vedas* alone are the supreme authority in the ascertainment of true religion—the *true conduct of life*. Whatever is enjoined by the *Vedas* we hold to be right; whilst whatever is condemned by them we believe to be wrong ... All men, especially the Aryas, should believe in the *Vedas* and thereby cultivate unity in religion.[86]

The Arya Samaj mimicked Protestantism in yet other ways. Dayanand accepted the characterization of Brahmins as sectarian and selfish 'popes', who fabricated false teachings and kept true revelation from the laity. He imagined a history of religious degeneration, mirroring the Protestant historiography of the medieval Church: 'As in Europe, so in India the *popery* appeared in a thousand different forms, and cast its net of hypocrisy and fraud, in other words, the Indian *popes* have kept the rulers and the ruled from acquiring learning and associating with the good.'[87]

This reproduced the orientalist version of Indian religious history. Like certain strands within the Reformation, this historiography invented

---

[84] Strachey (1911), p. 317.
[85] Dayanand Saraswati (1978), pp. 82–3.
[86] Dayanand Saraswati (1994), pp. 74–5.
[87] Dayanand Saraswati (1994), p. 336.

a primitive and true Hindu religion, corrupted by human additions over time. Now one had to return to the pure and primitive core:

> I believe in a religion based on universal and all-embracing principles which have always been accepted as true by mankind, and will continue to command the allegiance of mankind in the ages to come. Hence it is that the religion in question is called the *primeval eternal religion*, which means that it is above the hostility of all human creeds whatsoever.[88]

This restructuring of Hindu traditions introduced universal truth claims for a set of doctrines: 'The educated Hindus have now learned that the religion of their forefathers is founded on solid rock of truth.'[89] It also entailed the launch of a missionary movement. As one of the Samaj publications put it, funds were required so 'that our missionaries may be able to preach the Vedic religion even in the far distant nooks of the land and save the inhabitants thereof by taking them up, as it were, from the dark abyss of ignorance in which they are struggling.'[90] The newly converted threw their idols into the river or publicly smashed them in local markets.

Thus, this reform movement spread different elements of the Protestant-colonial model of religion in Indian society. In his work on the Arya Samaj, Kenneth Jones describes its impact on society. More and more, Christianity and Islam were viewed as rival religions, whose falsity had to be supplanted by Vedic truth. The Arya Samaj also attacked Sikhism as a degenerate rival. Consequently, several traditions in the urban Punjab of the 1880s entered into a strife over religious truth: 'In the years that followed, the streets of Lahore became dotted with preachers—Christian, Arya, Brahmo, Sikh, Muslim—each extolling his particular cause and condemning all others.'[91] The Arya Samaj also initiated stinging attacks on traditional pundits, who were chided for hardly knowing Sanskrit and the Vedas. Rather than realizing that these texts were marginal to many traditions, this ignorance was viewed as another confirmation of the corruption of popular religion in India. Hence, the Arya Samaj began to reform all traditions 'in strict accordance to Vedic principles.'[92]

---

[88] Dayanand Saraswati (1994), p. 772.

[89] *Arya Patrika*, April 13 (1886), cited in K.W. Jones (1976), p. 144.

[90] *Arya Patrika*, 31 August (1886), cited in Jones (1976), p. 123.

[91] K.W. Jones (1976), p. 47.

[92] K.W. Jones (1976), pp. 96–7.

Such moves generated opposition from traditional Hindus, who again adopted the new model. They invoked 'scriptural foundations' to claim the opposite of Arya Samaj doctrines. One of the first to do so was Pandit Din Dayal, who in a lecture 'is said to have proved by quotations from the Vedas, Puranas and the Smritis, that the worship of idols alone is the means of finding God'.[93] In 1915, the Scottish missionary John Nicol Farquhar noted that Din Dayal's association, the Bharata Dharma Mahamandala, even though it claimed to defend orthodox Hinduism, found 'itself driven to set forth the Hindu system as the religion for all mankind. To defend a religion which is but the religion of the Hindus is felt to be impossible for the modern mind'. He noted with satisfaction: 'Clearly, the freedom as well as the universality of Christianity is working with irresistible force within the very citadel of Hinduism.'[94]

By the mid-1890s, traditional Hindus united in Sanatan Dharma Sabhas in order to propound the 'eternal religion'. In their meetings also, 'the correct meaning' of the Vedas was presented as 'the basic scripture' of this religion. Here, the tenets of 'unity in diversity' and 'the Truth is only One', but 'different persons call it by different names' were formulated as Hindu religious teachings. Along with this message of Hindu tolerance, they stressed the national pride and unity of Aryan Hindus.[95]

Similar reform movements, such as the Prarthana Samaj in Bombay (present-day Mumbai), emerged in other parts of the subcontinent, with analogous social effects. From this moment grew a generation of intellectuals and politicians in India. Mahadev G. Ranade, Bal Gangadhar Tilak, Lala Lajpat Rai, Bipin Chandra Pal, and many others had all been involved in, or opposed to, these movements at some point. All of them would play significant roles in the development of Hindu nationalism.[96]

[93] From the *Arya Patrika*, 27 December (1887), cited in Jones (1976), p. 109.

[94] Farquhar (1915), pp. 321–2.

[95] The quotes are from a lecture delivered at the *Sanatan Dharma Sabha* of Sialkot, now in Pakistan, by Swami Rama Tirtha (1896), p. 2, pp. 10–34. See also Jones (1998).

[96] As Gould (2004) shows, a softer variant of Hindu nationalism developed within the Indian National Congress in the early twentieth century.

The Emergence of 'Hindu Fundamentalism'

The problem of so-called 'Hindu fundamentalism' is different than it is in Christianity or Islam. Before the nineteenth century, militant traditions existed within the Hindu fold but these did not aspire to found Indian society on a set of Hindu doctrines or principles.[97] No one text, teaching, or body of law was considered central to all Hindu traditions.[98]

In fact, early modern encounters between Europe and India present a striking fact: when Christian travellers denounced the native traditions as 'false religion' and preached conversion to 'true religion', non-Muslim and non-Christian Indians reacted with *incomprehension*. They failed to grasp how one religion could be true and others false.[99] To charges of falsity and idolatry, they replied that their ancestral traditions were very old and could not therefore be false.[100] Before the late eighteenth century, Hindus did not defend their traditions in terms of doctrinal truth or texts: the tendency to provide a foundation for ancestral practices in 'true' scriptures was largely absent.[101]

Yet, the history of Hindu nationalism reads as a quest for a common set of beliefs and values, around which all Hindus should unite. Moreover, its advocates argue that Muslim and Christian minorities should also accept these as members of the Indian nation. To call this movement 'Hindu fundamentalist' is problematic. However, it does harbour a tendency towards fundamentalism in the sense that it has often aspired to establish Indian society on the foundation of supposedly Hindu principles. The content of the principles has varied over time and this tendency is but one strand within Hindu nationalism. Still, we can isolate certain characteristic properties.

The first property lies in the pursuit of a discrete core that should unite followers of indigenous Indian traditions (*Hindutva* or 'Hindu-ness' includes Buddhist, Sikh, Jain, and tribal traditions). The main ideologue of the movement, V.D. Savarkar, identified this core in his *Hindutva: Who is a Hindu?* (1923).[102] As he put it in a 1937 presidential speech for the

---

[97]   See, for instance, Subrahmanyam (1996).

[98]   Dalmia and Von Stietencron (1995); R. King (1999); Oddie (2006).

[99]   For instance, see Bernier (1671), pp. 149–50; Craufurd (1790), pp. 131–2; Anonymous (1800), p. 6; and excerpts in Fox Young (1981).

[100]   Ziegenbalg (1719), p. 5, p. 15.

[101]   For analysis, see Balagangadhara (1994).

Hindu Mahasabha, an early Hindu-nationalist organization: 'Hindudom is bound and marked out as a people and a nation by themselves not only by the tie of a common Holy Land in which their religion took birth but by the ties of a common culture, a common language, a common history and essentially a common fatherland as well.'[103]

As a second property, this 'Hindudom' was taken to give these traditions a common identity and interests, which separate them from Muslims and Christians. The latter were 'excluded from claiming themselves as Hindus', since they had extraterritorial loyalties and lacked the true Hindu spirit.[104] This is not an ancient opposition. Medieval Sanskrit texts, for instance, did not even identify Muslims along religious lines.[105] Until today, traditions combining Hindu and Muslim practices continue to exist throughout the subcontinent.[106] Yet the drive of Hindu fundamentalism is to create an identity that separates Hindus from others. Religion becomes the marker of the 'religious brotherhood' of truly loyal Indians, as opposed to Christians and Muslims.[107]

This identity proved difficult to find: no practice or doctrine is shared by all Hindus. Many of their attitudes are common also among Indian Muslims and Christians. Hindu fundamentalism is unique in the sense that it cannot draw upon any dogma or holy book. Throughout its history, it has nevertheless tried to do so.[108] Noting the Christian call for religious revival, Hindu nationalist leader B.S. Moonje argued in 1944 that Hindus must develop the boldness to strive for the revival of their religion, and that 'the constitution of Hindustan, the land of the Hindus, should be based upon the Vedas as the constitutions of the lands of ... Christianity and Islam are to be based on the revival of these religions.'[109] Paradoxically, the project of Hindu nationalism tries to distinguish Hindu identity from that of Muslims and Christians, while modelling itself upon Islam and Christianity.

The third property is even more paradoxical. The lack of dogmas shared by Hindus gives rise to the claim that they hold principles of

[102] Savarkar (1969).
[103] Savarkar (1984), p. 8.
[104] Savarkar (1984), p. 9.
[105] Chattopadhyaya (1998).
[106] Burman (2002); Gilmartin and Lawrence (2000).
[107] Savarkar (1984), p. 9.
[108] Graham (1990), pp. 94–5; J. Sharma (2003), pp. 5–9.
[109] Mathur (1996), pp. 217–8.

'tolerance' in common.[110] The principles are variously called as 'Hindu tolerance', 'positive secularism', or 'equality of religions'.[111] These are traced to Sanskrit aphorisms, which become Hindutva teachings and are invoked to contrast Hindu identity to the fanatic theocratic nature of Islam and Christianity.[112] Subsequently, these principles are to be imposed on all Indians: 'In Indian thought, identity of underlying reality permits variety of surface custom or even philosophical view. But the difference or diversity or variety should not oppose the underlying reality. Difference should realise its common root in the identity.'[113] Therefore, religions can be accepted only in so far as they conform to this underlying identity. This inspires legal measures against proselytization, a practice regarded as a violation of religious equality. It is argued that Muslims should rewrite the Quran to accommodate the equality of religions and that Christians should 'Indianize' their churches.[114] Made into a principle, 'Hindu tolerance' becomes a ground for intolerance towards Islam and Christianity.

*   *   *

Any historical explanation of the phenomenon of so-called 'Hindu fundamentalism' needs to account for the emergence of the above paradox. How did the inclination to found the Hindu traditions in a common core of principles come into being? Why did followers of these traditions begin to perceive Islam and Christianity as rival religions with incompatible doctrines, if this experience was largely absent before the late eighteenth century?

Hindu fundamentalism emerged from the intervention of the liberal state. This state operates within a particular normative framework, which construes the indigenous traditions of India as variants of the same phenomenon as Islam and Christianity. Colonial policies of toleration and neutrality caused the Hindu traditions to transform themselves according

---

[110] Mathur (1996), p. 65.

[111] Madhok (1995); Graham (1990), p. 50.

[112] Two favourites are 'Sarva Dharma Sama Bhava' and 'Ekam Sat, Viprah Bahudha Vadanti', translated as 'equal respect for all religions' and 'truth is one; the sages call it by many names' respectively. See Golwalkar (1966), pp. 101–6; Chitkara (1997), p. 1; Mathur (1996), p. 113, p. 131; Savarkar (1984), pp. 14–15, p. 41, p. 49.

[113] M.A.V. Rao (1960), p. 6.

[114] V. Rao (1966), pp. i–xxxiv, p. xxix.

to this religious model. They identified scriptural foundations for their practices in order to survive under colonial rule. This inspired a series of movements in nineteenth-century India to embark on a quest for the true teachings of Hinduism. Originally, they turned to the Vedas and Shastras. Given the lack of consensus and diversity of traditions, however, the core of Hindu principles could not but become less precise. Eventually, the Hindutva movement located its unity in notions of 'Hindu tolerance'.

In other words, Hindu nationalists sustain and reproduce the transformation of Indian traditions instigated by the liberal state. Since the resulting model of religion locates Hindu identity in a shared set of principles and beliefs, Islam and Christianity are now inevitably viewed as rivals with incompatible doctrines. Accordingly, as Hindutva focused on principles of tolerance, Islamic and Christian intolerance towards other religions were identified as the central flaws of these minorities. From this perspective, in order to coexist with the Hindu nation, Indian Islam and Christianity have to conform themselves to its fundamental values.

As the liberal perspective sees it, the secular state and its principles of neutrality and toleration are antidotes to religious nationalism and fundamentalism. By tracing the historical emergence of the liberal secular state and its policy of religious toleration in colonial India, this chapter shows how liberal secularism and religious fundamentalism in India are two faces of the same coin. They are two mutually reinforcing moments of a mechanism that transforms the indigenous cultural traditions of India into variants of the religions of the Book.

This is *religious* toleration in a fundamental sense: the policies not only function within a religious framework that originates in Christianity, but also reproduce the conceptual structures of this framework. By placing the Hindu traditions into this normative framework, the liberal secular state in India and its principles of neutrality and toleration coerce communities to take a particular form. That is, it is forcing the cultural traditions of India to mould themselves along the lines of biblical religion.[115] The growth of the so-called 'Hindu fundamentalism' is a product of this straitjacket. This conclusion throws doubt on the common belief that liberal secularism is the only credible antidote to the forces of religious fundamentalism. If secularism feeds fundamentalism in one case, it may well do the same in other cases where similar conditions prevail.

[115] Balagangadhara and De Roover (2007).

7. Straitjackets of Secularism

ecularism is in crisis.' This proclamation has been reverberating through Indian public debate for decades now.[1] Various diagnoses are offered of the crisis, but these have generally failed to show a way out. In fact, the predominant impression left by the Indian secularism debate is one of intellectuals running in place. This chapter will examine why that is the case.

The first section scrutinizes the cultural asymmetry at the heart of the contemporary debates on secularism and toleration in India and elsewhere. It shows how this asymmetry takes the form of a normative disjunction: either a polity endorses the norms of liberal toleration, or it embodies their negation. This mode of reasoning is rooted in the religious soil from which the dominant Western discourse about Indian culture sprouted. However, this discourse did not remain confined to Western

---

[1] See, for example: Gudavarthy (2014); Nigam (2006); Tambiah (1998); Needham and Sunder Rajan (2007).

minds; its hegemony also generated a 'colonial consciousness' among the thinkers and leaders of post-Independence India.

As the second section shows, colonial consciousness functions as an iron frame that keeps in place certain conceptual limits inherited from centuries of orientalist discourse and liberal theorizing. Advocates of secularism reproduce accounts about India that transform its society into a deficient variant of that of Europe, with its own forms of religious conflict and oppression. Therefore, so the story goes, the country's survival depends on implementing secularism, with the necessary modifications adapted to the Indian context. Critics of secularism also reproduce the same conceptual language, which prevents them from exploring alternative modes of coexistence in Indian culture. Eventually, the straitjackets of secularism became so well entrenched in the political reasoning of Europe and India that the search for alternatives is facing a dead end.

False Religion and Political Salvation

The liberal model of secularism is normative in the sense that it revolves around a set of principles such as toleration, state neutrality, and religious freedom. These contain the moral ought: in a liberal secular state, all citizens *ought to* have equal rights irrespective of religious affiliation; they *ought to* be free to profess and practice the religion they prefer; and the state *ought not to* endorse any religious doctrine. Thus, liberal secularism does not just put forward heuristics for building peaceful societies, but also lays down unconditional principles claiming general validity.

Through the eyes of this model, the range of potential descriptions of any polity is limited: it is viewed either as an affirmation or as a negation of the norms of liberal secularism. It becomes either a reflection of, or deficiency vis-à-vis, *the way things ought to be.* On one hand, the polity could be judged as a secular state respecting toleration, neutrality, and religious freedom. It may have shortcomings but at least strives to uphold these principles. On the other hand, when rejected as a violation of liberal secularism, the polity is transformed into one that unites politics and religion, fails to create a secular public sphere, and disrespects the religious freedom and equal rights of all citizens.

These conceptual restrictions may seem obvious: after all, moral principles reflect obligations. When a set of acts falls under the scope of some principle but fails to obey it, these acts constitute violations of the principle, which are prohibited. This also seems to go for any state that violates liberal secular principles. When this way of reasoning is applied to actual cultures, however, it brings in its wake a basic problem.

The Deception of Normative Disjunction

Consider two cultures often taken as paradigms of tolerance: ancient Greco-Roman paganism and traditional India. Several authors argue that it is wrong to understand these cultures as inherently tolerant. A recent work suggests polytheism was pluralistic to some extent, but this should be qualified, for 'the Greco-Roman world was, after all, as intolerant and exclusive as any other culture'. The author adds: 'The inclusiveness of Greco-Roman polytheism more or less resembles the modern Hindu plurality of religions or the Japanese overlapping of religions that have traditionally had little to do with religious moderation.' Moreover, 'a secular society, in which religion is separated from other aspects of social and political life, was unimaginable and impossible in Greco-Roman antiquity'.[2]

Similar things are said about India. The traditional claim that Hinduism is tolerant, Romila Thapar suggests, 'is not borne out by historical evidence ... The extremity of intolerance implicit in the notion of untouchability was glossed over by regarding it as a function of caste and society'. In reality, intolerance towards certain groups is inherent to Hindu religion.[3] Similarly, Bhikhu Parekh aims to debunk 'the Hindu theory of tolerance' by saying that it allows adherents considerable freedom of belief but is extremely restrictive of their freedom of conduct: 'Hindus are expected to follow the dharma of their caste on pain of social ostracism and, under traditional Hindu kingdoms, of legal sanctions.' As for religious pluralism in which Hindus take great pride, it is not at all as benign and egalitarian as it appears', for it relies on a rigid hierarchy.[4]

Such claims are illustrative of a particular way of reasoning. First, it is noted that certain cultures accommodated a variety of traditions and groups. From this fact, some infer that such cultures are inherently tolerant in nature. Second, another fact is added: in Indian and Greco-Roman society, some groups were oppressed or persecuted. From this, it is inferred

[2] Kahlos (2009), p. 5.
[3] Thapar (1987), p. 15.
[4] Parekh (2003), pp. 50–1.

that the relevant cultures cannot have held values of toleration, equality, and religious freedom. Therefore, they remain 'as intolerant and exclusive as any other culture'. By implication, the contemporary world has little to learn from them, since we possess liberal secular values.

This mode of reasoning is problematic. Greco-Roman and Indian cultures indeed accommodated a degree of diversity that Christendom could not accept throughout its history. From this, it does not follow that they embodied values of religious toleration. They could well have accommodated this plurality in a completely different manner without relying on such principles. Similarly, from the fact that followers of these traditions also oppressed others, it does not follow that they did so because they are 'as intolerant and exclusive as any other culture'. It is not because they do not hold liberal values that they are by implication *intolerant of* other religions.

Within the liberal secular framework, however, there is no cognitive space for alternative forms of pluralism. It carves up the universe of political possibilities in terms of a normative disjunction: *either* one pursues secularism and toleration (as one ought to) *or* one ends up in religious oppression and conflict. This is flawed reasoning because the *absence* of the liberal model logically does not imply the *presence* of its negations. There may be modes of coexistence that amount neither to liberal toleration nor to its negation. Yet the liberal model is regarded as the normative standard from which ancient Greco-Roman or traditional Indian society deviates and does so to its own loss. This is the case because any society without liberal secular norms is descriptively transformed into one endorsing antithetical norms, namely, the unity of politics and religion, religious intolerance, and sacred hierarchy.

This approach prevents one from discovering how one could learn from other forms of coexistence. Once one accepts the liberal model, the only way to make sense of non-Western societies appears to be as deviations from its principles. Then the only route towards improvement is implementation of the model. This vicious circle effectively closes off liberal secularism from any potential discovery of viable alternatives to itself. As long as we remain within this framework, we are bound to reproduce the asymmetry of cultures.

This section traces the emergence of the problem of cultural asymmetry in the liberal secular reasoning about Indian society. What allows secularists to presuppose that there are only two options for India, either liberal secularism or political religion? Whence the false conviction that the absence of liberal secular virtues entails the presence of illiberal religious vices?

False Religion and Cultural Asymmetry

Even though it is often said today that 'Hinduism' is a modern construction and not the ancient religion of India, the implications of such statements are unclear.[5] The most cogent thesis in this debate is the claim that religions like 'Hinduism' and 'Buddhism' are fictitious entities, which exist in the books and minds of Western and Western-educated intellectuals but not among the people whose religions they are supposed to be.[6]

From the start, two tendencies played out in the European writings about Indian culture and society. On the one hand, there were observers who tried to fit the traditions of India into a biblical framework and thus transformed them into inferior variants of Christianity. On the other hand, some travellers, missionaries, and orientalists had highly insightful observations to offer concerning Indian culture and its traditions. [7]

In Europe, however, the reception of such reports regarding Indian culture and society took a particular form. When orientalists culled over the observations and reflections sent from India, they aimed to make these compatible and coherent with the topoi about religion and society that circulated among the European educated classes. In several senses, they 'digested' the ideas and descriptions presented in these reports. In effect, this implied a filtering and reconstitution of the available information through a grid of conceptual clusters deriving from a genericized Christian theology.

The Protestant Reformation produced some of the most significant of these conceptual clusters. In post-Reformation Europe, many citizens had accepted the characterization of the Church and medieval society as dens of corruption as though it were a truthful empirical description. In reality, this concerned a Protestant theological critique of false religion.[8] From the seventeenth century, the same template now began to give shape

---

[5] See several essays in Bloch, Keppens, and Hegde (2010); Dubuisson (2003); R. King (1999).

[6] Balagangadhara (1994) and (2010).

[7] See, for instance, Hastings (1846) and the work of James Henry Nelson (1877), (1881), and (1887).

[8] In fact, this popular understanding of the middle ages as a devoutly religious era ruled by the priestly hierarchy has been shown to be false. See Glover (1984), pp. 17–46.

to early modern descriptions of Indian culture and guided the dominant understanding of Hinduism in British India.[9]

Consider two extremely influential texts by very different authors: one by the evangelical Charles Grant (1746–1823), the other by the utilitarian philosopher-historian James Mill (1773–1836). Grant was a champion of missionary activity in British India, who later became chairman of the East India Company. In 1792, he published his *Observations on the State of Society among the Asiatic Subjects of Great Britain*, arguing that missionary work provided the only means for India to advance socially and morally.[10] Unlike Grant, his fellow Scotsman James Mill never travelled to India, even though his *History of British India* (1817) would become central to the training of British officials.[11]

Both texts offered a deeply normative description of Indian culture and society. In his *Observations*, Grant concluded that Hindus lacked all morality: whenever the distribution of justice had been committed to the natives in India, it had 'become a traffic in venality'. This corruption was caused by the Hindu character, composed of a mixture of absolute egotism, greed, shocking cruelty, want of benevolence, absence of affection and rational enjoyment in marriage, widespread promiscuity, and general depravity.[12] This character, Grant argued, had been formed by the despotism entrenched in Hindu society. And at the core of this despotic system lay the absolute power attributed to certain classes, particularly Brahmin priests.[13]

Grant was extremely critical of the caste system because it assigned fixed social positions to distinct groups. The evils flowing from this system were obvious: the frame of society cannot change; the highest orders 'pervert the use of power, become weak, arrogant and oppressive'; while the lowest rank 'is doomed to perpetual abasement' and has 'no relief against the most oppressive and insulting tyranny, no hope of ever escaping from its sufferings'. If 'the genius of a Newton should arise in that class, it could have no room to expand, nor if it had, could all its excellence deliver its possessor from the obligation of administering to the most ignorant and

---

[9] See Gelders and Derde (2003); Gelders (2009).
[10] See Embree (1962).
[11] See Plassart (2008).
[12] C. Grant (1970), pp. 21–2.
[13] C. Grant (1970), pp. 34–5.

vicious of the Brahmins'. The system discourages 'all liberal exertions'. Yet, Brahmin impostors had been able to institute it by means of the ruse of divine origin.[14]

One could perhaps mistake Grant's account for a set of rational objections to the caste hierarchy, similar to those of today's 'secularists'. However, the essentially theological nature of such descriptions must be clear. Grant argued that the code of Hindu law was the work of a crafty priesthood, which had feigned divine revelation and appointment in order to invest itself with absolute power. The immorality of the Hindu people, Grant continued, was caused by the purely religious part of their complex system. They believed in external ceremonies and pecuniary atonements for 'the expiation of the guilt of sin'.[15] Like Catholic believers, they had faith in 'works of supererogation', which they believed would give them eminence in the heavenly world.

It appeared obvious that Indians had developed the same theology of remission of sins and spiritual merit as the 'papists' in Europe: 'For the violations of conscience, which though smothered is not extinct; for the disregard of truth, of justice, and of mercy, their system has enabled them, without making any the slightest compensation to men, to give satisfaction to their gods'.[16] Such opinions about the divine being gave rise to equally depraved practices, for false religion always corrupted society. Consequently, all reprehensible practices in Indian society could be explained in terms of the false doctrines and scriptures at its foundation. Perhaps the central danger of the Hindu system was its omnipresence: 'The spirit of superstition extends among the Hindoos to every hour, and every business of life'.[17]

Grant's mode of reasoning about 'Hindu religion' and its 'caste hierarchy' reflected Reformation theology. Each human had a conscience to potentially access and obey God's will. Spiritual freedom entailed that this conscience should be liberated from human laws and priestly authority. Since each believer possessed the right to find his own place in God's plan, all occupations were potentially divine vocations and no one should be chained to a particular profession. In India, Grant saw a system

[14] C. Grant (1970), p. 35.
[15] C. Grant (1970), p. 46.
[16] C. Grant (1970), pp. 47–8.
[17] C. Grant (1970), p. 51.

of despotism and false religion isomorphous to the papacy: Brahmin priests had fabricated a system of rules and rites in order to subordinate the laity, smother the conscience, and establish a hierarchy with fixed occupations. Guided by Satan, they drew on the Indian's capacity to follow God only to misguide him into idolatry and immorality.

Even though Mill's description of Hindu society was couched in more 'secular' terms, it repeated the same story. Brahmins retained the role of priests controlling society and misguiding the flock of believers by means of fictitious laws and ceremonies. More than any priesthood, Mill argued, they had claimed a divine origin and authority over the people. Their privileges pervaded society:

> As the greater part of life among the Hindus is engrossed by the performance of an infinite and burdensome ritual, which extends to almost every hour of the day, and every function of nature and society, the Brahmens, who are the sole judges and directors in these complicated and endless duties, are rendered *the uncontrollable masters of human life*.[18]

According to Mill, ceremonies and rites bound and oppressed the Hindu people, and even prevailed over morality, because of the belief that these gained the favour of the Almighty.[19] He provided a variety of illustrations to drive home one crucial point: Hindus knew the ordinary precepts of morality but all-powerful priests had misguided them into external performances believed to delight the deities.[20]

Again, this point makes sense against the background of the relation between human works and divine grace in Protestant doctrine. Here, all humans are born with the capacity to obey God's laws, but truly virtuous acts can spring only from those whose souls have been transformed by the Spirit. Ceremonies divert attention away from spiritual reform. Thus, the Hindus are misguided: even though they possess the capacity to follow moral precepts, their religion is so corrupt that it confuses the conscience and oppresses the spirit.

Like Grant, Mill loathed 'the Hindu system of sacred law', because it failed to distinguish between the sphere of political and civil life and that of religion:

---

[18] Mill (1820), pp. 111–13; emphasis added.
[19] Mill (1820), p. 276.
[20] Mill (1820), pp. 277–8.

The doctrines and ceremonies of religion; the rules and practices of education; the institutions, duties, and customs of domestic life; the maxims of private morality, and even of domestic economy; the rules of government, of war, and of negotiation: all form essential parts of the Hindu codes of law, and are treated in the same style, and laid down with the same authority, as the rules for the distribution of justice.[21]

Mill's diatribe presupposed the principle of separating the two spheres of authority. Mixing these two spheres constituted a basic injustice of 'heathen society', according to him. It generated the worst system of despotism and priestcraft ever witnessed on earth and transformed the Hindus into the most enslaved portion of humanity.[22]

These accounts mirrored a body of orientalist descriptions of Indian culture. It is not that all descriptions were identical, or that there were no alternative attempts to understand this culture, but the dominant picture filtered out during the nineteenth century was largely invariant. Brahmins were viewed as priests or even as the local equivalent of the Levites or 'tribe of priests' of the Old Testament. Religion in India was imagined as the parallel of 'jewry' and 'popery'—a constricting body of rites and laws invented and imposed by a jealous and self-interested priesthood.[23]

At this first level, it must be clear how the asymmetry of cultures had been established. European descriptions transformed the very structures of Indian culture into expressions of false religion. Some attributed explicit predicates of falsity; others did not. But these authors generally imagined Hinduism in terms of the negation of certain normative doctrines, which derived from the opposition between true and false religion: opposed to spiritual freedom stood clerical tyranny; a fixed hierarchy denied the equality of all believers; the belief in works negated justification by faith alone.

The ploy of normative disjunction emerged here: either a society strove to fulfil certain norms or it would remain steeped in their negations. This mode of reasoning translated the disjunction between true and false religion into 'secular' terminology. Again, this shift generated intractable problems:

[21] Mill (1820), p. 133.

[22] Mill (1820), pp. 451–2.

[23] For some illustrations from different periods, see Lyall (1910), pp. xi–xii; Orme (1763), pp. 3–4; Thornton (1835), pp. 148–52; Whitehead (1924), p. 22.

it is problematic to claim that the absence of liberal norms implies the presence of antithetical norms. But this problem dissolves once one turns back to the theological original, for the absence of true religion *does imply* the presence of its negation, false religion. Wherever the Sovereign is not obeyed and the Spirit does not liberate, the lord of this world controls humankind. Wherever God is rejected, Satan pulls the strings.

Within this framework, it is equally obvious that false religion cannot offer alternatives to true religion. The true should displace the false but not the other way round. This is one reason why Western accounts of Indian culture continue to reproduce the asymmetry of cultures to this day: they build on the conceptual skeletons of earlier conceptions of false religion. The normativity of modern accounts of 'Hinduism' and 'caste' reflects the secularization of this disjunction between true and false religion, between the pure and the putrid, Satan and Saviour, divine will and demonic wiles, and so on.

Thus, orientalist discourse absorbed Indian culture into the normative dynamic that propelled both post-Reformation Christendom and liberal secularism. Like the earlier critiques of Catholicism and Judaism, the discourse about Hinduism and caste revolved around their alleged negation of the norms of Christian freedom and equality, either in explicitly theological or in secularized form. Consequently, Hinduism became the embodiment of tyranny and hierarchy.

Either Toleration or Ruin

In his textbook, *College History of India*, Talboys Wheeler contrasted 'Hindu despotisms' to the 'British liberties' brought by colonial rule.[24] According to Valentine Chirol's classic *Indian Unrest* (1910), the trouble in India was Brahmanism, which 'as a system represents the antipodes of all that British rule must stand for in India, and Brahmanism has from times immemorial dominated Hindu society ...' Indian unrest in general had as 'its mainspring ... a deep-rooted antagonism to all the principles upon which Western society, especially in a democratic country like England, has been built up.'[25] As Sir Alfred Lyall wrote, while the British were

---

[24] Wheeler (1888), pp. 107–8, p. 148. Wheeler also suggests that British rule 'established law, liberty, and order in Bengal'. See also Whitehead (1924), p. 3.

[25] Chirol (1910), p. 32, p. 37, p. 5.

'relying upon secular education and absolute religious neutrality to control the unruly affections of sinful men', Indian agitators combined 'primitive superstition' with modern politics: 'The mixture of religion with politics has always produced a highly explosive compound, especially in Asia.'[26] This was not primarily a justification of colonial rule, as contemporary critics of orientalism suggest. Rather, it was an *epistemic* consequence of the normative framework that constrained the colonial reasoning about Indian society.

This framework also formed the Indian intelligentsia of this period. Nineteenth-century reformers like Raja Rammohun Roy and Jotirao Phule had adopted the orientalist discourse about India as a veridical description. In Maharashtra, Phule campaigned for the destruction of the caste system, a system of 'slavery', which he regarded as falsehood fabricated by 'the deep cunning' of the Brahmin priests and deceitfully attributed to divine inspiration. He celebrated British rule as an act of divine providence liberating 'the shudras' from 'Brahmin thraldom'.[27]

Independence did not bring about major changes in this regard. India's first prime minister, Jawaharlal Nehru, had absorbed the 'Enlightenment values' of nineteenth-century Europe through his colonial education. In his autobiography, he wrote that the spectacle of organized religion filled him with horror for it always seemed to stand for 'blind belief and reaction, dogma and bigotry, superstition and exploitation, and preservation of vested interests.'[28] Similarly, in *The Discovery of India* (1946), he wrote that religion 'seemed to be closely associated with superstitious practices and dogmatic beliefs, and behind it lay a method of approach to life's problems which was certainly not that of science.'[29] Nehru's assessment did not result from his discovery of India but from the textbooks of Western liberal education. As he admitted, he had come to India via the West and therefore approached her 'almost as an alien critic', full of dislike for the present and the relics of the past, wishing to scrap much of her heritage and religion.[30]

---

[26] Lyall (2010), p. xv.
[27] Phule (2002), pp. 29–30, p. 44.
[28] Nehru (1941), p. 240.
[29] Nehru (1988a), p. 26.
[30] Nehru (1988a), p. 50.

From Nehru's perspective, superstition and the lack of 'scientific temper' lay at the root of central problems of Indian society. Hence, secular education needed to spread the latter and eradicate the former. This stance copied a crucial component of the colonial stance towards Indian society. Both British officials and missionaries had identified the absence of scientific reasoning as a major obstacle to the spread of 'rational religion' in India. Hindus, they claimed, could not grasp even the simplest rules of contradiction and inference, yet understanding Christian doctrine required such basic reasoning skills. Therefore, a programme of secular scientific education had to be instituted in British India. One should not proselytize but educate. Only thus would subjects come to see the truth and justice of Christianity as opposed to the falsity and injustice of Hinduism.[31]

In its glorification of the 'scientific temper', Nehruvian secularism built on the premises of the colonial education programme. Since this programme had operated under the assumption that Indian culture largely consisted of superstitious beliefs, it projected scientific education as a necessary step towards the decline of this culture and the rise of 'rational religion'. Even though Nehru did not have conversion to Christianity in mind, his urge to convert the Indian nation to 'the scientific temper' equally amounted to an attempt to root out the many aspects of Indian culture that he rejected as superstition and prejudice. Spreading the scientific temper would free the citizens of India from the spell of organized religion.

In this way, Nehru assumed, the problem of communal violence could also be addressed. After all, 'communalism' resulted from the work of corrupt leaders exploiting superstition and religion by mixing it with politics. Its only antidote was secularism: the privatization of religion and its separation from politics and the public sphere. From Nehru's perspective, then, there seemed to be only two potential forms of political organization. In a letter to the Nawab of Bhopal, he commented on recent developments in Pakistan as follows:

> One of the biggest obstacles to the creation of the atmosphere we seek is the repeated declaration that Pakistan is an Islamic State. That, I think, is an absurdity in the present world, at any rate for any progressive nation. If

---

[31] Claerhout (2010), pp. 325–80. On the relationship between the missionary endeavour and secular education in British India, see also Bellenoit (2007) and Seth (2007).

Pakistan insists on being what is called an Islamic State it will be backward, narrow-minded and unprogressive just as India, if its seeks to be a Hindu State, would be similarly backward and unprogressive.[32]

Throughout his writings, this restriction on Nehru's reasoning is striking: either a country establishes a progressive secular nation state or it becomes a backward religious one. In a 1947 speech, he asserted that India should never become a Hindu state: 'The very idea of a theocratic state is not only medieval but also stupid. In modern times the people may have their religion but not the State.'[33]

As Nehru bluntly put it in another speech, the alternatives were either 'Toleration or Ruin'.[34] Were one to define 'toleration' as 'the absence of violent conflict', this would amount to a truism. Yet Nehru did not have this tautology in mind. Toleration stood for a specific aim:

> The freedom of India can only be based on a recognition of this richly varied life bound together by an overriding unity, and by full opportunities being given to every section of the people for professing and practicing their religion and culture. The aim of the Congress has therefore been to develop this great country as *a democratic secular State which neither favours nor discriminates against any particular religion.*[35]

Here, Nehru leaves no doubt as to his endorsement of the liberal-democratic secular state. For him, this was the only reasonable option. However, his mode of reasoning did not live up to the basic demands of reason. He presupposed the truth of a proposition instead of demonstrating it: the disjunction of *either* a secular nation state *or* communal strife and the ruin of civilization.

Today, Nehru is both admired and scorned for introducing secularism as a tenet of the Indian Republic. His dream as India's first prime minister was to transform the country into a strong secular nation state. But this dream was built on quicksand. Nehru's analysis resulted neither from empirical research into Indian society nor from reasonable reflection on its problems. Instead, it embraced the flawed reasoning of normative

---

[32] Nehru (1988b), p. 8.
[33] Nehru (1986), pp. 107–9.
[34] Nehru (1986), pp. 101–2.
[35] Nehru (1986), emphasis added.

disjunction: he simply accepted the orientalist discourse about Indian culture as a veracious description and then sold normative models of Western political thinking as the only future for India.

The Reformation of Caste

Another advocate of secular reform was B.R. Ambedkar, a leader of the untouchables and chairman of India's Constituent Assembly Drafting Committee. His *Annihilation of Caste* (1936) put forward its goal in unambiguous terms: 'It is not possible to break Caste without annihilating the religious notions on which it, the Caste system, is founded.'[36] On what epistemic grounds did this reformer argue for his project of annihilation?

Ambedkar accepted the crux of the orientalist approach towards Indian culture. To understand its social structure, he looked into the texts of 'Hindu religion' and read these as 'scriptures' stating the religious rules and justifications of the caste system. This system he viewed as the creation of Brahmin priests who wished to control and manipulate Indian society. Since caste is a *religious* tyranny, Ambedkar argued, a Reformation was needed in India in order to ensure social justice. He believed that the evidence for this claim could be found in the account that transformed Indian culture into a variant of the 'corruption' of medieval Europe. According to him, the history of India illustrated that religion is the source of power, since the priest controls the common man and gives every political event a religious twist.

Much like Grant and Mill, Ambedkar believed the central flaw of Hinduism was its representation of caste as a divine order: 'The Hindus hold to the sacredness of the social order. Caste has a divine basis. You must therefore destroy the sacredness and divinity with which Caste has become invested.'[37] He also had no doubt as to the guilty party: 'Inequality is the official doctrine of Brahminism and the suppression of the lower classes aspiring to equality has been looked upon by them and carried out by them without remorse as their bounden duty ... There is no social evil and no social wrong to which the Brahmin does not give his support.'[38]

---

[36] Ambedkar (1989), p. 27.
[37] Ambedkar (1989), p. 69.
[38] Ambedkar (2004), p. 146.

Since liberty is the ideal and religion dictates Indian society, Ambedkar suggested, social and religious reform is necessary.[39] To show its urgency, he systematically described Indian society as the embodiment of deficiencies vis-à-vis European nation states. Caste prevents India from becoming a genuine nation.[40] Its anti-social spirit has caused conflict and prevented solidarity. Its effects on Hindu ethics must be clear: 'Caste has killed public spirit. Caste has destroyed the sense of public charity. Caste has made public opinion impossible.'[41]

Inevitably then, the annihilation of caste would also involve annihilating most of 'Hinduism'. What was fundamentally wrong with this religion? 'What is called Religion by the Hindus is nothing but a multitude of commands and prohibitions. Religion, in the sense of spiritual principles, truly universal, applicable to all races, to all countries, to all times, is not to be found in them.'[42] This was a critique of 'Hinduism' inherited from the orientalist discourse about this 'religion' and constituted by a set of background ideas concerning true and false religion.

As we saw, when European scholars constructed 'Hinduism' as a structural equivalent of Judaism and Catholicism, it became the object of a critique of the corruption of religion. This built on the early Christian idea that the coming of Christ had superseded Judaism and its multitude of commands and prohibitions. Gospel had displaced Law. According to the Reformers, the Roman Church once again falsely substituted Law for Gospel, until true spiritual religion returned in the form of the Protestant Reformation. From this perspective, 'Hinduism' was another religion of rules and rites. Therefore, it could equally be rejected as one that produced a divine basis for a social order and falsely put down commands and prohibitions for a particular group. Thus, it failed to provide universal spiritual principles for humanity. Ambedkar echoed such utterances as though they constituted an objective rational analysis of Hinduism; in reality, these were scraps of a theology of false religion now presented as facts about the world.

Unlike some of their predecessors, neither Nehru nor Ambedkar presented Christianity or colonialism as the way out for India. They had,

[39] Ambedkar (1989), p. 45.
[40] Ambedkar (1989), pp. 50–1.
[41] Ambedkar (1989), p. 56.
[42] Ambedkar (1989), p. 75.

however, accepted the colonial account of Indian society as evidence for the necessity of establishing a secular nation state. In brief, they argued that the values of secularism, liberty, and equality had to take the place of communal oppression and caste tyranny. Since they believed the latter two pervaded Indian society, the project of a secular India entailed a reform as wide in scope as the grandest dreams of the British colonizer.

Colonial Consciousness and Political Salvation

The writings of Nehru and Ambedkar throw into sharp relief the phenomenon of colonial consciousness conceptualized by Balagangadhara.[43] This type of consciousness came into being as a result of colonialism's aspirations to be an educational project. Colonial education attributed a scientific status to the colonizer's accounts of the culture and society of the colonized. Orientalist stories about 'all-pervasive Hindu religion', 'evil Brahmins', and 'the tyranny of caste' were taught in Europe and India as the epistemic equivalents of Newton's theory of gravitation or Lavoisier's explanation of combustion: true descriptions of the world.

Much like genuine educational projects, colonialism tries to transform the experience of the colonized by replacing the latter's cultural modes of thought with new conceptual schemes. But colonial education differs from genuine education in one crucial respect. When we educate children, the theories they are taught can be shown to be cognitively superior to their naive understanding of the world. In contrast, colonial education never demonstrated the cognitive superiority of its orientalist discourse vis-à-vis existing Indian modes of thought.

Instead, these accounts presupposed the normativity of Western culture and from this inferred that the colonized culture must be deficient. The resulting accounts were imposed onto the colonized. Lacking cogent arguments, the colonizer had to take recourse to other means: indoctrination and violence. Therefore, colonialism was not a genuine educational project, even though it claimed to be. In reality, it consisted of a vicious circle, which took Western liberal values as the beginning and end of civilization.

Through a mechanism consisting of three steps, the colonial educational project generates a specific kind of consciousness. The first step presupposes the validity of a particular normative framework from

[43] Balagangadhara (2012), pp. 95–120.

the West—a moral–political model that represents society *as it ought to be*. Its tenets are taken as axiomatic. The second step describes the factual situation of a non-Western society as deficient with respect to this model and its principles. This description leads to the third step, namely, the conclusion that the model should now be implemented in the society in question. That is, the factual situation should be reformed in terms of the normative model.

The third step pretends to have demonstrated that the moral structure should replace the immoral system of the colonized society. In reality, it commits the fallacy of *petitio principii* in an ingenious form. The reasoning of colonizer and colonized alike are captured in between the first and the third step. The only way to make sense of the colonized society is as a failure to realize the norms from the colonizer's culture. Consequently, an impoverishing disjunction imprisons our minds: *either the normative model or its negations*. This is how colonial consciousness constricts the thought and imagination of those caught in its grip.

The programme of Indian secularism mirrors the three moments of colonial consciousness. The first moment reflects the normative premises shared by Christian missionaries, European orientalists, and colonial officials. But its scope is wider: it is also the starting-point of reformers and secularists in postcolonial India, who endorse liberalism or some other political theory from the West.

In the second moment, the first party perceives Indian culture as a religious tyranny which gives rise to the injustice of caste and the violence of communalism. The secularists reproduce the topoi of this colonial account, but strip it of certain theological details and contribute new 'content'. In other words, they adopt the basic outlines of this normative conception of 'Hinduism' and 'the caste system' and then produce historical or social-scientific accounts of these 'facts' by drawing on modern European theorists from Marx to Foucault.

On the one hand, the third step had the missionaries strive for the destruction of 'false religion' and diffusion of 'true religion' in India, while colonial officials tried hard to replace 'native superstition and corruption' with scientific education and liberal values. On the other hand, the same step inspires Indian reformers and secularists to superimpose the normative framework of secularism onto their society and its people. In the eyes of this enclave of academics and activists, secularism truly is political salvation for India.

The Twilight of Secularism

Secularism is dead, or at least moribund, so Ashis Nandy declares in a recent obituary for the idea. Instead of trying to keep alive an incurable patient, he adds, we should now look toward a new generation of concepts.[44] This compulsion to search for alternative concepts is part of a more general predicament of social and political theorizing in Asia. In the attempt to theorize Asian cultures, it became abundantly clear that the dominant social–scientific paradigms and theories could not comprehend these forms of life. Yet, Asian thinkers had not succeeded at developing any credible alternatives. In the 1980s, this led Balagangadhara to a major question: Why is it that Asia did not see any major intellectual revolutions in the modern era, even though it had its share of social upheavals? In spite of its many brilliant men and women, why did it not produce any thinker or theory with substantial impact on the contemporary study of society?

In response, he argued that the basic heuristics and concerns behind the social theorizing of the West failed to make intuitive sense to Asian minds. Educated Asians had adopted a body of theories and ideas while having no access to the experiential world reflected by this conceptual apparatus. They started looking at their own cultures and societies the way the West looked at them. They came to know the West through its self-descriptions. 'We do not even know whether the world would look different, if we looked at it our way.'[45]

There are two sides to this state of affairs. On the one hand, the contemporary social sciences operate within the cognitive constraints of one particular culture, namely the West. Historically, the dominant theories developed as Western intellectuals reflected on their experience of the problems they faced. While doing so, they drew upon a particular body of heuristics and ideas. Conceptual patterns from Christian religion had become the commonplaces of European societies. These not only guided the process of conceptualizing concerns but also constituted the building blocks of the resulting theories. In other words, today's social sciences consist of oblique reflections on the Western cultural experience—a cultural experience structured by clusters of ideas, attitudes, and heuristics deriving from the secularization of Christianity.

---

[44] Nandy (2007), p. 112.
[45] Balagangadhara (1985), p. 74.

On the other hand, during the colonial period, the same cognitive framework began to dominate the education system and intellectual analysis of colonized societies. Asian thinkers not only adopted the conceptual apparatus of the Western intellectual traditions but also their descriptions of Asian societies. Thus, a discourse reflecting the Western cultural experience became the framework through which they approached both Asia and the West. As a result, these thinkers lost access to their own cultural experience. They tried to make an alien world their own, while their own world became alien to them.

This is the situation of India's secularists. They also reproduce the Western discourse about India and the West, but these sets of ideas fail to make intuitive sense to them because they cannot access the experiential world within which the ideas are embedded. Worse, the same discourse also prevents them from gaining insight into their own experiences and the world they live in, including Indian experiences of conflict and co-existence. This section argues that colonial consciousness continues to shape the reasoning of both advocates and opponents of secularism in India. In order to discover a new generation of concepts, we first have to grasp the constraints of the old generation. It is here that colonial consciousness poses major obstacles for secularists and anti-secularists alike.

Liberal Secularism and Religious Conflict

Secularism is indispensable for modern India, it is often said, because of the Hindu–Muslim 'communal' conflict that disrupted the country during the last six decades. Does this conclusion result from systematic reflection on the problem of Hindu–Muslim conflicts in Indian society? Has any thinker demonstrated a clear link between the structure of these conflicts and the political model of secularism?

Early modern European thinkers presented the principles of the secular state as antidotes to strife between Christian confessions and persecution of religious minorities. Under which conditions would it be plausible that these principles also offer solutions for Hindu–Muslim conflict? Only if the conflicts in India are variants of those in Europe, that is, both sets of conflicts should share some similar structure or relevant properties. The obvious route here is to suggest that the secular state is the political model required to contain all *religious* conflicts.

This would help if we could demonstrate that the conflicts between Hindus and Muslims in India, Protestants and Catholics in Europe, Christians and Muslims in Nigeria, and all other conflicts designated as *religious* conflicts indeed share a common structure, which renders them into this particular type of conflict. But, in its contemporary use, the predicate 'religious' does not refer to any such common structure in the phenomena it intends to describe. It functions as a self-explanatory tag, which generates the illusion that we have a deeper understanding of certain acts of violence.[46]

In fact, a superficial glance at the conflicts between Hindus and Muslims indicates that they are very different from the conflicts between Christian confessions in Europe. In a trivial sense, they are similar: violence and cruelty are part of both. However, characteristic of the conflicts in Europe was violence deriving from a mutual rivalry of claims to religious truth. Each confession claimed to be the only true representative of God's will for humanity and viewed the others as minions of the devil. This dimension distinguished the conflicts from purely political or socio-economic conflicts.

The same dimension is absent from Hindu–Muslim conflicts, which are not driven by a mutual clash of truth claims. In communal riots, Hindus do attack Muslims. But they do not do so because they want the latter to worship and believe in Shiva instead of Allah, or because they think all should accept the truth of the Vedas, or because they regard Muslims as heathens. From Alberuni's days, Muslim and Christian visitors to India were struck by the fact that local traditions did not enter into violent conflict to defend the truth of some set of dogmas. For Hindus, so the textbook story says, 'Dogmas cannot be eternal but only the transitory, distorting, and distorted images of a truth that transcends not only them but all verbal definition.'[47] Given such initial observations, one would expect advocates of secularism to examine how Hindu–Muslim conflicts are different from conflicts between Christian confessions (or, say, between Islam and Christianity). This kind of research would allow them to assess in how far the principles of secularism may offer solutions to both sets of conflicts.

[46] Cavanaugh (2009).
[47] Zaehner (1969), p. 4.

How can one argue that secularism is necessary because of the conflicts in Indian society, if one has not systematically examined the structure of these conflicts and its relation to the principles of secularism? Consider the work of the political philosopher Rajeev Bhargava. The case for secularism is 'over-determined', he believes, since the reasons in favour of the idea are 'overwhelming'.[48] Of these, he considers 'the argument from ordinary life' the most convincing.

Religious world views are constituted by ultimate ideals, this argument says, and when believers of different religions and non-believers live together, a clash of their ultimate ideals is always imminent. A clash of such ideals could deprive people of leading an ordinary life. Since it is the state's task to secure a minimally decent existence for its citizens, all ultimate ideals must be expunged from the affairs of the state. Therefore, politics and religion should be separated, and the two domains must keep a principled distance and respect each other's boundaries. 'To sum up', Bhargava says, 'ordinary life requires that an acceptable minimum standard exists and that it is barbaric to fall below it.' Political secularism is the only way to secure this minimum standard and avoid barbarism.[49]

This argument from ordinary life relies on a conception of a common predicament confronting human societies. Both in India and the West, Bhargava suggests, secularism consolidated in the face of irresolvable religious conflicts and in the aftermath of sectarian violence. More generally, 'Whenever conflicts became uncontainable and insufferable, something resembling a politically secular state simply had to emerge.'[50] This simply had to happen because human societies always harbour different conflicting sets of ultimate ideals. When these ideals clash, *humanity* either enters an escalating spiral of violence and cruelty or discovers that such ultimate ideals ought to be delimited:

> In short, it has recurrently stumbled upon something resembling political secularism. Political secularism must then be seen as a part of the family of views which arises in response to a fundamental human predicament. It is neither purely Christian nor peculiarly Western. It grows wherever there is a persistent clash of ultimate ideals perceived to be incompatible.[51]

[48] Bhargava (1998b), p. 488.
[49] Bhargava (1998b), p. 491.
[50] Bhargava (1998b), p. 497.
[51] Bhargava (1998b), pp. 497–8.

Although there is some ambiguity in this passage ('something *resembling* political secularism'), the author does not waver from his main point: all human societies are confronted with the same predicament and secularism is the answer they inevitably *stumble upon*.

When Bhargava claims that the secular state has to emerge whenever conflicts become uncontainable and insufferable, he cannot mean all conflicts, since this would imply that even fights between family members, lovers, or neighbours have secularism as their solution. He is referring to conflicts between groups holding different religions, and defines these conflicts in terms of 'a persistent clash of ultimate ideals'. But this is a vague notion: what makes some ideal into an ultimate ideal? The notion could well comprise gang-wars between Latinos and Blacks in Los Angeles, battles between hooligans of rival soccer teams in Europe, separatist struggles of ethnic minorities anywhere, and thousands of other conflicts. From this perspective, whenever some compromise emerges between conflicting parties, this is an instance of humanity solving 'the fundamental human predicament' by stumbling upon 'something resembling political secularism'.

Bhargava is keen on proving the universal scope of secularism, so he presents it as the indispensable solution to the predicament of diversity. Since he begins with the presupposition that this predicament is universal across human societies, he never poses the question as to what properties are characteristic of conflicts solved by secularism. Instead he takes recourse to an all-encompassing category, 'the clash of ultimate ideals', which cannot possibly refer to a well-defined set of conflicts with common traits. The same is true for the resulting notion of political secularism: if all non-violent compromises preventing barbarism between groups holding different 'ultimate ideals' are termed 'secularism', the term becomes so all-encompassing that it loses its meaning. Thus, Bhargava's argument from ordinary life intends to give secularism its due by stating that all civilized pluralism in human societies is due to secularism.

Such problems are predictable when colonial accounts of Indian society are reproduced as truthful descriptions and when theological topoi are sold as self-evident principles. As noted in Chapter 4, the liberal model of secularism comes with an inbuilt conception of religious plurality: a clash of communities holding conflicting beliefs and values. This template defined how British officials and orientalists perceived conflicts in Indian society. Mutatis mutandis, the predicament of confessional strife in post-Reformation Europe was taken as a model for characterizing conflicts and tensions between Hindus and Muslims and other groups.

The resulting conceptual framework carves up Indian society into distinct communities of believers or practitioners (Hindus, Sikhs, Jains, Muslims, and such like), understood as followers of so many competing religions. Colonial authors presented religious bigotry and conflict between people of different religious persuasions as typical characteristics of Indian society. They described a variety of conflicts in terms of antagonism between 'Hindus' and 'Muslims', even when such conflicts had nothing to do with religion.[52] Similarly, orientalists characterized Sikhism as a religion distinct from, and conflicting with, Hinduism, which then led reformers to declare the Sikhs a separate religious community that should assert its independence from the Hindu community.[53]

In Europe, the belief that politics ought to be separated from religion had in part resulted from a particular understanding of confessional strife: it was caused by sinful men who abused religion for worldly ends; to do so, they invented human doctrines sold as religious truth; this divided Christendom into factions, each claiming to be the true religion, which in turn led to conflict between competing religious confessions. After being rid of its saliently theological features, this conceptual framework shaped the colonial account of 'communalism' in Indian society. The continuing background presence of this account unto this day makes it appear obvious that secularism is a question of survival for India.

Totalizing Religion?

'Secularism is the dream of a minority that wishes to shape the majority in its own image, that wishes to impose its will upon history but lacks the power to do so under a democratically organized polity.'[54] The sociologist T.N. Madan uttered these words at the 1987 annual conference of the Association for Asian Studies. During the 1980s, several Indian intellectuals had launched a critique of secularism. The ideology of separating religion from political life, they argued, did not suit the societies of the

[52]   Pandey (1990), pp. 23–4, p. 44.
[53]   Mandair (2009).
[54]   Madan (1998), p. 297.

Subcontinent. It was a 'gift' of Western culture, which had been imposed onto a deeply religious majority by a powerful educated minority.

In his lecture, Madan insists that secularism is impossible as a shared credo of life in South Asia, since the great majority of the people are active adherents of some religious faith. As a blueprint for the future, it would also fail, for it is incapable of countering religious fundamentalism. The contradiction between the secularization of daily life and the rise of religious fundamentalism was noted before, Madan adds: 'But surely these phenomena are only apparently contradictory, for in truth it is the marginalization of religious faith, which is what secularization is, that permits the perversion of religion. There are no fundamentalists or revivalists in traditional society.'[55]

Some of Madan's points are substantial. 'Paradoxically', he notes, 'the uniqueness of the history of modern Europe lies, we are asked to believe, in its generalizability.' Indeed, the elements that had converged historically to constitute modern life in Europe from the sixteenth century were being presented as a paradigm with universal applicability. Thus, secularism was falsely represented as the product of the general rejection of religion and the rise of rationalism, which should be embraced by any people wishing to leave behind superstition and theocracy. In reality, Madan points out, 'secularism as an ideology has emerged from the dialectic of modern science and Protestantism' and cannot be transferred to non-Western societies 'without regard for the character of their religious traditions or for the gifts that these might have to offer.'[56]

Yet, it is when Madan turns to the character of these traditions that the limits of his analysis come to the surface. Rather than reflecting on the incompatibility between the Asian traditions and the model of secularism, he turns to old orientalist bromides that shut off all reflection. South Asia's major religious traditions (Buddhism, Hinduism, Islam, and Sikhism), he argues, 'are totalizing in character, claiming all of a follower's life, so that religion is constitutive of society.'[57] Now, remember where this idea originated. Initially, Christian thinkers had argued that false religion encompassed all of society and the idolater's life. More generally, they suggested, politics had failed to become independent from religion in the heathen world. Later, European scholars continued to argue that religion

[55] Madan (1998), p. 298, p. 300.
[56] Madan (1998), pp. 307–8.
[57] Madan (1998), p. 302.

permeated all of Indian society, even though they possessed no criteria for distinguishing the religious from the non-religious.

Madan adopts this conception of 'all-encompassing religion' wholesale as he begins to examine the relationship between the categories of the 'religious' and the 'secular' in South-Asian religions. In Hinduism, the relationship between 'spiritual authority' and 'temporal power' is hierarchical: 'It would seem that originally the two functions were differentiated, but they were later deliberately brought together, for the regnum (kshatra) could not subsist on its own without the sacerdotium (brahma) that provided its principle of legitimacy.'[58] The terminology is familiar; yet the peculiarity of Madan's claims should not escape us.

The relationship between spiritual authority and temporal power reflects the age-old Christian division of the world into two spheres. The notions of regnum (the royal) and sacerdotium (the priestly) had been introduced by the early medieval pope Gelasius I to delimit the power of kings in relation to the priest's authority to mediate between humanity and the Deity. These distinctions in turn rely on the Bible and its division of the cosmos into a temporal and a spiritual world. But now an Indian sociologist accepts these theological terms as though they constitute a theory-neutral observational language. Next, Madan presumes with his orientalist predecessors that there is an obvious semantic equivalence between these terms and certain Sanskrit words, like 'kshatra' and 'brahma.'[59]

Thus, in spite of his criticism, this critic of secularism himself accepts that particular historical developments of medieval Christendom— namely, the distinction between spiritual power and temporal authority and regnum and sacerdotium—are uniquely generalizable to all societies. Finally, this allows him to analyse 'Hinduism' in terms of the relation between priest and king: 'What is more, the priest and the king are united, as husband is to wife, and they must speak with one voice.'[60]

---

[58] Madan (1998), p. 303.

[59] Turning to a Sanskrit–English dictionary (like Monier Monier-Williams' popular dictionary) to translate these terms does not offer a way out, since these dictionaries embody the very same problems: they use a Christian conceptual language as though it is a neutral language to translate terms from the Hindu traditions and thus map the terms 'brahma' and 'kshatra' onto the Christian-theological distinction between priestly and civil authority.

[60] Madan (1998), p. 304.

This is precisely how 'Hinduism' had been imagined through the framework guiding the reasoning and experience of authors like Grant and Mill. In contrast to true religion, Hindu religion had failed to separate religious from secular authority and allowed the Brahmin priesthood to rule every aspect of life. This underlying generic theology of false religion also determined how orientalists had translated Sanskrit terms and sentences and how they had described the structures of 'Hindu religion'— translations and descriptions now wholeheartedly adopted by Madan.

In other words, once he turns to examining the cultures of India, it becomes clear that Madan's objections to secularism fail to escape the cognitive framework behind this political model. He adopts its basic conceptual vocabulary and, for this reason, cannot but replicate its conclusions. He cannot enter into a sustained exploration of his intuition that secularism is unfit for Indian culture and its traditions, since he reproduces the framework of colonial consciousness and just attempts to make minor modifications. In the end, the modifications are limited to an altered evaluative judgement about the merits of secularism. Madan's critique of secularism is then reduced to an almost trivial conclusion: in its current form, this ideology does not suit societies where religion is all encompassing; therefore, a different form of secularism is required.

The Tragedy of Anti-Secularism

In comparison to Madan, Ashis Nandy's critique is more radical. He rejects secularism as the manifestation of a peculiar form of imperialism of categories, whereby concepts produced in the West turn hegemonic to such an extent that the original conceptual domains vanish from awareness. Thus, secularism has colonized the domain of ethnic and religious tolerance in India—a conceptual domain that should now be recovered.[61]

The moral of Nandy's story is the following: rather than count on the ideology of a culturally alienated elite, one should explore the modes of tolerance present in South-Asian traditions and 'hope that the state systems in South Asia may learn something about religious tolerance from everyday Hinduism, Islam, Buddhism, or Sikhism, rather than wish that ordinary Hindus, Muslims, Buddhists, and Sikhs will learn tolerance from

---

[61] Nandy (1998a), p. 321.

the various fashionable secular theories of statecraft.[62] This is a compelling idea. As Nandy insists, secularism has little to say about cultures. It is 'ethnophobic' and often 'ethnocidal' for it only tolerates cultures insofar as these accept the role of ornaments subservient to the nation state. Yet, it is precisely traditional cultural forms of co-existence that could offer the resources for alternatives to secularism.

When Nandy turns to the current state of Indian culture and its traditions, however, the poverty of the available conceptual language also distorts his insights. Each religion in India, he suggests, is split into two: 'religion-as-faith' and 'religion-as-ideology'. These are inappropriate terms, he admits, but they have private meanings here: 'By faith I mean religion as a way of life, a tradition that is definitionally non-monolithic and operationally plural.' Ideology refers to religion as an identifier of groups contesting for political or socio-economic interests. 'Such religions-as-ideologies usually get identified with one or more texts which, rather than ways of life of the believers, then become the final identifiers of the pure forms of the religions.'[63] Consequently, they work with well-bounded and mutually exclusive identities.

Faith, according to Nandy, always encompasses and endorses a theory and experience of transcendence, whereas ideology bypasses such theories and experiences except when they can be used for secular purposes. The modern secular state prefers to deal with religion-as-ideology because it finds the inchoate ways of life unmanageable. From the secularist's perspective, 'Religion is an ideology in opposition to the ideology of modern statecraft and, therefore, needs to be contained.' This perspective cannot allow that religion-as-faith has its own relevant principles of tolerance, 'for that claim denies the state and the middle-class ideologues of the state the right to be the ultimate reservoir of sanity and the ultimate arbiter among different religions and communities.'[64]

Does this contrast between religion-as-faith and religion-as-ideology work as a conceptual tool? Consider religions like Christianity and Islam. If we follow Nandy, such religions are supposed to identify groups contesting for political or socio-economic interests only when they take the form of ideology. Then, they are identified in terms of texts taken to

[62] Nandy (1998a), p. 338.
[63] Nandy (1998a), p. 322.
[64] Nandy (1998a), pp. 322–4.

represent the pure form of the religion in question, rather than in terms of the ways of life of the believers. In contrast, as faiths, these religions are non-monolithic ways of life endorsing a theory and experience of transcendence.

The first problem here is that the ways of life of Christian and Islamic believers are necessarily shaped by scriptures containing 'the Word of God'. That is, Islam and Christianity revolve around submission to God's will, which is expressed in the respective holy books of these religions. Faith here refers to absolute trust in, and complete surrender to, God or Allah. But such faith cannot come into being without genuine belief in the Bible or the Quran as His revelation. Moreover, His Word or revelation necessarily reflects the pure form of the religion, which becomes impure accordingly as human beings add their own inventions to religion. In other words, the basic structure of these religions and their conception of faith appear to correspond to what Nandy calls religion-as-ideology.

What about the theory and experience of transcendence? Since God coincides with the transcendent (indeed His spiritual realm is the only sensible referent of the term 'transcendence'), His Word and purpose are what the theory and experience of transcendence are all about. If religion-as-ideology identifies the pure form of religion in terms of certain texts, then it certainly cannot bypass transcendence here, since the surest way of understanding the theory and experience of transcendence (God and His eternal spiritual realm) is constituted by the 'ideology' found in those texts. Moreover, the truly Islamic or Christian community is characterized by its faith in God's purpose *as revealed in Scripture*. In this sense, its way of life is determined by a text identifying the pure form of the religion. To see the point, just try to imagine a Christian 'way of life' without the Bible or a Muslim 'way of life' without the Quran.

All of this shows how the contrast between religion-as-faith and religion-as-ideology fails to make sense of these religions. The difficulty cannot be deflected by qualifying the distinction, as Nandy does: 'The two categories are not mutually exclusive; they are like two axes on which could be plotted the state of contemporary religions.'[65] In these religions, 'religion-as-faith' and 'religion-as-ideology' coincide. The more the believer has faith, the more he lives according to the Christian or Islamic ways of life, and the more he conforms to what Nandy calls religion-as-ideology.

[65] Nandy (1998a), p. 322.

Faith and ideology then cannot possibly be two separate axes on which the state of these religions can be plotted.

What remains of Nandy's distinction is one suggestion: religion-as-ideology is a sort of mask for the pursuit of political and socio-economic interests, which draws on the experience of transcendence only for secular purposes and thus generates rivalry between groups. Interestingly, this moral judgement is virtually identical to that of anti-clerical theology: when clerics and rulers abuse religion for worldly politi-cal or economic purposes, it is corrupted and causes conflict. True faith is spiritual and not political (it is a 'way of life' constituted by 'the experience of transcendence'), this theology insists, and therefore does not revolve around detailed doctrines ('ideology') invented by clerics, who claim to give the one correct interpretation of Scripture ('texts which become the final identifiers of the pure forms of the religions'), but actually carve up the communion of believers into competing confessions ('well-bounded, mutually exclusive identities').[66]

Now consider a reformulation: Nandy is grappling with the differences between religion and tradition as two distinct phenomena. Traditions are plural and flexible, since they do not revolve around doctrines but around the inherited practices of a community. Religions, in contrast, need to demarcate the community of believers and identify the true doctrine and correct interpretation of God's will as expressed in Scripture. In Indian society, for reasons we do not yet grasp, Christianity and Islam often took the form of traditions similar to other Indian traditions: to a large extent, they lost the fixation on distinguishing between true and false religion and the resulting proselytizing drive. Because of the reli-gious framework it has inherited, however, the secular state cannot cope with traditions without attempting to transform them into religions. Consequently, it has *created* conflicting 'religious' communities rather than resolving conflicts in Indian society as an impartial arbiter.

What prevents Nandy from exploring this route is the deep-rooted presupposition that Islam and Christianity on the one hand, and the Hindu, Buddhist, Jain, and Sikh traditions on the other hand, are mani-festations of religion and involve clerics, doctrines, sacred texts, and faith. From this, he concludes that these are isomorphic phenomena with two conflicting tendencies: religion-as-faith and religion-as-ideology. In this

[66] Nandy (1998a), pp. 322–5.

way, he reinforces 'the imperialism of categories' that he wishes to undo. In other words, he ends up adopting the conceptual language of colonial consciousness, even though he is one of its major critics.

The tragedy of anti-secularism is that it fails to draw on the resources of Indian culture, even where it explicitly aims to do so. Colonial consciousness keeps in place the European discourse about India as a descriptive framework that filters even the anti-secularist's understanding of his own society. Because of this conceptual screen, Indian thinkers lose access to the intellectual traditions and experiential world of their own culture. Drawing on Sanskrit terminology or Indian philosophy does not help here, for the roots of the problem go far deeper: the same conceptual framework constrains how the relevant terms and sentences are translated and interpreted today.

This state of affairs also explains the intellectual poverty of Hindu nationalism, a movement very different from Nandy's anti-secularism.[67] The consistent rejection of 'backward Hinduism' by colonial and postcolonial elites led to an equally aggressive response from Indians attached to their cultural traditions. They deride the secularism of state ideologues as a 'pseudo-secularism' that privileges minorities and disadvantages Hindu communities. Yet the resulting movement conceives of itself as 'Hindu nationalism', which by implication transforms it into the mirror image of 'secular nationalism'.

This move could occur because Hindu nationalists generally reproduce the orientalist account about Hinduism, merely adding another value judgement. They may believe they are fighting the secularists; in fact, they are also prisoners of colonial consciousness. That is, the Western discourse about India also functions as the framework through which Hindu nationalists understand themselves and their culture. They also accept that Indian culture is constituted by a religion with its own sacred scriptures, gods, revelations, and doctrines. When they abjure these specific terms, they fall back onto other elements of the same discourse, such as the notion of nationhood or the connection between nation, territory, and religion.

The dominant framework posits a struggle of secular nationalism versus religious nationalism, and the Hindu nationalists have conformed

---

[67] The intellectual poverty of the Sangh Parivar is analysed by Elst (2001), pp. 225–70.

to this prefabricated template. They may object that theirs is a *cultural* nationalism, or that Hindu *rashtra* reflects a different notion of nation, or that a Hindu state would be truly *secular*, but these are so many icings on a rotten cake. They have succumbed to the very discourse they sought to challenge and failed to develop any sound alternative.

*   *   *

The straitjackets of secularism not only restrict the reasoning of secularists but also restrain opposition to this model. The precondition for developing a new generation of concepts is that we leave behind the constraints of colonial consciousness. But the only way to succeed is to first get a hold on the conceptual limits shared by the liberal model of secularism and the orientalist discourse about India.

One of the major obstacles here is the peculiar dogmatism characteristic of Indian secularism. From the perspective of your average secularist, anyone who dares question the concepts and principles of secularism must either be a romantic revivalist or a Hindu nationalist in disguise. Critics of secularism are accused of denying the reality of violence and injustice in Indian society. This stream of thinking reveals an inability to imagine ways of theorizing the problems of Indian society other than through the conceptual language of 'religion', 'communalism', and 'caste'. It is as though the movements of Hindu nationalists and Islamic jihadists can be conceptualized only as instances of one common phenomenon of 'political religion' or 'religious fundamentalism'. Similarly, within the bounds of this framework, it appears as though acts of violence and injustice by members of one *jati* (caste or subcaste) against members of another jati can be understood solely as 'the caste system' in action.

The dominant discourse about Indian society has become one of those forms of thought 'which are so familiar that we take their outlines to be the outlines of the world itself'.[68] Today's secularists ignore the distinction between a phenomenon and its description. They conflate the structures of Indian society with the conceptual structures of *their particular understanding* of this society. As a result, the core conception of Indian culture and society inherited from European colonialism is protected

[68]   Feyerabend (1970), p. 36.

from refutation at all cost, even though it reproduces orientalist ideas and topoi inherited from the secularization of Protestant Christianity.

The result is the dead end we have reached today. The options are few: the separation of politics and religion or its normative negation, either secularism or communal violence and caste discrimination. This is how the deception of normative disjunction operates in the dominant thinking about postcolonial India. It seems unthinkable that the framework of secularism could be flawed at its very core. Opposition is permitted only *within* its theoretical constraints. In this manner, the iron frame of colonial consciousness continues to make the world appear as though no reasonable alternatives to secularism could exist.

Conclusion

W
hat is the alternative?' This question is often raised as an objection to any critique of dominant beliefs and entrenched ideas. In the contemporary study of India, however, it points to a peculiar dimension of our current predicament. In order to say what Indian culture and society are like, we first have to say what they are *not* like. That is, we are compelled to uncover the outlines of the dominant discourse about India and show how these reflect the constraints of the Western cultural experience and its intellectual traditions. We need to get a grip on the limitations of the dominant set of ideas before we can even think of developing an alternative.

In the case of the liberal model of religious toleration and the secular state, we confront a similar challenge. We are in urgent need of an alternative political theory of pluralism and better heuristics for coping with cultural diversity. But many routes that appear to lead towards such alternatives actually consist of pitfalls and dead ends. Travelling along these routes would take us right back into the straitjackets of secularism.

Hence, this study has aimed to clear the ground for the search for alternatives by explaining the cognitive limits of the liberal model and the cultural dynamics behind its development.

Inevitably, then, this work has its own set of limitations. Even though a new generation of ideas is much needed today, we first need to study the cultures of the non-Western world in a new light before we can turn to developing alternative political models for our time. As I said in the Introduction, an international research group is working on this alternative kind of research and its results are under way. In anticipation of these results, this conclusion will review the major points of the story told so far and point out the routes we should avoid in the pursuit of alternatives to liberal secularism.

The Search for the Secular

The story told in this book started out with the puzzle of the two spheres: How can one identify the sphere of religion and separate it from the political sphere in jurisprudence and policymaking? Which criteria allow one to distinguish between the public and the private? For decades now, these questions have kept scholars busy. We discovered that liberal political theory fails to provide any consistent answer, even though it presupposes the distinction between the religious and the political and that between the public and the private. In fact, no political or legal theory has succeeded at developing sound criteria to systematically distinguish between the two spheres.

But there is one theoretical framework where the distinction between the realm of religion and that of politics is coherent: the theology of Christian freedom and the two kingdoms. The conceptual constituents of this theology emerged from centuries of Christian reasoning about human existence and politics. The Bible postulates a division between the eternal spiritual world (the religious) and the temporal material world (the secular). Human beings have a body and a soul or flesh and spirit.

When the early medieval monasteries began to develop a process to give shape to the life of the true Christian, this division between the spiritual and the temporal played a central role. The monastic process of *conversio* consisted of a turning away from the temporal world of the flesh towards the spiritual world of God. The sinful monk underwent a purification of the soul that resulted from his never-ceasing attempt to live up to God's will. While his flesh remained corrupt, his soul was gradually freed from the clutches of the devil, even in this temporal world.

During the Papal Revolution, the spiritual–temporal distinction played a crucial role in determining the right relations between the authority of the papal hierarchy and that of the secular rulers. The Church had been reformed according to the model of the monastery. The priest joined the monk in living the truly religious life of conversion. As a result of this monasticization of the Church, the priesthood became the religious estate, which had gained spiritual freedom and the associated authority over the temporal estate, including lay rulers. Consequently, the Papal reformers argued, the Church and its priestly hierarchy had to be free from the rule of secular powers.

By setting in motion the monasticization of daily life, the Protestant Reformation took this dynamic some steps further. Every believer should now go through the process of conversion and gain the spiritual freedom that is its result. Neither priest nor prince could have authority in the realm of religion and the soul. Only God could rule in this spiritual realm. Consequently, Protestant theologians systematically developed the theory of the two kingdoms as the framework of reference for debates about religion, freedom, and political authority.

By the seventeenth century, its basic ideas had become commonplaces of educated Europe: human beings can rule only in the political kingdom; all believers are free from secular authority and human laws in the spiritual kingdom; mixing these two spheres is equivalent to the corruption of religion; the coercion of the conscience is evil; our iniquity and fallibility prevent us from imposing our own understanding of God's will onto others. Over the next few centuries, this framework was gradually transformed into the core structure of the liberal model of secularism and religious toleration, accordingly as it lost more and more of its explicitly theological elements.

Consequently, the conceptual language of this model, this work has argued, is 'secular' only in so far as it secularized the tropes of Christian political theology into the topoi of liberal political theory. The term 'secular' here refers to a *Christian* secular world produced by this religion. In this world, the separation of 'the religious' from 'the political' is self-evident because it builds on centuries of theological reflection. The same goes for notions such as religious freedom and liberty of conscience. All these notions presuppose specific conditions of intelligibility: to a significant extent, they depend on a Christian-theological anthropology or, at least, on a set of attitudes and ideas embedded in this background framework.

This also goes for the Enlightenment and its principles of toleration and freedom of conscience. In spite of its ambitions to free humankind from the tutelage of religion, the Enlightenment never succeeded at cutting loose such principles from the religious clusters of ideas that sustain them. The philosophes reproduced old terms from anticlerical theology—'the conscience', 'religious freedom', 'this world' and 'the other world', 'the religion of the priest'—without developing any alternative non-theological framework to interpret these terms and relate them to each other in a systematic way. Thus, if one wishes to argue that the radical Enlightenment's notions of toleration are independent from Christian-theological reasoning, one should demonstrate how that is the case rather than presupposing it is.

The same type of proof is also required for the latest avatars of the liberal model. These claim to be political and not metaphysical. Political liberalism presents itself as a freestanding conception independent from any comprehensive doctrines or substantive conceptions of the good. But we saw that the conceptual core of this liberal model of toleration and the secular state is in fact deeply metaphysical. It continues to depend on a conception of the person and human social life that secularizes Protestant-Christian ideas by transforming them into topoi of political thought.

This hypothesis about the secularization of Christian freedom has specific consequences for the Western world. The liberal democracies of Europe and North America are now home to groups of people coming from many different parts of the world, from Asia to Africa. Many of these citizens do not share the common-sense attitudes and ideas generated by the secularization of Christianity. How can liberal democracies truly accommodate such groups, if the toleration model of these states implicitly reproduces and imposes a particular theological conception of human existence that lacks intelligibility to them?

The hypothesis also downsizes the importance of research that presumes itself 'secular' and 'universal', while being theological in a crucial sense. Instead, it calls upon political theorists to look for other, non-religious solutions to the problems of diversity by studying how cultures other than the West have tackled and solved the problem of pluralism. In short, if we desire to find new solutions to the growing diversity of our multicultural societies, it is advisable to stop approaching the political domain through a Christian-secular perspective.

This is not to say that all ideas generated by the secularization of Christianity have no role to play in the search for alternatives. Some of these could remain valuable and helpful. For instance, it is possible that some specific ideas of liberal secularism can serve as useful heuristics in coming to reasonable policies and judgements. However, to make such a case, we need to examine these ideas and rethink their status, instead of selling them as normative principles that offer the only rational foundation for coexistence. The utility of 'liberal' ideas and attitudes cannot be decided a priori, but only on the basis of research into the role they have played in the past and into their relationship to a culture-specific background framework.

What has become clear is that we cannot count on topoi such as religious freedom, liberty of conscience, and the separation of religion and politics in order to develop viable models of coexistence for the twenty-first century. We cannot allow our political models to rely on ideas that are intuitively self-evident only to people raised in the Western-Christian culture. Unless we can reformulate these ideas in new ways accessible to all cultural groups living in today's liberal democracies, they will have to be replaced by other ideas and models.

The Normativity of Toleration

During the nineteenth and twentieth centuries, writings about the history of toleration often took the form of 'Whig historiography'. They presented the rise of toleration or religious freedom as a progressive expansion of its scope. Critics of this type of account point out that the development of toleration did not follow a rising path towards a predetermined telos. Moreover, they suggest, the liberal state and liberal toleration come with their own forms of intolerance.

As I suggested, these two perspectives constitute a challenge for any account of the emergence of the liberal model of toleration and the secular state. On the one hand, such an account should explain why Western culture remains distinctly intolerant of differences in comparison to certain other cultures. Liberal secular states do show intolerance towards many practices and groups, even though these are not obviously harmful. On the other hand, however, the account cannot deny the experience of many thousands of Westerners that their culture has witnessed a progressive rise of toleration and freedom. Instead of discounting this perception as some kind of illusion, it should save the phenomena by making sense of them.

The account presented in this book tries to live up to this condition. The perception of systematic progress derives from a specific historical dynamic that propelled the emergence of toleration. This dynamic goes back to early Christianity. From the start, the church or communion of believers was viewed as simultaneously human and divine: it had to embody God's will, even though it consisted of human beings. Christianity also claims that the will of God unites the factual and the normative, the 'is' and the 'ought'. Consequently, the Church had to strive to embody this unity of the factual and the normative. But this unity is not accessible to human beings. Therefore, fact and norm or 'is' and 'ought' always fell apart and this caused ever-recurring attempts to realize their unity.

Once anticlerical Christians identified freedom of conscience as God's will for humanity, this dynamic began to push forward the emergence of toleration in Europe. While the confessional movement identified the divine order with a particular system of doctrine and discipline, its anti-confessional counterpart argued that the community had to embody the charity of ecumenical unity and religious freedom. But every empirical attempt to do so failed. From the Remonstrants in the Dutch Republic to the Puritans in England and America, each failure generated new attempts to realize the norms of religious freedom and toleration. The Whig view of the rise of toleration reproduces this Christian dynamic without relating it to divine providence. The endless attempt to unite the factual and the normative continues to guide liberal states in Europe and America, even though many liberals left God's will out of the equation.

However, this same normative dynamic also accounts for the intolerance at the heart of liberal toleration. The identification of religious freedom as God's will went hand in hand with an anticlerical theology that viewed the Catholic Church, Protestant confessions, and other religions as the devil's inventions and violations of God's will. This framework represented these religions as negations of the norms of toleration and freedom of conscience: they had allegedly corrupted religion by uniting it with politics, imposed all kinds of human rites and rules in the realm of religion, and stifled the freedom of conscience and spirit.

Driven by its normative dynamic, the liberal model of toleration and secularism never lost this dimension of deep intolerance. For a long time, it represented Judaism and Catholicism in explicitly theological terms as 'jewry' and 'popery': human institutions that impose their own fabricated doctrines and laws as though these are necessary to salvation. The Enlightenment secularized the normative model of Christian freedom but retained its intolerance. Now, all 'religions of the priest' were rejected because they supposedly constituted threats to the public order. Because such religions claimed authority in the secular realm and over the conscience of citizens, they were rejected as illegitimate rivals to the modern nation state and its claim of exclusive authority.

In fact, this imposed Protestant structures onto all religious and traditional communities in the name of secular raison d'état. The extent to which even the Roman-Catholic Church began to accept such claims indicates how Protestantism won the wars of religion by taking on a secular guise. Whether in Europe or in India, liberal secularism continues to reject certain traditions and groups in society as the negations of its own norms of toleration, religious freedom, and the separation of state and religion. It then opposes itself to these negations as the only rational model for living together peacefully. Today, the same tendency continues in the form of a clash between liberal secularism and the movements it perceives as its normative negations: for instance, 'political Islam' and 'Hindu nationalism'. This perspective has reduced our options to an impoverishing normative disjunction: either liberal secularism or political religion.

A genuine alternative to liberal secularism cannot take the form of a similar normative model, simply because this would again bring such forms of intolerance in its wake. It would aim for a radical discarding of liberal secular states. Instead, the challenge is to start from the factual situation in some society and then devise heuristics (or instructions for action) that aim to incrementally improve this situation by generating peaceful coexistence. In this sense, it would be a pragmatic political theory consisting of practical heuristics, rather than a normative model built on axioms and principles.

Doctrines of Coexistence

Another pitfall is to try and create a foundation for coexistence in a system of shared beliefs or values. This is what the Hindu nationalists have tried to do in contemporary India. Under colonial rule, Hindu reformers and their 'conservative' opponents had both adopted a particular model of religion from the British colonial state and its toleration policy. If a practice was to be tolerated, the colonized had to produce proof of its religious nature by showing its scriptural sanctions and doctrinal foundations. Basically, this model had the effect of transforming all traditions into variants of the religions of the Book.

Much like the secularists in India, the Hindu nationalists did not escape from the colonial framework but adopted the Orientalist discourse about their own culture. They started looking for the common beliefs and values of their religion. Consequently, instead of examining how Indian forms of pluralism work, they postulated a Hindu doctrine of tolerance or 'positive secularism'. This is often formulated in terms of the belief in 'the equality of all religions'. However, such doctrines of religious equality cannot but be unacceptable to Islam and Christianity, because these religions necessarily claim to be God's one true revelation. To give up this claim would condemn these religions to self-destruction. Hence, the result of this notion of 'Hindu tolerance' is intolerance towards Islam and Christianity. From the Hindu nationalist perspective, these religions either have to adapt to 'Hindu tolerance' by adopting its values, or they should leave India because they are alien to its values.

This doctrine of Hindu tolerance stands in conflict with the Indian cultural modes of pluralism that have existed for centuries. After all, the pluralism of Indian society allowed for the coexistence of a variety of groups on the subcontinent, including religions like Islam and Christianity. There were conflicts. But there is no historical evidence for systematic persecution or demands that Muslims and Christians rewrite the Quran and the Bible in order to conform to the 'equality of religions'. Indeed, Indian culture has shown a striking capacity to accommodate diversity, but to attribute this to some doctrine of Hindu tolerance is to miss the power of its pluralism.

At this point, Balagangadhara's theory of cultural difference comes in again. As he argues, human coexistence is the domain of practical knowledge and it cannot be founded in reason. It does not have its foundation in theoretical knowledge and doctrines. Instead, reason plays the role of reflecting on human practice and improving it where possible. In the pursuit of alternative modes of pluralism, we should focus on practical knowledge and systematic reflection on human practice. We need to examine existing practices of coexistence in different parts of the world. We should not only study the pluralism of Indian culture, but also look closer at the prudential modes of tolerance that crystallized elsewhere.

Only thus can we generate the heuristics of coexistence that we need so urgently today.

Breaking the Spell

Perhaps the most urgent task is to break the spell of colonial conscious-ness and its asymmetry of cultures. Both in the Western world and in former colonies like India, colonialism has put in place this harmful form of consciousness. It takes a normative framework developed in modern Europe as the dominant framework for describing all non-Western cultures. Consequently, it also views the traditions of India and other Asian cultures as negations of liberal secular norms. Maximally, it can look at some of these traditions (say, Ashoka's Buddhism or Akbar's rule) as immature approximations of secularism.

In India, both secularists and Hindu nationalists embrace the frame-work of colonial consciousness and continue to reproduce its discourse about India in some way or the other. Their value judgements may dif-fer, but their basic ideas do not. The normativity of this discourse has tragic consequences. The social sciences and humanities in India are now hijacked by an acerbic ideological conflict. On the one hand, Hindu nationalists advocate their ideology of Hindutva and attack its critics as 'pseudo-seculars' or 'sickularists'. On the other hand, secularists see 'Hindu fascists' around every corner. They dogmatically defend their ideology and dismiss any alternative perspective as another instance of Hindu national-ism or revivalism.

In Europe, the normative dimension of colonial consciousness leads to an implicit denial of the global shifts of the twenty-first century. When Western commentators look at India, they see widespread immorality: caste discrimination, corruption, religious persecution, systematic rape, gender inequality, and what have you. Consequently, they conclude that the denial of freedom, equality, and fraternity is rampant in India. This sustains a sense of moral superiority: 'Economically, Asia may be on the rise, but civilizationally we are still on top.' In the words of John Gray, Europeans and North Americans are thus weaving 'a comfort blanket against an unfamiliar world'.[1] This keeps in place the asymmetry of

---

[1]   Gray (2009).

cultures, which continues to shape the general views and media reporting about countries like India. Such a comfort blanket may temporarily blind us to reality but it can never make the real world go away.

The twenty-first century urgently needs a new perspective, which allows cultures to meet as alternative forms of life on an equal footing. Such a perspective should enable the many rich cultures of humanity to help solve each other's problems, to correct each other's shortcomings, and to experiment with and learn from the different kinds of knowledge each of them has developed. This is the promise that the twenty-first century offers to humanity; it is up to us to make the promise come true.

Bibliography

Abray, Lorna J. 1985. *The People's Reformation: Magistrates, Clergy, and Commons in Strasbourg, 1500–1598*. Ithaca, NY: Cornell University Press.

Adams, Geoffrey. 1991. *The Huguenots and French Opinion, 1685–1787: The Enlightenment Debate on Toleration*. Waterloo, Ontario: Wilfrid Laurier University Press.

Ahmed, A.F. Salahuddin. 1965. *Social Ideas and Social Change in Bengal 1818–1835*. Leiden: Brill.

Almond, Philip C. 1996. 'The Heathen in His Blindness?', *Cultural Dynamics* 8(2): 137–45.

Ambedkar, B.R. 1989. *Dr. Babasaheb Ambedkar: Writings and Speeches, Vol. 1*. Bombay: Education Department, Government of Maharashtra.

———. 2004. 'Caste, Class and Democracy'. In *The Essential Writings of B. R. Ambedkar*, edited by Valerian Rodrigues, 132–48. New Delhi: Oxford University Press.

Andreescu, Gabriel and Liviu Andreescu. 2010. '"The European Court of Human Rights" Lautsi Decision: Context, Contents, Consequences'. *Journal for the Study of Religions and Ideologies* 9(26): 47–74.

Anonymous. 1578. *Ordonnance et Declaration Nouvelle du Roy sur l'entretenement de la Pacification de Gand*. Antwerp.

Anonymous. 1579. *Discours Contenant le Vray Entendement de la Pacification de Gand, de L'union des Estats et Aultres Traictez Y Ensuyuiz, Touchant le Faict de la Religion*, s. l.

Anonymous. 1652. *Zeal Examined: Or, a Discourse for Liberty of Conscience in Matters of Religion*. London.

Anonymous. 1688a. *Old Popery as Good as New*. s. l.

Anonymous. 1688b. *An Expedient for Peace: Perswading an Agreement amongst Christians from the Impossibility of their Agreement in the Matters of Religion*. London.

Anonymous. 1800. 'The History of British India'. In *The Asiatic Annual Register ... For the Year 1799*. London.

Anonymous. 1804. 'Peculiar Customs of the Hindus'. In *The Asiatic Annual Register ... For the Year 1803*, vol. 5. London.

Anonymous. 1856. 'Our Indian Empire'. *Blackwood's Edinburgh Magazine* 80(494): 636–59.

Anonymous. 2004. 'Laïcité: bandanas et barbes interdits'. *Le Nouvel Observateur*. 22 January 2004. http://tempsreel.nouvelobs.com/politique/20040120. OBS2814/laicite-bandanas-et-barbes-interdits.html (last accessed 25 June 2015).

Arminius, James. 1956. *The Writings of James Arminius*. Grand Rapids: Baker Book House.

Arnoldi Vander Linde, Henricus. 1629. *Vande Conscientiedwangh*. Delft.

Asad, Talal. 2003. *Formations of the Secular: Christianity, Islam, Modernity*. Stanford: Stanford University Press.

Ashcraft, Richard. 1996. 'Religion and Lockean Natural Rights'. In *Religious Diversity and Human Rights*, edited by Irene Bloom, J. Paul Martin, and Wayne Proudfoot, 115–213. New York: Columbia University Press.

Augustine. 1995a. 'A Treatise on the Spirit and the Letter'. In *Nicene and Post-Nicene Fathers, First Series, Volume 5: Augustin: Anti-Pelagian Writings*, edited by Philip Schaff, 301–394. Peabody, MA: Hendrickson.

———. 1995b. 'Treatise on Rebuke and Grace'. In *Nicene and Post-Nicene Fathers, First Series, Volume 5: Augustin: Anti-Pelagian Writings*, edited by Philip Schaff, 1286–1347. Peabody, MA: Hendrickson.

———. 2000. *The City of God*. New York: The Modern Library.

Bailey, Joe. 2002. 'From Public to Private: The Development of the Concept of "Private"'. *Social Research* 69(1): 15–32.

Bainton, Ronald, ed. 1935. *Concerning Heretics*. New York: Columbia University Press.

Bajpai, Rochana. 2002. 'The Conceptual Vocabulary of Secularism and Minority Rights in India'. *Journal of Political Ideologies* 7(2): 179–97.

Bakshi, P.M. 2011. *The Constitution of India*. New Delhi: Universal Law Publishing.

Balagangadhara, S.N. 1985. "'...We Shall Not Cease From Exploration...": An invitation disguised as a position paper composed at the behest of Arena for the theme "Decolonizing Social Sciences", mimeo.

———. 1988. 'Comparative Anthropology and Moral Domains'. *Cultural Dynamics* 1(1): 98–128.

———. 1994. *'The Heathen in His Blindness ...': Asia, the West and the Dynamic of Religion*. Leiden and New York: Brill.

———. 2005a. *'The Heathen in His Blindness ...': Asia, the West and the Dynamic of Religion*, second edition. New Delhi: Manohar.

———. 2005b. 'How to Speak for the Indian Traditions?' *Journal of the American Academy of Religion* 73(4): 987–1013.

———. 2010. 'Orientalism, Postcolonialism and the "Construction" of Religion'. In *Rethinking Religion in India: The Colonial Construction of Hinduism*, edited by Esther Bloch, Marianne Keppens, and Rajaram Hegde, 135–163. London and New York: Routledge.

———. 2012. *Reconceptualizing India Studies*. Delhi: Oxford University Press.

Balagangadhara, S.N. and Jakob De Roover. 2007. 'The Secular State and Religious Conflict: Liberal Neutrality and the Indian Case of Pluralism'. *Journal of Political Philosophy* 15(1): 67–92.

Barry, Brian. 2001. *Culture & Equality*. Cambridge: Polity.

Basham, A.L. 1969. *The Wonder that Was India: A Survey of the Culture of the Indian Subcontinent before the Coming of the Muslims*. London: Sidgwick & Jackson.

Bayle, Pierre. 2005. *A Philosophical Commentary on These Words of the Gospel, Luke 14:23, 'Compel Them to Come in, Thay My House May Be Full'*. Indianapolis: Liberty Fund.

Been, Wouter de. 2011. 'Lautsi: A Case of 'Metaphysical Madness'?' *Religion and Human Rights* 6: 231–5.

Bejczy, Istvan. 1997. 'Tolerantia: A Medieval Concept'. *Journal of the History of Ideas* 58(3): 365–84.

Bellenoit, Hayden J.A. 2007. *Missionary Education and Empire in Late Colonial India, 1860–1920*. London: Pickering & Chatto.

Benedict, Philip. 2002. *Christ's Churches Purely Reformed: A Social History of Calvinism*. New Haven: Yale University Press.

Beneke, Chris. 2006. *Beyond Toleration: The Religious Origins of American Pluralism*. Oxford and New York: Oxford University Press.

Berkvens-Stevelinck, Christine, Jonathan I. Israel, and G.H.M. Posthumus Meyjes, eds. 1997. *The Emergence of Tolerance in the Dutch Republic*. Leiden: E.J. Brill.

Berman, Harold J. 1983. *Law and Revolution: The Formation of the Western Legal Tradition*. Cambridge, MA: Harvard University Press.

Bernier, François. 1671. *A Continuation of the Memoires of Monsieur Bernier concerning the Empire of the Great Mogol, Tome III & IV*. London.

Beteille, Andre. 1994.'Secularism and Intellectuals'. *Economic and Political Weekly* 29(10): 559–66.

Bethke Elshtain, Jean. 2008. *Sovereignty: God, State, and Self*. New York: Basic Books.

Bhargava, Rajeev, ed. 1998a. *Secularism and Its Critics*. Delhi: Oxford University Press.

———. 1998b.'What is Secularism For?' In *Secularism and Its Critics*, edited by Bhargava, 486–520. Delhi: Oxford University Press.

———. 2007. 'The Distinctiveness of Indian Secularism'. In *The Future of Secularism*, edited by T.N. Srinivasan, 20–53. New Delhi: Oxford University Press.

———. 2008.'Introduction'. In *Politics and Ethics of the Indian Constitution*, edited by Rajeev Bhargava. New Delhi: Oxford University Press.

———. 2010. *What is Political Theory and Why Do We Need It*. New Delhi: Oxford University Press.

Bharucha, Rustom. 1998. *In the Name of the Secular: Contemporary Cultural Activism in India*. New Delhi: Oxford University Press.

Bhattacharyya-Panda, Nandini. 2008. *Appropriation and Invention of Tradition: The East India Company and Hindu Law in Early Colonial Bengal*. New Delhi: Oxford University Press.

Bloch, Esther, Marianne Keppens, and Rajaram Hegde, eds. 2010. *Rethinking Religion in India: The Colonial Construction of Hinduism*. London and New York: Routledge.

Blumenberg, Hans. 1983. *The Legitimacy of the Modern Age*, translated by Robert M. Wallace. Cambridge, MA: MIT Press.

Bossy, John. 1985. *Christianity in the West, 1400–1700*. Oxford: Oxford University Press.

Bou-Habib, Paul. 2003. 'Locke, Sincerity and the Rationality of Persecution'. *Political Studies* 51(4): 611–26.

Bowen, John R. 2007. *Why the French Don't Like Headscarves: Islam, the State and Public Space*. Princeton: Princeton University Press.

Brandt, Geeraerdt. 1677. *Historie Der Reformatie en Andere Kerkelyke Geschiedenissen in en Omtrent de Nederlanden*. Amsterdam.

Brass, Paul R. 1999. 'Secularism Out of Its Place'. In *Tradition, Pluralism and Identity*, edited by V. Das, D. Gupta, and P. Uberoi, 359–80. New Delhi: Sage.

———. 2003. *The Production of Hindu-Muslim Violence in Contemporary India*. Delhi: Oxford University Press.

Brown, Wendy. 2006. *Regulating Aversion: Tolerance in the Age of Identity and Empire*. Princeton: Princeton University Press.

Bucer, Martin. 1969. '*De Regno Christi*' (1550). In *Melanchthon and Bucer*, edited by Wilhelm Pauck, 174–394. Philadelphia: The Westminster Press.

Buchanan, Allen E. 1989. 'Assessing the Communitarian Critique of Liberalism'. *Ethics* 99(4): 852–82.

Burchardt, Marian, Monika Wohlrab-Sahr, and Ute Wegert. 2013. '"Multiple Secularities": Postcolonial Variations and Guiding Ideas in India and South Africa'. *International Sociology* 28(6): 612–28.

Burman, J.J. Roy. 2002. *Hindu-Muslim Syncretic Shrines and Communities*. New Delhi: Mittal.

Buruma, Ian. 2010. *Taming the Gods: Religion and Democracy on Three Continents*. Princeton: Princeton University Press.

Busher, Leonard. 1966. 'Religions Peace: Or a Plea for Liberty of Conscience'. In *Tracts on Liberty of Conscience and Persecution, 1614–1661*, edited by Edward B. Underhill, 14–81. New York: Burt Franklin.

Butterfield, Herbert. 1965. *The Whig Interpretation of History*. New York and London: Norton.

———. 1977. 'Toleration in Early Modern Times'. *Journal of the History of Ideas* 38: 573–84.

Cady, Linell E. and Elizabeth Shakman Hurd, eds. 2010. *Comparative Secularisms in a Global Age*. New York: Palgrave Macmillan.

Caird, Edward. 1894. *The Evolution of Religion: The Gifford Lectures*, 2 vols. Glasgow: James Maclehose and Sons.

Calvin, John. 1960. *Institutes of the Christian Religion*. Edited by John T. McNeill. Louisville: Westminster John Knox Press.

Carlin, Norah. 1996. 'Toleration for Catholics in the Puritan Revolution'. In *From Persecution to Toleration: The Glorious Revolution and Religion in England*, edited by Ole P. Grell, Jonathan I. Israel, and Nicholas Tyacke, 216–230. Oxford: Clarendon Press.

Carson, Penny. 2001. 'The British Raj and the Awakening of Evangelical Conscience: The Ambiguities of Religious Establishment and Toleration, 1698–1833'. In *Christian Missions and the Enlightenment*, edited by Brian Stanley, 47–70. Grand Rapids, MI: Eerdmans.

Casanova, Jose. 1992. 'Private and Public Religions'. *Social Research* 59(1): 17–58.

Castellio, Sebastian. 1971. *De l'Impunité des Hérétiques*. Genève: Droz.

Cavanaugh, William T. 2009. *The Myth of Religious Violence: Secular Ideology and the Roots of Modern Conflict*. New York: Oxford University Press.

Chadwick, Henry. 1953. *Origen: Contra Celsum*. Cambridge: Cambridge University Press.

Chandhoke, Neera. 1999. *Beyond Secularism: The Rights of Religious Minorities*. Delhi: Oxford University Press.

Chandra, Bipan. 1994. *Ideology and Politics in Modern India*. New Delhi: Har-Anand.

Chandra, Bipan, Mridula Mukherjee, and Aditya Mukherjee. 2000. *India After Independence, 1947–2000*. New Delhi: Penguin Books.

Chareyre, Philippe. 1994. "'The Great Difficulties One Must Bear to Follow Jesus Christ": Morality at Sixteenth-Century Nîmes'. In *Sin and the Calvinists: Morals Control and the Consistory in the Reformed Tradition*, edited by Raymond A. Mentzer, 63–97. Kirksville, MO: Sixteenth Century Journal Publishers.

Chatterjee, Partha. 1998. 'Secularism and Tolerance'. In *Secularism and Its Critics*, edited by Rajeev Bhargava, 345–79. New Delhi: Oxford University Press.

Chatterji, P.C. 1995. *Secular Values for Secular India*. New Delhi: Manohar.

Chattopadhyaya, Brajadulal. 1998. *Representing the Other? Sanskrit Sources and the Muslims (Eighth to Fourteenth Century)*. New Delhi: Manohar.

Chiriyankandath, James. 2000. "'Creating a Secular State in a Religious Country": The Debate in the Indian Constituent Assembly'. *Commonwealth & Comparative Politics* 38(2): 1–24.

Chirol, Valentine. 1910. *Indian Unrest*. London: Macmillan.

Chitkara, M.G. 1997. *Hindutva*. New Delhi: APH.

Claerhout, Sarah. 2010. '*Losing my Tradition*': Conversion, Secularism and Religious Freedom in India, unpublished doctoral dissertation, Ghent University.

Cloots, André, Stijn Latré, and Guido Vanheeswijck. 2013. 'The Future of the Christian Past: Marcel Gauchet and Charles Taylor on the Essence of Religion and its Evolution'. *The Heythrop Journal*, 6 November (Early View): 1–17.

Coffey, John. 1998. 'Puritanism and Liberty Revisited: The Case for Toleration in the English Revolution'. *The Historical Journal* 41(4): 961–85.

———. 2000. *Persecution and Toleration in Protestant England 1558–1689*. Harlow: Pearson.

———. 2008. 'Milton, Locke and the New History of Toleration'. *Modern Intellectual History* 5(3): 619–32.

Cohn, Bernard S. 1996. *Colonialism and Its Forms of Knowledge: The British in India*. Princeton, NJ: Princeton University Press.

Coornhert, Dirck V. 1579. *Vanden Aengheheven Dwangh Inder Conscientien Binnen Hollandt*, s.l.

———. 1582a. *Proeve vande Nederlandtsche Catechismo*. Haarlem.

———. 1582b. *Synodus vander Conscientien Vryheidt*. Vryburgh.

———. 1589. *Dolinghen der Catechismi*, s.l.

———. 1597. *Justificatie des Magistraets tot Leyden in Hollant*. Amsterdam.

———. 1630. *Wercken*. Amsterdam.

Coornhert, Dirck V. and Justus Lipsius. 1590. *Proces vant Ketterdoden ende Dwang der Conscientien*. Gouda.

Corbet, John. 1668. *A Second Discourse of the Religion of England*. London.

Cossman, Brenda and Ratna Kapur. 1996. 'Secularism: Bench-Marked by Hindu Right'. *Economic and Political Weekly* 31(38): 2613–30.

Coward, Harold. 1987. 'Introduction'. In *Modern Indian Responses to Religious Pluralism*, edited by Harold Coward, ix–xii. Albany: State University of New York Press.

Craufurd, Quintin. 1790. *Sketches Chiefly Relating to the History, Religion, Learning, and Manners of the Hindoos*. London.

Creppell, Ingrid. 1996. 'Locke on Toleration: The Transformation of Constraint'. *Political Theory* 24(2): 200–40.

Croope, J. 1656. *Conscience-Oppression*. London.

Dallmayr, Fred R. 2004. 'Beyond Monologue: For a Comparative Political Theory'. *Perspectives on Politics* 2(2): 249–57.

Dalmia, Vasudha and Heinrich Von Stietencron, eds. 1995. *Representing Hinduism: The Construction of Religious Traditions and National Identity*. New Delhi: Manohar.

Dandekar, R.N. 1971. 'Hinduism'. In *Historia Religionum: Handbook for the History of Religions, vol. 2, Religions of the Present*, edited by E. Jouco Bleeker and Geo Widengren, 237–43. Leiden: Brill.

Das Gupta, Amlan. 2005. 'Universality of Religion'. *The Book Review*, 29(12): 15–6.

Davis, Derek H. 2003. 'Thomas Jefferson and the "Wall of Separation" Metaphor'. *Journal of Church and State* 45(1): 5–14.

Dayanand Saraswati. 1978. *Autobiography of Dayanand Saraswati*. New Delhi: Manohar.

———. 1994. *Light of Truth or an English Translation of the Satyarth Prakash*, translated by Chiranjiva Bharadwaja. New Delhi: Sarvadeshik Arya Pratinidhi Sabha.

De Doyar, Pierre. 1782. *Eclaircissement sur la Tolérance, ou Entretiens D'une dame et de Son Cure*. Rouen.

Dees, Richard H. 1997. 'The Justification of Toleration'. In *Philosophy, Religion, and the Question of Intolerance*, edited by Mehdi A. Razavi and David Ambuel, 134–57. Albany, NY: State University of New York Press.

Dell, William. 1646. *Right Reformation*. London.

De Marneffe, Peter. 1990. 'Liberalism, Liberty, and Neutrality'. *Philosophy and Public Affairs* 19(3): 253–74.

De Roover, Jakob. 2003. 'An Unhappy Lover of Theology: Feuerbach and Contemporary Religious Studies'. *Journal of the American Academy of Religion* 71(3): 615–35.

———. 2014. 'Incurably Religious? *Consensus Gentium* and the Cultural Universality of Religion'. *Numen: International Review of the History of Religions* 61(1): 5–32.

De Roover, Jakob and Sarah Claerhout. 2010. 'The Colonial Construction of What?' In *Rethinking Religion in India: The Colonial Construction of Hinduism*, edited by Esther Bloch, Marianne Keppens, and Rajaram Hegde, 164–83. London and New York: Routledge.

De Roover, Jakob, Sarah Claerhout, and S.N. Balagangadhara. 2011. 'Liberal Political Theory and the Cultural Migration of Ideas: The Case of Secularism in India'. *Political Theory* 39(5): 571–99.

Derrett, J.D.M. 1968. *Religion, Law and the State in India*. New York: Free Press.

Dhavan, Rajeev and Fali Nariman. 2000. 'The Supreme Court and Group Life: Religious Freedom, Minority Groups, and Disadvantaged Communities'. In *Supreme but Not Infallible: Essays in Honour of the Supreme Court of India*, edited by B.N. Kirpal, Ashok H. Desai, Rajeev Dhavan, and Raju Ramachandran, 256–87. New Delhi: Oxford University Press.

Diderot, Denis. 1992. *Political Writings*. Cambridge: Cambridge University Press.

Dirks, Nicholas B. 2001. *Castes of Mind: Colonialism and the Making of Modern India*. Princeton: Princeton University Press.

———. 2006. *The Scandal of Empire: India and the Creation of Imperial Britain*. Cambridge, MA: Harvard University Press.

Donteclock, Reginald. 1608. *Proeve des Gouschen Catechismu*. Delft.

Dow, Alexander. 1970. 'A Dissertation Concerning the Customs, Manners, Language, Religion and Philosophy of the Hindoos'. In *The British Discovery of Hinduism*, edited by P.J. Marshall, 107–39. Cambridge: Cambridge University Press.

Dubuisson, Daniel. 2003. *The Western Construction of Religion: Myths, Knowledge, and Ideology*. Baltimore: The Johns Hopkins University Press.

Dunn, John. 1969. *The Political Thought of John Locke: An Historical Account of the Argument of the 'Two Treatises of Government'*. Cambridge: Cambridge University Press.

———. 1991. 'The Claim to Freedom of Conscience, Freedom of Speech, Freedom of Thought, Freedom of Worship?' In *From Persecution to Toleration: The Glorious Revolution and Religion in England*, edited by Ole P. Grell, Jonathan I. Israel, and Nicholas Tyacke, 171–93. Oxford: Clarendon Press.

Dworetz, Steven. 1990. *The Unvarnished Doctrine: Locke, Liberalism, and the American Revolution*. Durham, NC: Duke University Press.

Dworkin, Ronald. 1985. *A Matter of Principle*. Cambridge, MA: Harvard University Press.

Dyzenhaus, David. 1992. 'John Stuart Mill and the Harm of Pornography'. *Ethics* 102(3): 534–51.

Eire, Carlos. 1982. *War Against the Idols: The Reformation of Worship from Erasmus to Calvin*. New Haven: Yale University Press.

Eisgruber, Christopher L. and Lawrence G. Sager. 2007. *Religious Freedom and the Constitution*. Cambridge, MA and London: Harvard University Press.

Elm, Kaspar. 1993. 'Antiklerikalismus im Deutschen Mittelalter'. In *Anticlericalism in Late Medieval and Early Modern Europe*, edited by Peter A. Dykema and Heiko A. Oberman, 3–18. Leiden: E.J. Brill.

Elst, Koenraad. 2001. *Decolonizing the Hindu Mind: Ideological Development of Hindu Revivalism*. New Delhi: Rupa Publications.

Embree, Ainslie T. 1962. *Charles Grant and British Rule in India.* New York: Columbia University.

Episcopius, Simon and Johannes Uytenbogaert. 1621. *Belijdenisse ofte Verklaringhe Van 't ghevoelen der Leeraren, die in de Gheunieerde Nederlanden Remonstranten worden ghenaemt, over de voornaemste Articulen der Christelijcke Religie*, s.l.

Estes, James M., ed. 1994. *Whether Secular Government Has the Right to Wield the Sword in Matters of Faith: A Controversy in Nürnberg in 1530 over Freedom of Worship and the Authority of Secular Government in Spiritual Matters.* Toronto: Centre for Reformation and Renaissance Studies.

Evans, Malcolm D. 2011. 'Lautsi v. Italy: An Initial Appraisal'. *Religion and Human Rights* 6(3): 237–44.

Farquhar, John Nichol. 1915. *Modern Religious Movements in India.* New York: Macmillan.

Farr, James R. 2003. 'Confessionalization and Social Discipline in France, 1530–1685'. *Archiv für Reformationsgeschichte* 94: 276–93.

Faulkner, Robert K. 2003. 'Political Philosophy'. In *Encyclopedia of the Enlightenment*, vol. 3, edited by Alan Charles Kors, 314–23. Oxford: Oxford University Press.

Ferry, Patrick T. 1997. 'Confessionalization and Popular Preaching: Sermons against Synergism in Reformation Saxony'. *Sixteenth Century Journal* 28(4): 1143–66.

Feyerabend, Paul. 1970. 'Against Method: Outline of an Anarchistic Theory of Knowledge'. In *Minnesota Studies in the Philosophy of Science*, vol. 4, edited by M. Radner and S. Winokur, 17–130. Minneapolis: University of Minnesota Press.

Fish, Stanley. 2011. 'Crucifixes and Diversity: The Odd Couple'. *New York Times*, 28 March 2011.

Flood, Gavin. 1996. *An Introduction to Hinduism.* Cambridge: Cambridge University Press.

Forst, Rainer. 2013. *Toleration in Conflict: Past and Present.* Cambridge: Cambridge University Press.

Forster, Greg. 2005. *John Locke's Politics of Moral Consensus.* Cambridge: Cambridge University Press.

Fox Young, Richard. 1981. *Resistant Hinduism: Sanskrit Sources on Anti-Christian Apologetics in Early Nineteenth-Century India.* Vienna: De Nobili Research Foundation.

Freedman, Jane. 2004. 'Secularism as a Barrier to Integration? The French Dilemma'. *International Migration* 42(3): 5–27.

Fuller, C.J. 2012. 'Review of Rethinking Religion in India: The Colonial Construction of Hinduism'. *Pacific Affairs* 85(3): 664–6.

Galanter, Marc. 1971. 'Hinduism, Secularism, and the Indian Judiciary'. *Philosophy East and West* 21(4): 467–87.

Galloway, Archibald. 1825. *Observations on the Law and Constitution of India*. London: Kingsbury, Parbury, and Allen.

Ganguly, Sumit. 2003. 'The Crisis of Indian Secularism'. *Journal of Democracy* 14(4): 11–25.

Gasché, Rodolphe. 2014.'The Remainders of Faith: On Karl Löwith's Conception of Secularization'. In *The Multidimensionality of Hermeneutic Phenomenology*, edited by B. Babich and D. Ginev, 339–58. Cham: Springer.

Gauchet, Marcel. 1999. *The Disenchantment of the World: A Political History of Religion*. Princeton: Princeton University Press.

Gaustad, Edwin S. 1998.'Thomas Jefferson, Religious Freedom, and the Supreme Court'. *Church History* 67(4): 682–94.

Gedicks, Frederick M. 2006. 'Religious Exemptions, Formal Neutrality, and *Laïcité*'. *Indiana Journal of Global Legal Studies* 13(2): 473–92.

Gelders, Raf. 2009.'Genealogy of Colonial Discourse: Hindu Traditions and the Limits of European Representation'. *Comparative Studies in Society and History* 51(3): 563–89.

Gelders, Raf and Willem Derde. 2003. 'Mantras of Anti-Brahminism: Colonial Experience of Indian Intellectuals'. *Economic and Political Weekly* 38(43): 4611–17.

Gensichen, Hans-Werner. 1967. *We Condemn: How Luther and 16th-Century Lutheranism Condemned False Doctrine*. St. Louis, MI: Concordia.

Gillespie, Michael Allen. 2008. *The Theological Origins of Modernity*. Chicago: The University of Chicago Press.

Gilmartin, David and Bruce D. Lawrence, eds. 2000. *Beyond Turk and Hindu: Rethinking Religious Identities in Islamicate South Asia*. Gainesville: University Press of Florida.

Glover, Willis B. 1984. *Biblical Origins of Modern Secular Culture: An Essay in the Interpretation of Western History*. Macon: Mercer University Press.

Goertz, Hans-Jürgen. 1993.'"What a Tangled and Tenuous Mess the Clergy Is!" Clerical Anticlericalism in the Reformation Period'. In *Anticlericalism in Late Medieval and Early Modern Europe*, edited by Peter A. Dykema and Heiko A. Oberman, 499–520. Leiden: E.J. Brill.

Golwalkar, M.S. 1966. *Bunch of Thoughts*. Bangalore: Vikrama Prakashan.

Gopal, Sarvepalli. 1993.'Introduction'. In *Anatomy of a Confrontation: Ayodhya and the Rise of Communal Politics in India*, edited by Sarvepalli Gopal, 11–21. London and New Jersey: Zed Books.

Gordon, Robert. 1675. *Spiritual Order and Christian Liberty Proved To Be Consistent in the Churches of Christ and Impositions Upon the Consciences of Believers in Religious Practices Found To Be Antichristian and Destructive to Both*, s.l.

Gould, William. 2004. *Hindu Nationalism and the Language of Politics in Late Colonial India*. Cambridge: Cambridge University Press.

Graham, Bruce D. 1990. *Hindu Nationalism and Indian Politics: The Origins and Development of the Bharatiya Jana Sangh*. Cambridge: Cambridge University Press.

Graham, Michael F. 1996. *The Uses of Reform: 'Godly Discipline' and Popular Behavior in Scotland and Beyond, 1560–1610*. Leiden: E.J. Brill.

Grant, Charles. 1970. 'Observations on the State of Society among the Asiatic Subjects of Great Britain (1792)'. In *British Parliamentary Papers—Colonies East India, Vol. 5: 1831–1832*. Shannon: Irish University Press.

Grant, Ruth W. 1987. *John Locke's Liberalism*. Chicago and London: The University of Chicago Press.

Gray, John. 1983. *Mill on Liberty: A Defense*. London: Routledge and Kegan Paul.

———. 2009. 'The End of a Dream'. *New Statesman*, 10 December 2009.

Greenawalt, Kent. 1984. 'Religion as a Concept in Constitutional Law'. *California Law Review* 72(5): 753–816.

———. 2006. *Religion and the Constitution, vol. 1: Free Exercise and Fairness*. Princeton and Oxford: Princeton University Press.

Gudavarthy, Ajay. 2014. 'Debating the Secular-Communal Divide'. *Hindu*, 25 March 2014.

Guthrie, Stewart. 1996. 'Theories of Religion'. *American Anthropologist* 98(1): 162–3.

Halhed, Nathaniel B. 2000. 'A Code of Gentoo Laws or, Ordinations of the Pundits'. In *Representing India: Indian Culture and Imperial Control in Eighteenth-Century British Orientalist Discourse*, edited by Michael J. Franklin. London and New York: Routledge.

Haliczer, Stephen. 1990. *Inquisition and Society in the Kingdom of Valencia 1478–1834*. Berkeley: University of California Press.

Hamburger, Philip. 2002. *The Separation of Church and State*. Cambridge, MA: Harvard University Press.

Harcourt, Bernard. 1999. 'The Collapse of the Harm Principle'. *Journal of Criminal Law & Criminology* 90(1): 109–95.

Harris, Ian. 1994a. *The Mind of John Locke: A Study of Political Theory in Its Intellectual Setting*. Cambridge: Cambridge University Press.

———. 1994b. 'The Politics of Christianity'. In *Locke's Philosophy: Content and Context*, edited by G.A.J. Rogers, 198–205. Oxford: Clarendon Press.

Hasan, Mushirul. 1996. 'The Changing Position of the Muslims and the Political Future of Secularism in India'. In *Region, Religion, Caste, Gender and Culture in Contemporary India*, edited by T.V. Sathyamurthy, 200–28. Delhi: Oxford University Press.

Hastings, Warren. 1846. 'Introduction'. In *The Bhagavat-Geeta, or Dialogues of Krishna and Arjoon; in Eighteen Lectures*, edited by Rev. J. Garrett, v–xi. Bangalore.

Hastings, Warren. 1968. 'Minute of Evidence (1813)'. In *Minutes of Evidence—British Parliamentary Papers, Vol. 4 (1812–1813)*. Shannon: Irish University Press.

Headley, John M., Hans J. Hillerbrand, and Anthony Papalas, eds. 2004. *Confessionalization in Europe, 1555–1700*. Aldershot: Ashgate.

Helwys, Thomas. 1612. *A Shorte Declaration of the Mistery of Iniquity*. Amsterdam.

Herbert of Cherbury. 1663. *De Religione Gentilium*. Amsterdam.

———. 1768. *A Dialogue between a Tutor and His Pupil*. London.

Hibbard, Scott W. 2010. *Religious Politics and Secular States: Egypt, India, and the United States*. Baltimore: The Johns Hopkins University Press.

Hudson, W.D., ed. 1969. *The Is/Ought Question: A Collection of Papers on the Central Problem in Moral Philosophy*. Basingstoke: Macmillan.

Hume, David. 1976. *The Natural History of Religion (1757)*. Oxford: Clarendon Press.

Inden, Ronald. 1990. *Imagining India*. Oxford: Basil Blackwell.

Irschick, Eugene F. 1994. *Dialogue and History: Constructing South India, 1795–1895*. Berkeley and Los Angeles: University of California Press.

Irwin, Robert. 2007. *For Lust of Knowing: The Orientalists and Their Enemies*. London: Penguin Books.

Israel, Jonathan I. 2001. *Radical Enlightenment: Philosophy and the Making of Modernity 1650–1750*. Oxford: Oxford University Press.

———. 2004. 'Bayle, Enlightenment, Toleration and Modern Western Society'. *Pierre Bayle Lezing 2004*. Rotterdam, 10 December 2004. Available at: http://vorige.nrc.nl/krant/article1606378.ece, last accessed 26 July 2015.

———. 2006. *Enlightenment Contested: Philosophy, Modernity, and the Emancipation of Man 1670–1752*. Oxford: Oxford University Press.

Jacobsohn, Gary. 2003. *The Wheel of Law: India's Secularism in Comparative Constitutional Context*. Princeton and Oxford: Princeton University Press.

Jacoby, Susan. 2004. *Freethinkers: A History of American Secularism*. New York: Henry Holt & Co.

Jakobsen, Janet R. and Ann Pellegrini, eds. 2008. *Secularisms*. Durham and London: Duke University Press.

Jefferson, Thomas. 1903. *The Writings of Thomas Jefferson*, vol. 16. Washington DC: Thomas Jefferson Memorial Association of the United States.

———. 1955. *Notes on the State of Virginia*. Chapel Hill, NC: University of North Carolina Press.

Jenkins, Philip. 2003. *The New Anti-Catholicism: The Last Acceptable Prejudice*. New York: Oxford University Press.

Jensen, Tim. 2011. 'When is Religion, Religion, and a Knife, a Knife—and Who Decides? The Case of Denmark'. In *After Secular Law*, edited by W.F. Sullivan, R. Yelle, and M. Taussig-Rubbo, 341–62. Stanford: Stanford University Press.

Jha, Shefali. 2002. 'Secularism in the Constituent Assembly Debates, 1946–1950'. *Economic and Political Weekly* 37(30): 3175–80.

Jones, Kenneth W. 1976. *Arya Dharm: Hindu Consciousness in 19th-Century Punjab*. Berkeley: University of California Press.

———. 1998. 'Two *Sanatan Dharm* Leaders and Swami Vivekananda: A Comparison'. In *Swami Vivekananda and the Modernization of Hinduism*, edited by William Radice. New Delhi: Oxford University Press.

Jones, William. 1970. *The Letters of Sir William Jones*, 2 vols. Oxford: Clarendon Press.

———. 2000. 'Institutes of Hindu Law or, the Ordinances of Menu'. In *Representing India: Indian Culture and Imperial Control in Eighteenth-Century British Orientalist Discourse*, edited by Michael J. Franklin. London and New York: Routledge.

Jordan, W.K. 1965. *The Development of Religious Toleration in England*, 4 vols. Gloucester, MA: Peter Smith.

Juergensmeyer, Mark. 2008. *Global Rebellion: Religious Challenges to the Secular State, from Christian Militias to al Qaeda*. Berkeley and Los Angeles: University of California Press.

J.V.C.O. 1663. *Amsterdam: Toleration, or No Toleration in a Discourse between Conformists, Non-Conformists, Papists, Anabaptists, Quakers, &c*. London.

Kahlos, Maijastina. 2009. *Forbearance and Compulsion: The Rhetoric of Religious Tolerance and Intolerance in Late Antiquity*. London: Duckworth.

Kantorowicz, Ernst H. 1997. *The King's Two Bodies: A Study in Mediaeval Political Theology*. Princeton, NJ: Princeton University Press.

Kaplan, Benjamin J. 1994. '"Remnants of the Papal Yoke": Apathy and Opposition in the Dutch Reformation'. *Sixteenth Century Journal* 25(3): 653–69.

———. 1995. *Calvinists and Libertines: Confession and Communion in Utrecht, 1578–1620*. Oxford: Clarendon Press.

———. 2007. *Divided by Faith: Religious Conflict and the Practice of Toleration in Early Modern Europe*. Cambridge, MA: Harvard University Press.

Karant-Nunn, Susan C. 1994. 'Neoclericalism and Anticlericalism in Saxony, 1555–1675'. *Journal of Interdisciplinary History* 24(4): 615–37.

———. 1997. *The Reformation of Ritual: An Interpretation of Early Modern Germany*. London and New York: Routledge.

Kaye, John W. 1859. *Christianity in India: An Historical Narrative*. London: Smith, Elder, and Co.

———. 1898. *The Suppression of Human Sacrifice, Suttee, and Female Infanticide*. London and Madras: Christian Literature Society for India.

Keen, Ralph. 1996. 'Political Authority and Ecclesiology in Melanchthon's "De Ecclesiae Autoritate"'. *Church History* 65(1): 1–15.

Kelly, P.J. 1991. 'John Locke: Authority, Conscience and Religious Toleration'. In *John Locke: A Letter Concerning Toleration in Focus*, edited by John Horton and Susan Mendus, 125–46. London and New York: Routledge.

Kendall, E.A. 1822. 'On the Burning of Hindoo Widows'. *Asiatic Journal* 13(May 1822): 446–56.

Khan, Mumtaz A. 1994. 'Islam's Encounter with Hinduism in Secular India'. *Journal of Dharma* 19: 370–83.

Khilnani, Sunil. 2007. 'Secularism: Western and Indian'. In *The Secular State and Islam in Europe*, edited by Kurt Almqvist, 71–85. Stockholm: Axel and Margaret Axson Johnson Foundation.

Killian, Caitlin. 2003. 'The Other Side of the Veil: North African Women in France Respond to the Headscarf Affair'. *Gender & Society* 17(4): 567–90.

King, Peter. 1999. *Western Monasticism: A History of the Monastic Movement in the Latin Church*. Kalamazoo, MI: Cistercian Publications.

King, Preston. 1976. *Toleration*. London: George Allen & Unwin.

King, Richard. 1999. *Orientalism and Religion: Post-Colonial Theory, India and 'the Mystic East'*. London and New York: Routledge.

Kingdon, Robert M. 1972. 'The Control of Morals in Calvin's Geneva'. In *The Social History of the Reformation*, edited by Lawrence P. Buck and Jonathan W. Zophy, 3–16. Columbus: Ohio State University Press.

Knox, John. 1842. *Writings of the Rev. John Knox*. Philadelphia: Presbyterian Board of Publication.

Kolakowski, Leszek. 1987. *Chrétiens sans Église: La Conscience Religieuse et le Lien Confessional au XVIIe siècle*. Paris: Gallimard.

Kolb, Robert. 1982. 'God, Faith and the Devil: Popular Lutheran Treatments of the First Commandment in the Era of the Book of Concord'. *Fides et Historia* 15(1): 71–89.

———. 1991. *Confessing the Faith: Reformers Define the Church, 1530–1580*. St. Louis: Concordia.

———. 1996. *Luther's Heirs Define His Legacy: Studies on Lutheran Confessionalization*. Aldershot: Variorum.

Kolb, Robert and Timothy J. Wengert, eds. 2000. *The Book of Concord: The Confessions of the Evangelical Lutheran Church*. Minneapolis: Fortress Press.

Kooi, Christine. 2000. *Liberty and Religion: Church and State in Leiden's Reformation, 1572–1620*. Leiden: E.J. Brill.

Kyle, Richard. 1986. 'John Knox and the Purification of Religion: The Intellectual Aspects of His Crusade against Idolatry'. *Archiv für Reformationsgeschichte* 77: 265–80.

Kuttner, Stephan. 1980. *The History of Ideas and Doctrines of Canon Law in the Middle Ages*. London: Variorum.

Labrousse, Elisabeth. (1963–4). *Pierre Bayle*, 2 vols. The Hague: Martinus Nijhoff.

Laclear, George F. 1859. *The Christian Statesman and Our Indian Empire*. Cambridge.

La Crequinière. 1705. *The Agreement of the Customs of the East-Indians, With Those of the Jews, and Other Ancient People*. London.

Lacroix de Marlès, M. 1828. *Histoire Générale de l'Inde Ancienne et Moderne*, 6 vols. Paris: Emler Frères.

Ladner, Gerhart B. 1967. *The Idea of Reform: Its Impact on Christian Thought and Action in the Age of the Fathers*. New York: Harper & Row.

Lariviere, Richard W. 1989.'Justices and Panditas: Some Ironies in Contemporary Readings of the Hindu Legal Past'. *The Journal of Asian Studies* 48(4): 757–69.

Larmore, Charles. 1990.'Political Liberalism'. *Political Theory* 18(3): 339–60.

———. 1999. 'The Moral Basis of Political Liberalism'. *Journal of Philosophy* 96(12): 599–625.

Larson, Gerald J. 1997. Review of '*The Heathen in His Blindness ...*': *Asia, the West, and the Dynamic of Religion*, by S.N. Balagangadhara. *Philosophy East and West* 47(3): 433–5.

———, ed. 2001. *Religion and Personal Law in Secular India: A Call to Judgment*. Bloomington and Indianapolis: Indiana University Press.

Latré, Stijn. 2010. 'Jean-Claude Monod and the Historical Heritage of Secularization Theory'. *Bijdragen: International Journal in Philosophy and Theology* 71(1): 27–50.

Leclerc, Joseph. 1955. *Histoire de la Tolérance au Siècle de la Réforme*, 2 vols. Paris: Aubier.

Levine, Alan. 1999.'Introduction: The Prehistory of Toleration and Varieties of Skepticism'. In *Early Modern Skepticism and the Origins of Toleration*, edited by Alan Levine, 1–16. Lanham: Lexington.

Likhovski, Assaf. 1999.'Protestantism and the Rationalization of English Law: A Variation on a Theme by Weber'. *Law & Society Review* 33(2): 365–91.

Lilla, Mark. 2008. *The Stillborn God: Religion, Politics, and the Modern West*. New York: Vintage Books.

Llewellyn, Jack E., ed. 2005. *Defining Hinduism: A Reader*. London: Equinox.

Locke, John. 1690. *A Second Letter Concerning Toleration*. London.

———. 1692. *A Third Letter for Toleration*. London.

———. 1997a. 'First Tract on Government'. In *Locke: Political Essays*, edited by Mark Goldie, 3–53. Cambridge: Cambridge University Press.

———. 1997b. 'Civil and Ecclesiastical Power'. In *Locke: Political Essays*, edited by Mark Goldie, 216–21. Cambridge: Cambridge University Press.

———. 1997c. 'An Essay on Toleration'. In *Locke: Political Essays*, edited by Mark Goldie, 134–59. Cambridge: Cambridge University Press.

Locke, John. 2003. *Two Treatises of Government and a Letter Concerning Toleration.* New Haven and London: Yale University Press.

Lord, Henry. 1630. *A Discoverie of the Banian Religion and the Religion of the Persees.* London.

Löwith, Karl. 1949. *Meaning in History.* Chicago and London: The University of Chicago Press.

Luther, Martin. 1989. *Martin Luther's Basic Theological Writings.* Minneapolis: Fortress Press.

———. 1999. *Luther's Works, vol. 21: The Sermon on the Mount and the Magnificat.* Saint Louis: Concordia Publishing House.

———. 1999. *Luther's Works, vol. 35: Word and Sacrament I.* Edited by J. J. Pelikan, H.C. Oswald, and H.T. Lehmann. Philadelphia: Fortress Press.

Lyall, Alfred C. 1910. 'Introduction'. In *Indian Unrest,* by Valentine Chirol, vii–xvi. London: Macmillan.

MacDonald, John. 1822. 'On the Hindoo Laws Respecting the Burning of Widows'. *Asiatic Journal* 13(March 1822): 220–6.

Macfie, Alexander Lyon, ed. 2000. *Orientalism: A Reader.* New York: New York University Press.

MacNaghten, Francis W. 1824. *Considerations on the Hindoo Law as It is Current in Bengal.* Serampore: Mission Press.

Macnaughten, W.H. 1829. *Principles and Precedents of Hindu Law,* vol. 1. Calcutta: The Baptist Mission Press.

Madan, T.N. 1987. 'Secularism in Its Place'. *The Journal of Asian Studies* 46(4): 747–59.

———. 1997. *Modern Myths, Locked Minds: Secularism and Fundamentalism in India.* Delhi: Oxford University Press.

———. 1998. 'Secularism in Its Place'. In *Secularism and Its Critics,* edited by R. Bhargava, 297–320. Delhi: Oxford University Press.

Madhok, Balraj. 1995. 'Secularism: Genesis and Development'. In *Secularism in India: Dilemmas and Challenges,* edited by M.M. Sankhdher, 110–22. New Delhi: Deep and Deep Publications.

Mahajan, Gurpreet. 2002. 'Secularism as Religious Non-Discrimination: The Universal and the Particular in the Indian Context'. *India Review* 1(1): 33–51.

Mahbubani, Kishore. 2008. *The New Asian Hemisphere: The Irresistible Shift of Global Power to the East.* New York: PublicAffairs.

Major, Andrea. 2006. *Pious Flames: European Encounters with Sati 1500–1830.* New Delhi: Oxford University Press.

Majumdar, J.K., ed. 1988. *Raja Rammohun Roy and Progressive Movements in India.* New Delhi: Anmol.

Malcolm, John. 1833. *The Government of India.* London: J. Murray.

Malik, Shiv. 'Muslim Boys Told Their Beards Breach School Rules'. *Guardian*. 3 October 2013. http://www.theguardian.com/world/2013/oct/03/muslim-boys-beards-breach-school-rules (last accessed 4 October 2013).

Mandair, Arvind-Pal Singh. 2009. *Religion and the Specter of the West: Sikhism, India, Postcoloniality, and the Politics of Translation*. New York: Columbia University Press.

Mani, Lata. 1998. *Contentious Traditions: The Debate on Sati in Colonial India*. Berkeley and Los Angeles: The University of California Press.

Mansfield, John H. 1984. 'The Religion Clauses of the First Amendment and the Philosophy of the Constitution'. *California Law Review* 72(5): 847–907.

March, Andrew F. 2009. 'What is Comparative Political Theory?' *The Review of Politics* 71(4): 531–65.

Markus, Robert A. 1988. *Saeculum: History and Society in the Theology of St. Augustine*. Cambridge: Cambridge University Press.

———. 1990. *The End of Ancient Christianity*. Cambridge: Cambridge University Press.

———. 2006. *Christianity and the Secular*. Notre Dame, IN: University of Notre Dame Press.

Marshall, John. 1994. *John Locke: Resistance, Religion and Responsibility*. Cambridge: Cambridge University Press.

Massie, Allan. 2012. 'When Will We See an Islamic Enlightenment'. *Telegraph*, 21 March.

Mathur, Sobhag. 1996. *Hindu Revivalism and the Indian National Movement: A Documentary Study of the Ideals and Policies of the Hindu Mahasabha, 1939–45*. Jodhpur: Kusumanjali Prakashan.

McClure, Kirstie. 1990. 'Difference, Diversity and the Limits of Toleration'. *Political Theory*, 18(3): 361–91.

McIntosh, Terence. 2004. 'Confessionalization and the Campaign against Prenuptial Coitus in Sixteenth-Century Germany'. In *Confessionalization in Europe, 1555–1700*, edited by John M. Headley, Hans J. Hillerbrand, and Anthony Papalas, 155–74. Aldershot: Ashgate.

McLoughlin, William G. 1991. *Soul Liberty: The Baptists' Struggle in New England, 1630–1833*. Hannover and London: Brown University Press.

Mehta, Pratap Bhanu. 2008. 'On the Possibility of Religious Pluralism'. In *Religious Pluralism, Globalization, and World Politics*, edited by Thomas Banchoff, 65–88. Oxford: Oxford University Press.

Melanchthon, Philip. 1969. 'Loci Communes Theologici' (1521). In *Melanchthon and Bucer*, edited by Wilhelm Pauck, 3–150. Philadelphia: The Westminster Press.

Mendus, Susan. 1989. *Toleration and the Limits of Liberalism*. Basingstoke: Macmillan.

Mentzer, Raymond A. 1987.'Disciplina Nervus Ecclesiae: The Calvinist Reform of Morals at Nimes'. *Sixteenth Century Journal* 18(1): 89–116.

——, ed. 1994. *Sin and the Calvinists: Morals Control and the Consistory in the Reformed Tradition*. Kirksville, MO: Sixteenth Century Journal Publishers.

——. 1996.'The Persistence of "Superstition and Idolatry" among Rural French Calvinists'. *Church History* 65(2): 220–33.

——. 2000. 'Morals and Moral Regulation in Protestant France'. *Journal of Interdisciplinary History* 31(1): 1–20.

——. 2004. 'Fashioning Reformed Identity in Early Modern France'. In *Confessionalization in Europe, 1555–1700*, edited by John M. Headley, Hans J. Hillerbrand, and Anthony Papalas. Aldershot: Ashgate.

Michaels, Axel. 2004. *Hinduism: Past and Present*. Princeton: Princeton University Press.

Mill, James. 1820. *The History of British India in 6 vols*, vol. 1. London: Baldwin, Cradock and Joy.

Mill, John Stuart. 1987. *On Liberty*. Harmondsworth: Penguin Books.

Milton, John. 1646. 'On the New Forcers of Conscience under the Long Parliament'. In *John Milton: Complete Shorter Poems*, edited by Stella Revard, 314–15. Oxford: Wiley Blackwell.

——. 1659. *A Treatise of Civil Power in Ecclesiastical Causes*. London.

Monod, Jean-Claude. 2002. *La Querelle de la Sécularisation—De Hegel à Blumenberg*. Paris: J. Vrin.

Monter, E. William. 1976.'The Consistory of Geneva, 1559–1569'. *Bibliothèque d' Humanisme et Renaissance* 38: 467–84.

Moore, R.I. 1987. *The Formation of a Persecuting Society: Power and Deviance in Western Europe, 950–1250*. Oxford: Basil Blackwell.

——. 1994. *The Origins of European Dissent*. Toronto: University of Toronto Press.

——. 1995. *The Birth of Popular Heresy*. Toronto: University of Toronto Press.

Morris, Colin. 1989. *The Papal Monarchy: The Western Church from 1050 to 1250*. Oxford: Clarendon Press.

Morrison, Karl F. 1992. *Understanding Conversion*. Charlottesville: University of Virginia Press.

Moss, Ann. 1996. *Printed Commonplace-Books and the Structuring of Renaissance Thought*. Oxford: Oxford University Press.

Mout, M.E.H.N. 1997. 'Limits and Debates: A Comparative View of Dutch Toleration in the Sixteenth and Early Seventeenth Centuries'. In *The Emergence of Tolerance in the Dutch Republic*, edited by C. Berkvens-Stevelinck, Jonathan I. Israel, and G.H.M. Posthumus Meyjes, 37–48. Leiden: E.J. Brill.

Munro, Thomas. 1968.'Minute of Evidence (1813)'. In *Minutes of Evidence—British Parliamentary Papers, Vol. 4 (1812–1813)*. Shannon: Irish University Press.

Mushir-Ul-Haq. 1972. *Islam in Secular India.* Shimla: Indian Institute of Advanced Study.

Nandy, Ashis. 1985. 'An Anti-secularist Manifesto'. *Seminar* 314: 14–24.

———. 1998a. 'The Politics of Secularism and the Recovery of Religious Tolerance'. In *Secularism and Its Critics*, edited by Rajeev Bhargava, 321–44. Delhi: Oxford University Press.

———. 1998b. 'The Twilight of Certitudes: Secularism, Hindu Nationalism and Other Masks of Deculturation'. *Postcolonial Studies* 1(3): 283–98.

———. 2007. 'Closing the Debate on Secularism: A Personal Statement'. In *The Crisis of Secularism in India*, edited by Anuradha Dingwaney Needham and Rajeswari Sunder Rajan, 107–17. Durham and London: Duke University Press.

Nandy, Ashis, Shikha Trivedy, Shail Mayaram, and Achut Yagnik. 1998. *Creating a Nationality: The Ramjanmabhumi Movement and Fear of the Self.* Delhi: Oxford University Press.

Nederman, Carey J. 2000. *Worlds of Difference: European Discourses of Toleration, c. 1100–1550.* University Park, PA: The Pennsylvania State University Press.

Needham, Anuradha Dingwaney and Rajeswari Sunder Rajan, eds. 2007. *The Crisis of Secularism in India.* Durham and London: Duke University Press.

Nehru, Jawaharlal. 1941. *Toward Freedom: The Autobiography of Jawaharlal Nehru.* New York: John Day Company.

———. 1986. *Selected Works of Jawaharlal Nehru, Second Series*, vol. 4. New Delhi: Jawaharlal Nehru Memorial Fund.

———. 1988a. *The Discovery of India.* New Delhi: J. Nehru Memorial Fund and Oxford University Press.

———. 1988b. *Selected Works of Jawaharlal Nehru, Second Series*, vol. 7. New Delhi: Jawaharlal Nehru Memorial Fund.

Nelson, J.H. 1877. *A View of the Hindu Law as Administered by the High Court of Judicature at Madras.* Madras: Higginbotham and Co.

———. 1881. *A Prospectus of the Scientific Study of the Hindû Law.* London: C. Kegan Paul & Co.

———. 1887. *Indian Usage and Judge-Made Law in Madras.* London: Kegan Paul, Trench, & Co.

Nigam, Aditya. 2006. *The Insurrection of Little Selves: The Crisis of Secular-Nationalism in India.* New Delhi: Oxford University Press.

Nijwahan, P.K. 1995. 'Secularism: A New Paradigm'. In *Secularism in India: Dilemmas and Challenges*, edited by M.M. Sankhdher, 159–88. New Delhi: Deep and Deep Publications.

Nischan, Bodo. 1984. 'The "Fractio Panis": A Reformed Communion Practice in Late Reformation Germany'. *Church History* 53(1): 17–29.

Nischan, Bodo. 1997. 'Demarcating Boundaries: Lutheran Pericopic Sermons in the Age of Confessionalization'. *Archiv für Reformationsgeschichte* 88: 199–216.

———. 1999. *Lutherans and Calvinists in the Age of Confessionalism*. Aldershot: Variorum.

Oddie, Geoffrey A. 2006. *Imagined Hinduism: British Protestant Missionary Constructions of Hinduism, 1793–1900*. New Delhi: Sage.

Orme, Robert. 1763. *A History of the Military Transactions of the British Nation in Hindostan from the Year 1745, To Which is Prefixed a Dissertation on the Establishment made by Mahomedan Conquerors in Indostan*, vol. 1. London.

Overton, Richard. 1645. *The Araignement of Mr. Persecution*. Europe.

Ozment, Steven. 1991. *Protestants: The Birth of a Revolution*. New York: Doubleday.

Pandey, Gyanendra. 1990. *The Construction of Communalism in Colonial North India*. Delhi: Oxford University Press.

Pantham, Thomas. 1997. 'Indian Secularism and Its Critics: Some Reflections'. *The Review of Politics* 59(3): 523–40.

Parekh, Bhikhu. 2003. 'Some Reflections on the Hindu Theory of Tolerance'. *Seminar*, January 2003: 48–53.

Parel, Anthony J. 1992. 'The Comparative Study of Political Philosophy'. In *Comparative Political Philosophy: Studies under the Upas Tree*, edited by Anthony J. Parel and Ronald C. Keith. 11–28. New Delhi: Sage.

Parker, Geoffrey. 1994. 'The "Kirk by Law Established" and Origins of "The Taming of Scotland": Saint Andrews, 1559–1600'. In *Sin and the Calvinists: Morals Control and the Consistory in the Reformed Tradition*, edited by Raymond A. Mentzer, 159–97. Kirksville, MO: Sixteenth Century Journal Publishers.

Parker, Charles H. 2001. 'Two Generations of Discipline: Moral Reform in Delft Before and After the Synod of Dort'. *Archiv für Reformationsgeschichte* 92: 215–31.

Parker, Kim I. 2004. *The Biblical Politics of John Locke*. Waterloo, ONT: Wilfred Laurier Press.

Peggs, James. 1830. *India's Cries to British Humanity*. London.

Pelikan, Jaroslav and Valerie Hotchkiss, eds. 2003. *Creeds and Confessions of Faith in the Christian Tradition, vol. 2: Reformation Era*. New Haven and London: Yale University Press.

Penn, William. 1685. *Considerations Moving to a Toleration and Liberty of Conscience*. London.

———. 1687. *The Reasonableness of Toleration, and the Unreasonableness of Penal Laws and Tests*. London.

———. 1971. 'The Great Case of Liberty of Conscience' (1670). In *The Select Works of William Penn*, vol. 2. New York: Kraus Reprint Company.

Perry, Richard, ed. 1952. *Sources of Our Liberties: Documentary Origins of Individual Liberties in the United States Constitution and Bill of Rights.* Chicago: American Bar Foundation.

Phule, Jotirao. 2002. 'Slavery'. In *Selected Writings of Jotirao Phule*, edited by G.P. Deshpande, 25–46. New Delhi: LeftWord.

Piatigorsky, Alexander. 1985. 'Some Phenomenological Observations on the Study of Indian Religion'. In *Indian Religion*, edited by Richard Burghart and Audrey Cantile, 208–58. London: Curzon Press.

Plassart, Anna. 2008. 'James Mill's Treatment of Religion and the History of British India'. *History of European Ideas* 34(4): 526–34.

Po-Chia Hsia, R. 1989. *Social Discipline in the Reformation: Central Europe 1550–1750.* London and New York: Routledge.

Po-Chia Hsia, R. and Henk van Nierop, eds. 2002. *Calvinism and Religious Toleration in the Dutch Golden Age.* Cambridge: Cambridge University Press.

Poynder, John. 1827. *Human Sacrifices in India.* London: J. Hatchard and Son.

Preus, Samuel. 1987. *Explaining Religion: Criticism and Theory from Bodin to Freud.* New Haven: Yale University Press.

Puppinck, Gregor. 2010. 'Lautsi v. Italy: An Alliance Against Secularism'. *L'Osservatore Romano*: 28 July 2010.

———. 2012. 'The Case of Lautsi v. Italy: A Synthesis'. *Brigham Young University Law Review* 2012(3): 873–927.

Rai, Alok. 1989. 'Addled Only in Parts: Strange Case of Indian Secularism'. *Economic and Political Weekly* 24(50): 2770–3.

Rao, Badrinath. 2006. 'The Variant Meanings of Secularism in India: Notes Toward Conceptual Clarifications'. *Journal of Church and State* 48(1): 47–81.

Rao, M.A. Venkata. 1960. 'Jana Sangh, Islam & Humayun Kabir'. *Organiser*: 1 August 1960.

Rao, Venkata. 1966. 'Introduction'. In *Bunch of Thoughts*, edited by M.S. Golwalkar, i–xxxiv. Bangalore: Vikrama Prakashan.

Rawls, John. 1985. 'Justice as Fairness: Political Not Metaphysical'. *Philosophy and Public Affairs* 14(3): 223–51.

———. 1996. *Political Liberalism.* New York: Columbia University Press.

Reinhard, Wolfgang. 1983. 'Zwang zur Konfessionalisierung? Prolegomena zu einer Theorie des konfessionellen Zeitalters'. *Zeitschrift für Historische Forschung* 10(3): 257–77.

Remer, Gary. 1996. *Humanism and the Rhetoric of Toleration.* University Park: The Pennsylvania State University Press.

Reventlow, Henning Graf. 1984. *The Authority of the Bible and the Rise of the Modern World.* London: SCM Press.

Rex, Walter. 1965. *Essays on Pierre Bayle and Religious Controversy.* The Hague: Martinus Nijhoff.

Richardson, Samuel. 1966. 'The Necessity of Toleration in Matters of Religion'. In *Tracts on Liberty of Conscience and Persecution, 1614–1661*, edited by Edward B. Underhill, 235–85. New York: Burt Franklin.

Riley, Patrick. 1986. *The General Will before Rousseau: The Transformation of the Divine into the Civic*. Princeton: Princeton University Press.

Rogge, H.C. 1856–8. *Caspar Janszoon Coolhaes: De Voorlooper van Arminius en der Remonstranten*, 2 vols. Amsterdam: H.W. Mooij.

Romilly, Jean-Edmé. 1986. 'Tolérance'. In *Encyclopédie ou Dictionnaire Raisonné Des Sciences, Des Arts et Des Métiers*, vol. 2, edited by D. Diderot and J.L. d'Alembert, 335–7. Paris: Flammarion.

Ronchi, Paolo. 2011. 'Crucifixes, Margin of Appreciation and Consensus: The Grand Chamber Ruling in Lautsi v Italy'. *Ecclesiastical Law Journal* 13(3): 287–97.

Roodenburg, Herman. 1990. *Onder Censuur: De Kerkelijke Tucht in De Gereformeerde Gemeente Van Amsterdam, 1578–1700*. Hilversum: Verloren.

Rosemont, Henry, Jr. 1988. 'Against Relativism'. In *Interpreting Across Boundaries: New Essays in Comparative Philosophy*, edited by G. Larson and E. Deutsch, 36–70. Princeton: Princeton University Press..

Rousseau, Jean-Jacques. 2002. *The Social Contract and The First and Second Discourses*. New Haven and London: Yale University Press.

Rushdie, Salman. 1990. 'In Good Faith'. *Independent*, 4 February 1990.

Roy, Rammohun. 1982. *The English Works of Raja Rammohun Roy*, vol. 1. New Delhi: Cosmo.

Said, Edward W. 1978. *Orientalism: Western Conceptions of the Orient*. London: Vintage.

Saltmarsh, John. 1992. 'Smoke in the Temple (1646)'. In *Puritanism and Liberty: Being the Army Debates (1647–49) from the Clarke Manuscripts*, edited by A.S.P. Woodhouse. London: J.M. Dent & Sons.

Sandberg, K.C. 1964. 'Pierre Bayle's Sincerity in His Views on Faith and Reason'. *Studies in Philology* 61(1): 77–84.

Sandel, Michael J. 1998. *Liberalism and the Limits of Justice*. Cambridge: Cambridge University Press.

Sankhdher, M.M. 1995. 'Understanding Secularism'. In *Secularism in India: Dilemmas and Challenges*, edited by M.M. Sankhdher, 1–16. New Delhi: Deep and Deep Publications.

Savarkar, V.D. 1969. *Hindutva: Who Is a Hindu?*. Bombay: S.S. Savarkar.

———. 1984. *Hindu Rashtra Darshan*. Bombay: Veer Savarkar Prakashan.

Scherer, Matthew. 2013. *Beyond Church and State: Democracy, Secularism, and Conversion*. New York: Cambridge University Press.

Schilling, Heinz. 1987. '"History of Crime" or "History of Sin"? Some Reflections on the Social History of Early Modern Church Discipline'. In *Politics and*

Society in Reformation Europe, edited by E.I. Kouri and Tom Scott, 289–310. Basingstoke: Macmillan.

Schilling, Heinz. 1991. *Civic Calvinism in Northwestern Germany and The Netherlands*. Kirksville, MO: Sixteenth Century Journal Publishers.

———. 1992. *Religion, Political Culture and the Emergence of Early Modern Society*. Leiden: E.J. Brill.

Schillings, Jan. 1997. *Het Tolerantiedebat in de Franstalige Geleerdentijdschriften, Uitgegeven in de Republiek der Verenigde Provinciën in de Periode 1684–1753*. Amsterdam and Maarssen: APA—Holland Universiteits Pers.

Schmitt, Carl. 1985. *Political Theology: Four Chapters on the Concept of Sovereignty*. Cambridge, MA: MIT Press.

Schneewind, J.B. 1997. 'Bayle, Locke, and the Concept of Toleration'. In *Philosophy, Religion, and the Question of Intolerance*, edited by Mehdi Aman Razavi and David Ambuel, 3–15. Albany: State University of New York Press.

Schochet, Gordon. 2003. 'Toleration'. In *Encyclopedia of the Enlightenment*, edited by Alan Charles Kors, 165–70. Oxford: Oxford University Press.

Schwartzmann, Micah. 2005. 'The Relevance of Locke's Religious Arguments for Toleration'. *Political Theory* 33(5): 678–705.

Scott, James C. 1999. *Seeing like a State: How Certain Schemes to Improve the Human Condition Have Failed*. New Haven: Yale University Press.

Sehat, David. 2011. *The Myth of American Religious Freedom*. Oxford and New York: Oxford University Press.

Sen, Amartya. 1996. 'Secularism and Its Discontents'. In *Unravelling the Nation: Sectarian Conflict and India's Secular Identity*, edited by Kaushik Basu and Sanjay Subrahmanyam. New Delhi: Penguin Books.

Sen, Amiya P. 1993. *Hindu Revivalism in Bengal, 1872–1905: Some Essays in Interpretation*. New Delhi: Oxford University Press.

Sen, Ronojoy. 2010. *Articles of Faith: Religion, Secularism, and the Indian Supreme Court*. New Delhi: Oxford University Press.

Seth, Sanjay. 2007. *Subject Lessons: The Western Education of Colonial India*. Durham: Duke University Press.

Shah, Prakash. 2010. 'Comparatively Indian: Living with Legal Plurality'. *Zeitschrift für Vergleichende Rechstwissenschaft* 109(3): 314–26.

———. 2014. 'Critiquing the Western Account of India Studies within a Comparative Science of Cultures'. *International Journal of Hindu Studies* 18(1): 67–72.

Shakman Hurd, Elizabeth. 2007. *The Politics of Secularism in International Relations*. Princeton: Princeton University Press.

Sharma, Arvind. 2003. 'What is Hinduism?' In *The Study of Hinduism*, edited by Arvind Sharma, 1–19. Columbia, SC: University of South Carolina Press.

Sharma, Jyotirmaya. 2003. *Hindutva: Exploring the Idea of Hindu Nationalism.* New Delhi: Penguin.

Simonutti, Luisa. 1996. 'Between Political Loyalty and Religious Liberty: Political Theory and Toleration in Huguenot Thought in the Epoch of Bayle'. *History of Political Thought* 17(4): 523–54.

Skipper, Robert. 1993. 'Mill and Pornography'. *Ethics* 103(4): 726–30.

Smith, Donald E. 1963. *India as a Secular State.* Bombay: Oxford University Press.

———. 1998. 'India as a Secular State'. In *Secularism and Its Critics,* edited by Rajeev Bhargava, 177–234. Delhi: Oxford University Press.

Smith, Graeme. 2008. *A Short History of Secularism.* London: I.B. Tauris.

Smith, Steven D. 1995. *Foreordained Failure: The Quest for a Constitutional Principle of Religious Freedom.* Oxford and New York: Oxford University Press.

———. 2010. *The Disenchantment of Secular Discourse.* Cambridge, MA: Harvard University Press.

Spencer, Herbert. 1898. *The Principles of Sociology, in Three Volumes.* New York: D. Appleton.

Srikanth, H. 1994. 'Secularism versus Pseudo-secularism: An Indian Debate'. *Social Action* 44: 39–54.

Stanford Reid, William. 1988. 'John Knox's Theology of Political Government'. *Sixteenth Century Journal* 19(4): 529–40.

Stanton, Timothy. 2006. 'Locke and the Politics and Theology of Toleration'. *Political Studies* 54(1): 84–102.

Steinberger, Peter J. 1999. 'Public and Private'. *Political Studies* 47(2): 292–313.

Stietencron, Heinrich von. 2001. 'On the Proper Use of a Deceptive Term'. In *Hinduism Reconsidered,* edited by G.D. Sontheimer and H. Kulke, 11–27. New Delhi: Manohar.

Steele, Arthur. 1868. *The Law and Custom of Hindoo Castes within the Dekhun Provinces Subject to the Presidency of Bombay, Chiefly Affecting Civil Suits.* London: W.H. Allen and Co.

Stock, Eugene. 1899. *The History of the Church Missionary Society: Its Environment, Its Men and Its Work,* vol. 2. London: Church Missionary Society.

Stolzenberg, Nomi. 2007. 'The Profanity of Law'. In *Law and the Sacred,* edited by Austin Sarat, Lawrence Douglas, and Martha Merrill Umphrey, 29–90. Stanford: Stanford University Press.

Strachey, Sir John. 1911. *India: Its Administration and Progress.* London: Macmillan and Co.

Sturgion, John. 1966. 'A Plea for Toleration of Opinions and Persuasions in Matters of Religion'. In *Tracts on Liberty of Conscience and Persecution, 1614–1661,* edited by Edward B. Underhill, 309–41. New York: Burt Franklin.

Subrahmanyam, Sanjay. 1996. 'Before the Leviathan: Sectarian Violence and the State in Pre-Colonial India'. In *Unravelling the Nation: Sectarian Conflict and*

India's Secular Identity, edited by Kaushik Basu and Sanjay Subrahmanyam, 44–80. New Delhi: Penguin.

Sudarshan, K.S. 1995. 'Secularism and Distortions'. In *Secularism in India: Dilemmas and Challenges*, edited by M.M. Sankhdher. New Delhi: Deep and Deep Publications.

Sullivan, Winnifred Fallers. 2007. *The Impossibility of Religious Freedom*. Princeton: Princeton University Press.

Swami Rama Tirtha. 1896. *On Sanatan Dharma*. Lucknow.

Sweetman, Will. 2003. '"Hinduism" and the History of "Religion": Protestant Presuppositions in the Critique of the Concept of Hinduism'. *Method & Theory in the Study of Religion* 15(4): 329–53.

Synge, Edward. 1698. *A Gentleman's Religion in Three Parts*. London.

Tambiah, Stanley. 1998. 'The Crisis of Secularism in India'. In *Secularism and Its Critics*, edited by Rajeev Bhargava, 418–53. Delhi: Oxford University Press.

Taylor, Charles. 1995. 'Two Theories of Modernity'. *The Hastings Center Report* 25(2): 24–33.

———. 1998. 'Modes of Secularism'. In *Secularism and Its Critics*, edited by Rajeev Bhargava, 31–53. Delhi: Oxford University Press.

———. 2007. *A Secular Age*. Cambridge, MA: Harvard University Press.

Taylor, Jeremy. 1648. *The Liberty of Prophesying*. London.

Teignmouth, Lord. 1968. 'Minute of Evidence (1813)'. In *Minutes of Evidence— British Parliamentary Papers, Vol. 4 (1812–1813)*. Shannon: Irish University Press.

Tejani, Shabnum. 2008. *Indian Secularism: A Social and Intellectual History, 1890–1950*. Bloomington and Indianapolis: Indiana University Press.

Tellenbach, Gerd. 1991. *Church, State and Christian Society at the Time of the Investiture Contest*. Toronto: Toronto University Press.

———. 1993. *The Church in Western Europe from the Tenth to the Early Twelfth Century*. Cambridge: Cambridge University Press.

Temperman, Jeroen, ed. 2012. *The Lautsi Papers: Multidisciplinary Reflections on Religious Symbols in the Public School Classroom*. Leiden: Martinus Nijhoff.

Tertullian. 1987. *De Idololatria*. Edited by. J.H. Waszink and J.C.M. van Winden. Leiden and New York: E.J. Brill.

Thapar, Romila. 1987. *Cultural Transaction and Early India: Tradition and Patronage*. Delhi: Oxford University Press.

Thayer, Anne T. 2002. *Penitence, Preaching and the Coming of the Reformation*. Aldershot: Ashgate.

Thomas, Elaine R. 2006. 'Keeping Identity at a Distance: Explaining France's New Legal Restrictions on the Islamic Headscarf'. *Ethnic and Racial Studies* 29(2): 237–59.

Thomas, Megan C. 2010. 'Orientalism and Comparative Political Theory'. *The Review of Politics* 72(4): 653–77.

Thornton, Edward. 1835. *India, Its State and Prospects*. London: Parbury, Allen & Co.

Tierney, Brian. 1964. *The Crisis of Church and State 1050–1300, with Selected Documents*. Englewood Cliffs, NJ: Prentice-Hall.

Tomaselli, Sylvana. 2000. 'Intolerance, the Virtue of Princes and Radicals'. In *From Persecution to Toleration: The Glorious Revolution and Religion in England*, edited by Ole P. Grell, Jonathan I. Israel, and Nicholas Tyacke, 86–101. Oxford: Clarendon Press.

Trautmann, Thomas R. 1997. *Aryans and British India*. Berkeley: University of California Press.

Tuck, Richard. 1988. 'Scepticism and Toleration in the Seventeenth Century'. In *Justifying Toleration: Conceptual and Historical Perspectives*, edited by Susan Mendus, 31–60. New York: Cambridge University Press.

Tuckness, Alex. 2002. 'Rethinking the Intolerant Locke'. *American Journal of Political Science* 46(2): 288–98.

Tupper, Charles L. 1893. *Our Indian Protectorate: An Introduction to the Study of the Relations Between the British Government and Its Indian Feudatories*. London: Longmans, Green and Co.

Tylor, Edward. 1970. *Religion in Primitive Culture*. Gloucester, MA: Peter Smith.

Vanaik, Achin. 1997. *Communalism Contested: Religion, Modernity and Secularization*. New Delhi: Vistaar Publications.

Van Drielenburch, Vincent. 1616. *Proefken oft Staelken Van Iohanis Wtenbogaerts ende Iacobi Taurini Onderlinghe Verdraeghsaemheyt*. Amsterdam.

Vandrunen, David. 2004. 'The Context of Natural Law: John Calvin's Doctrine of the Two Kingdoms'. *Journal of Church and State* 46(3): 503–26.

Van Duffel, Siegfried. 2007. 'Sovereignty as a Religious Concept'. *The Monist* 90(1): 126–42.

Vanheeswijck, Guido. 2008. *Tolerantie en Actief Pluralisme: More, Erasmus, Gillis en de Uitdaging van Het Actief Pluralisme*. Kampen: Klement.

Van Loon, Hendrik W. 1926. *The Liberation of Mankind: The Story of Man's Struggle for the Right to Think*. London: George Harrap & Company.

Vernon, Richard. 1996. 'John Stuart Mill and Pornography: Beyond the Harm Principle'. *Ethics* 106(3): 621–32.

———. 2013. 'Lockean Toleration: Dialogical Not Theological?' *Political Studies* 61(1): 215–30.

Voltaire. 1994. *A Treatise on Toleration and Other Essays*. Amherst, NY: Prometheus Books.

———. 1998. 'Philosophical Dictionary'. In *Religious Pluralism in the West: An Anthology*, edited by David G. Mullan, 187–93. Malden, MA: Blackwell.

Waldron, Jeremy. 1988. 'Locke: Toleration and the Rationality of Persecution'. In *Justifying Toleration: Conceptual and Historical Perspectives*, edited by Susan Mendus, 61–86. Cambridge: Cambridge University Press.

————. 2002. *God, Locke, and Equality: Christian Foundations in Locke's Political Thought*. Cambridge: Cambridge University Press.

Walker, Leslie. 1911. 'Divine Providence'. In *The Catholic Encyclopedia, vol. 12*. New York: Robert Appleton Company.

Wallace, Robert M. 1981. 'Progress, Secularization and Modernity: The Löwith-Blumenberg Debate'. *New German Critique* 22: 63–79.

Walwyn, William. 1647. *A Still and Soft Voice From the Scriptures*. London.

Warner, Michael, Jonathan VanAntwerpen, and Craig Calhoun. 2010. 'Editors' Introduction'. In *Varieties of Secularism in a Secular Age*, edited by M. Warner, J. VanAntwerpen, and C. Calhoun, 1–31. Cambridge, MA: Harvard University Press.

Warnock, Mary. 1987. 'The Limits of Toleration'. In *On Toleration*, edited by Susan Mendus and David Edwards, 123–40. Oxford: Oxford University Press.

Weeks, Andrew. 2000. *Valentin Weigel (1533–1588): German Religious Dissenter, Speculative Theorist, and Advocate of Tolerance*. Albany, NY: State University of New York Press.

Weintraub, Jeff. 1997. 'The Theory and Politics of the Public/Private Distinction'. In *Public and Private in Thought and Practice: Perspectives on a Grand Dichotomy*, edited by Jeff Weintraub and Krishan Kumar, 1–42. Chicago: The University of Chicago Press.

Wheeler, James Talboys. 1888. *College History of India: Asiatic and European*. London: Macmillan and Co.

Whitehead, Henry. 1924. *Indian Problems in Religion, Education, Politics*. London: Constable & Co.

Whitford, David. 2004. 'Cura Religionis or Two Kingdoms: The Late Luther on Religion and the State in the Lectures on Genesis'. *Church History* 73(1): 41–62.

Wilhelm, Anthony G. 1999. 'Good Fences and Good Neighbors: John Locke's Positive Doctrine of Toleration'. *Political Research Quarterly* 52(1): 145–66.

Williams, Bernard. 1996. 'Toleration: An Impossible Virtue?' In *Toleration: An Elusive Virtue*, edited by David Heyd, 18–27. Princeton: Princeton University Press.

Williams, Roger. 1643. *A Key into the Languages of America*. London.

————. 1644. *The Bloudy Tenent of Persecution*. London.

Witte, John, Jr. 2002. *Law and Protestantism: The Legal Teachings of the Lutheran Reformation*. Cambridge: Cambridge University Press.

Wolfe, Alan. 1997. 'Public and Private in Theory and Practice: Some Implications of an Uncertain Boundary'. In *Public and Private in Thought and Practice:*

Perspectives on a Grand Dichotomy, edited by Jeff Weintraub and Krishan Kumar, 182–203. Chicago: The University of Chicago Press.

Wolfson, Adam. 1996. 'Two Theories of Toleration'. *Perspectives on Political Science* 25(4): 192–8.

Wolseley, Charles. 1668. *Liberty of Conscience, the Magistrates Interest*. London.

Woodhouse, A.S.P. ed. 1992. *Puritanism and Liberty: Being the Army Debates (1647–49) from the Clarke Manuscripts*. London: J.M. Dent & Sons.

Yelle, Robert A. 2005. 'Bentham's Fictions: Canon and Idolatry in the Genealogy of Law'. *Yale Journal of Law & the Humanities* 17(2): 151–79.

Zaehner, Richard. 1969. *Hinduism*. Oxford: Oxford University Press.

Zastoupil, Lynn and Martin Moir. 1999. 'Introduction'. In *The Great Indian Education Debate: Documents Relating to the Orientalist-Anglicist Controversy, 1781–1843*, edited by Lynn Zastoupil and Martin Moir, 1–72. Richmond: Curzon Press.

Zeeden, Ernst W. 1985. *Konfessionsbildung: Studien zur Reformation, Gegenreformation und Katholischen Reform*. Stuttgart: Klett-Cotta.

Ziegenbalg, Bartholomeus. 1719. *Thirty Four Conferences Between the Danish Missionaries and the Malabarian Bramans … in the East Indies, Concerning the Truth of the Christian Religion*. London.

Zijlstra, Samme. 2002. 'Anabaptism and Tolerance: Possibilities and Limitations'. In *Calvinism and Religious Toleration in the Dutch Golden Age*, edited by R. Po-Chia Hsia and Henk van Nierop, 112–31. Cambridge: Cambridge University Press.

Zuckert, Michael. 2002. *Launching Liberalism: On Lockean Political Philosophy*. Lawrence, KA: University Press of Kansas.

Index

About the Author

Jakob De Roover is Assistant Professor, Department of Comparative Science of Cultures at Ghent University, Belgium. His research focuses on the comparative study of politics and political thought in Europe and India, with a particular interest in issues of cultural difference, secularism, and religion. It is part of a larger research programme, called Comparative Science of Cultures, which argues that the currently dominant conceptualizations of Asian cultures and societies consist of oblique reflections upon the Western cultural experience. De Roover is embedded in an international research group that seeks to decolonize the social sciences and humanities. He is the author of a series of essays on the role of Christianity in the shaping of our contemporary thinking about politics, society, and religion.